ORGANISATION, PROCESSING AND USE OF INFORMATION IN THE DIGITAL ERA

ORGANISATION, PROCESSING AND USE OF INFORMATION IN THE DIGITAL ERA

Prof. M. Parameswaran Festschrift

Edited by

Dr. Jalaja V.

Veeran M.C.K.

Dineshan Koovakkai

Ess Ess Publications

4837/24, Ansari Road, Darya Ganj,
New Delhi-110002
✆ : 23260807
Fax : 23274173
E-mail: info@essessreference.com
url:http://www.essessreference.com

First Published 2004

ISBN : 81-7000-418-7

Price : Rs. 650/-

Published by :

Ess Ess Publications

4837/24, Ansari Road, Darya Ganj,
New Delhi - 110 002
Phone : 23260807
Fax : 23274173
E-mail: info@essessreference.com
url:http://www.essessreference.com

Printed at :
Print Line

Prof. M. Parameswaran

Head, Department of Library and Information Science
University of Calicut, Kerala
(Retires on 31st March 2004)

PREFACE

The present work is a collection of essays which have been collected for publication as a felicitation volume to Prof. M. Parameswaran, Professor and Head of the Department of Library and Information Science, University of Calicut, who is retiring from Calicut University service on 31st March 2004.

Prof. M. Parameswaran is a person with many faceted talents. He is a good teacher, eloquent speaker, experienced librarian, committed organizer, versatile scholar and a known poet in Malayalam.

Prof. Parameswaran has developed the Department of Library and Information Science of the University of Calicut during the last twenty five years with his untiring effort. He was also instrumental for the development of Calicut University Library (now known as C.H.Mohammed Koya Library) in its early phase. He has a very significant role in the organization of libraries and in popularizing library education in the northern part of Kerala during the last thirty years.

We, the colleagues and students of Prof. M. Parameswaran wished that we should bring out a felicitation volume in a befitting manner to honour him. That wish has been now materialized with the publication of this volume.

When the felicitation committee started planning for the publication of a collection of essays, it was decided that the publication should be restricted to cover certain interrelated areas of library and information science which are relevant in the electronic era. Thus the following areas were chosen. i) Digitization and electronic libraries. ii) Copyright and I PR issues in the digital environment. iii) Resource sharing and networking in the electronic environment. iv) Information processing in the electronic environment.

Among these four interrelated areas the last one – information processing – is of special interest to Prof. M. Parameswaran. He has contributed significantly to this area.

In this book there are 24 papers distributed in the following manner: ten papers in part I, six papers in part 2, four papers each in part 3 and 4.

In Part I there are ten papers on digitization and electronic libraries.

Prof. (Dr.) M. P. Satija interprets the five laws of library science in the context of the electronic era. Prof. C.A. Augustine discusses the content of Library Science curriculum in the context of digital libraries. Rejashekhar D. Kumbar examines the impact of I.T. on libraries in general. G. Dhanasegaran discusses the recent trends in computerisation of library operations. Dineshan Koovakkai and Jalaja V. examine the user side of IT application in the university libraries of Kerala state. P. Mounisami examines the impact of electronic journals. Dr. N.S. Harinarayana, Sunil M.V. and Namratha G.R. present a case study of digitization of project reports. Prof. (Dr.) G. Devarajan tries to establish that the digital divide divides the society into two J.P. S. Kumaravel discusses the problems involved in the preservation of digital information. Dr. P. Naushad Ali and Atiya Masood present a bibliometric study of I.T. literature in library and information science.

In part 2 copy right and IPR issues are considered from various perspectives- Dr. P. Venkata Ramana from legal perspective, M.C.K. Veeran and T.M. Vasudevan in global perspective, Meena V. with reference to digital libraries and Prof. (Dr) S. Seetharama with reference to academic institutions-. G. Hemachandran Nair presents his research findings about Ayurveda in the context of globalization, patent and IPR issues. Sudha A. discusses the issues relating to information security and privacy.

Part 3 resource sharing and networking in the electronic

environment includes 4 papers. M.G. Sreekumar, T. Sunitha and P. Sreejaya give an account of their experience in IIMK library related to electronic journal subscription and resource sharing in digital environment through networking. Dr. Rabinarayan Mishra explains the trends in information network and examines its role in libraries. A.K. Shobhana Devi discusses certain basic issues of resource sharing in digital environment. Dr. Humayun Kabir presents a proposal for resource sharing and networking in libraries in Kannur District.

Part 4 includes 4 papers on information processing in the electronic environment. Veerankutty C. discusses user interface design in Web OPAC. K.S. Chudamani and H.C. Nagarathna discuss the current trends in automatic classification with reference to DDC. T.M. Vasudevan and Jesbira M. present the results of a study conducted in CHMK Library on user behaviour towards catalogue. Manzoor Babu V. considers OPAC as an effective tool for distance learning.

The contributors to this felicitation volume include senior Professors, experienced teachers of library science, veteran librarians and research scholars. All of them are either friends, colleagues or former students of Prof. M. Parameswaran. We wish to express our sincere gratitude to all the contributors.

We also wish to thank Sri. Sumith Sethi, the Managing Director of ESS ESS publications who has readily agreed to publish this work. There are also other people who have helped us in many ways to bring out this publication. We are grateful to the Research Scholars and Data Entry Operators of the Department of Library and Information Science, University of Calicut for their help in typing and preparing the manuscript.

We dedicate this volume to Prof. M. Parameswaran in our appreciation for his life long efforts in the field of library and information science.

EDITORS

List of Contributors

Atiya Masood
Ex-Student Department of Library Science
A.M.U Aligarh-202 002

Augustine, C.A. (Prof.)
Former Head
Department of Library and Information Science
University of Kerala
Thiruvananthapuram

Chudamani, K.S.
JRD Tata Memorial Library
Indian Institute of Science
Bangalore-12

Devarajan, G. (Dr.)
Head, Dept. of Library & Information Science &
Director, College Development Council
University of Kerala
Thiruvananthapuram-34

Dhanasegaran, G.
Deputy Librarian,
Dr.T.P.M.Library
M.K.University
Madurai – 625 021.

Dineshan Koovakkai
Professional Assistant
University Library
University of Calicut
e-mail: dineshkoovakkai@yahoo.co.in

Harinarayana, N.S. (Dr.)
Lecturer,
Department of Library and Information Science
University of Mysore
Mysore

Hemachandran Nair, G.
Technical Assistant,
Kerala University Campus Library,
Kariavattom
Email: ghnair@yahoo.com

Humayoon Kabir, S. (Dr.)
Project Officer Kerala Women's Commission
Trivandrum - 14

Jalaja, V. (Dr.)
Reader
Department of Library and Information Science
University of Calicut

Jesbira, M.
MLISc Student
Department of Library and Information Science
University of Calicut

Kumaravel, J.P.S.
Information Scientist
Dr.T.P.M.Library
Madurai Kamaraj University
Madurai – 625 021
E-mail: jpskumar@yahoo.com

Kumbar, Rajashekhar D.
Librarian Jansons School of Business
Karumathampatti
Coimbatore – 641 659

Manzoor Babu, V.
Research Scholar
Department of Library and Information Science
University of Calicut
Meena, V.
Research Scholar
Department of Library of Information
University of Calicut

Mounissamy, P.
Assistant Librarian
National Institute of Technology
Tiruchirappalli
Tamil Nadu
e-mail: moun@nitt.edu.in

Nagarathna, H.C.
JRD Tata Memorial Library
Indian Institute of Science
Bangalore-12

Namratha, G.R.
Student, II Year MLISc
Department of Library and Information Science
University of Mysore
Mysore

Naushad Ali, P.M. (Dr.)
Lecturer
Department of Library Science
A.M.U Aligarh-202 002
Email:pmnali@hotmail.com

Rabinarayan Mishra (Dr.)
P G Dept. of Lib.& Inf.Science
Sambalpur University
Jyoti Vihar- 768 019 (Orissa)

Satija, M.P.
G.N.D. University
Amritsar - 143005

Seetharama, S.
(DRTC, Bangalore)
17 Varadarajulu Street
Chennai – 600 008

Sobhana Devi, A.K.
Assistant Librarian
Cochin University

Sreejaya, P.
Indian Institute of Management Kozhikode
Kunnamangalam
Calicut - 673 571

Sreekumar, M.G.
Librarian
Indian Institute of Management
Kozhikode Kunnamangalam
Calicut - 673 571

Sudha, A.
Assistant Librarian
Kannur University Central Library
Kannur-670002

Sunil, M.V.
Librarian
SDM Institute of Management Development
Mysore

Sunitha, T.
Indian Institute of Management Kozhikode
Kunnamangalam
Calicut - 673 571

Vasudevan, T.M.
Lecturer
Department of Library and Information Science
University of Calicut

Veeran, M.C.K.
Assistant Librarian (Sel.Grade)
C.H.M.K.Library
University of Calicut
Calicut University P.O.-673635

Veerankutty Chelatayakkot
Junior Librarian
Cochin University of Science and Technology

Venkata Ramana, P. (Dr.)
Assistant Librarian
JNTU School of Planning & Architecture
Maheever Marg
Masab Tank
Hyderabad-500 028

CONTENTS

PART II: COPYRIGHT AND IPR ISSUES IN THE DIGITAL ENVIRONMENT

PART III: RESOURCE SHARING AND NETWORKING IN THE ELECTRONIC ENVIRONMENT

PROF. M. PARAMESWARAN :
A Biographical Sketch

M.C.K. Veeran

EARLY PERIOD

Prof. M.Parameswaran was born at Trivandrum on the 11th of February, 1944. His birth star was Pooram (Poorva Phalguni) which fell on the 29th of Makaram 1119 according to Malayalam Era (Kollavarsham). M. Parameswaran had his school education in the Model High School, Trivandrum. Parameswaran comes from a Tamil Brahmin family (Iyer) and he is the grandson of Mahakavi Ullur S. Parameswara Iyer, one of the three great poets of Malayalam. From early childhood Parameswaran had an aptitude for literature. Even as a child he used to read as many books as he can from the personal library of his grand father which consisted of thousands of books. This reading habit had tremendous influence on him.

Parameswaran passed Pre-University from Intermediate College, Trivandrum (now known as Govt. Arts College) in 1961. He did his graduation from the University College, Trivandrum with geology as optional Subject.

After graduation Parameswaran took B.Lib.Sc degree in 1965 and M.Sc in geology in 1967 from the University of Kerala.

STUDY AT DRTC

In March 1968 Parameswaran joined Kerala University Library as an Assistant Librarian. In 1970 he took leave and did the Associateship in Documentation at the Prestigious Documentation Research & Training Centre, Bangalore. During this period he had the unique opportunity to study under Prof. A. Neelameghan, Prof. G. Bhattacharyya and Prof. M.A. Gopinath. S.R.Ranganathan, the founder Professor of DRTC was nominated as National Professor in Library Science by the Government of India and was continuing his relation with DRTC as its Honorary Professor at that time.

Prof. S. Seetharama had joined as Research Assistant to the National Professor and Dr. I.K.Ravichandra Rao had joined as Research Assistant in DRTC after his M.Stat. from Indian Statistical Institute.

Thus Parameswaran had the unique opportunity to establish contacts with all these giants of Library Profession. He always remembers the 14 months spent in DRTC from April 1970 to June 1971 which shaped his thinking process and laid foundation to his professional life. The annual and mid-year seminars organized in DRTC also helped him to present papers and actively participate in discussions. These seminars also gave opportunities to be acquainted with great personalities like Prof. Pauline Authorton, Professor of Library Science, Syracuse University (USA) and Dr. Suseela Kumar, Director, British Library, Madras.

BEGINNING OF PROFESSIONAL CAREER AND LITERARY CONTRIBUTIONS

Parameswaran returned to Kerala University Library and continued there till 1974. He passed the Associateship in documentation in 1972 with distinction which was a unique honour. In Kerala University Library he had the opportunity to work under Prof.K.A.Isaac, Professor of Library Science and University Librarian who is the Godfather of library profession in Kerala. Parameswaran had mastered the skills of library management from here and started contributing papers to professional journals. He also published a series of popular articles in library science in Malayalam journals like Granthalokam and Vijnanakairali. This period also saw the beginning of the budding poet in Parameswaran. He started publishing poems and critical studies in Malayalam journals during this period.

LECTURER IN CHARGE OF THE CALICUT UNIVERSITY LIBRARY

Prof. A.P. Srivastava was appointed as Professor of Library Science and University Librarian in the University of Calicut. M.Parameswaran joined as Lecturer in Library Science in the University of Calicut in November 1974 when Prof. A.P. Srivastava was developing the University Library.

Soon Prof. A.P. Srivastava left the University of Calicut to join as Librarian in I I I, Kanpur who later became the University Librarian of Delhi University.

M.Parameswaran had the responsibility of developing the Calicut University Library as the Lecturer in charge in its infantile stage with the able support of a limited number of professional staff for about two years, until Dr. M. Bavakutty was appointed as Deputy Librarian in March 1977.

UNTIRING WORK AS THE HEAD OF THE DEPARTMENT

The University of Calicut started the BLISc course in 1977 and the course was conducted with the help of the professional staff of the Department with the Deputy Librarian being in charge of the course. However Parameswaran's contribution was most significant in developing the syllabi and curriculum of BLISc.

In May 1985 when M. Parameswaran was appointed as Reader and Head of the Department of Library and Information Science he had great challenges to meet. Even though Library and Information Science Department was separated from Calicut University Library and declared as a full fledged Department, it did not have any infra structure facility. Parameswaran's untiring and ardent work as the Head, enabled the Library and Information Science Department to develop as one of the well known Library Science Departments in South India.

In 1986 Prof. K.A. Isaac, the pioneer of Library Science in Kerala joined Calicut University as visiting professor for one year under UGC scheme after his retirement from Kerala University. Prof. Isaac gave Parameswaran tremendous guidance and support in developing the new department from its toddling stage. This was followed by the appointments of two more efficient visiting Professors for one year each- Prof.A.B.George retired University Librarian of Cochin University and Prof. M.N.Ramakrishnan Nair, Retired Professor of Library Science, Kerala University. With the support of these experienced Professors, Sri. M. Parameswaran got over many problems in the development of the Department.

During October 1987 Parameswaran had to leave his Department for higher studies at Britain when he was selected for the Technical Co-operation Training Programme of the Govt of India. This Programme provides a scholarship for one year to study in a University at United Kingdom for a P.G. Course. Under this Programme Parameswaran did M. Sc Course in Library and Information Studies in the Prestigious Loughborough University of Technology in England. This period gave Parameswaran an opportunity to observe library education and library services in U.K. He visited many important libraries of U.K. during this period, such as the British Museum Library and the university libraries of Oxford and Cambridge.

Parameswaran returned to Calicut University with more confidence gained from his British experience in October 1988. The University had appointed two lectures in the Department. With the support of two more full time teachers in the Department, it was easier for Parameswaran to concentrate on further development of the Department. The last decade of 20th Century was very significant in the history of the Department of Library and Information Science in the University of Calicut. Under the able leadership of M.Parameswaran the Department conducted self financed BLISc evening courses from 1993 to 1999.

In 1994 MLISc course was started in the Department as a self financed evening course. Regular day-time MLISc course also was started from the next academic year. Even though self financed evening courses were conducted very efficiently, these had to be stopped due to lack of understanding on the part of the authorities. The Department also started full-time Ph.D. Programme and developed a Computer Laboratory.

NATIONAL SEMINARS AND REFRESHER COURSES

The Department of Library and Information Science organized four Annual National Seminars co-sponsored by CHMK Library (The Calicut University Library) from 1999 to 2002. The seminars held were on the following topics:

1. National Seminar on Management of Libraries in the 21st Century. 28th – 29th May, 1999.
2. National Seminar on Organisation of Libraries and Information Centres in the 21st Century. 26th – 27th May, 2000.
3. National Seminar on Library Cooperation in a Networked World. 25th – 26th May, 2001.
4. National Seminar on Information Access, Management and Exchange in the Technological Age. 28 – 29 May, 2002.

M.Parameswaran had a key role in the organization of these national seminars. He further served as the Director of the third National Seminar. Prof. Parameswaran organized a series of Refresher Courses in Library and Information Science with Information Technology as the thrust area under the aegis of the Academic Staff College. As Head of the Department and coordinator he had a key role in organizing these refresher courses.

RECOGNITION COMING LATE

M.Parameswaran was promoted as Professor under career advancement scheme of the UGC with retrospective effect from March 2002, on the basis of evaluation of publications. Due to some administrative delay, the order was served only in February 2004, one month before the retirement of Parameswaran. Thus leaving behind the trails of his untired efforts, Prof.

M.Parameswaran is retiring on 31st Of March 2004 to concentrate on more productive works, such as writing books on Library Science and to be absorbed in literary activities.

PUBLICATIONS

Prof. M. Parameswaran has published 3 books in Malayalam and two in English. He has also published more than 30 papers in English and about that much literary articles in Malayalam. His professional articles have appeared in both national and international journals. He has participated and presented papers in national and international conferences. Even though his papers have covered various aspects of Library Science, his special interest is in Library Classification, Cataloguing and Indexing.

By this time Prof. Parameswaran had established as a poet in Malayalam. His ability to translate Classical Tamil Literature into simple Malayalam language was also widely appreciated. He published a poetry collection entitled Desatanakkili(Migrating bird).

EXPERTISE IN LIBRARY AND INFORMATION SCIENCE

Prof. Parameswaran has served as paper setter and examiner in almost all Universities of South India. He has also served as Member of Board of Studies in various universities of Kerala. He is at present serving as Chairman of the Board of Studies and Member of Faculty of Humanities and Academic Council in the University of Calicut. He has completed one term as Member of Senate. The universities of Cochin and Kannur also have benefitted in many ways from his expertise. The students of Parameswaran remember that his classes are unique experiences. His ability to explain even complicated subjects in a simple manner with utmost clarity has been acknowledged by students and colleagues alike. His soft speaking nature has earned many friends to him but his frankly speaking nature has also earned a few enemies. Prof. Parameswaran is retiring from the

University Service but not from active Professional and literary activities which he wants to continue as long as he can.

FAMILY LIFE

Prof. Parameswaran is blessed with a happy family life. His wife Radha hails from a family which migrated from Palghat (Palakkad) to Madras (Chennai) and later settled in Bangalore. He has a son and a daughter. His daughter Sindhu and her husband Santhosh are computer engineers settled in the Virginia State of USA. His son Mahesh is an electrical engineer in a multinational company in Bangalore.

SOCIAL COMMITMENT

Prof. Parameswaran is a person of uncompromising social Commitment. He has participated in all social, cultural and literary movements on campus and at Calicut region. Translation Forum, Linguistics Forum and Calicut University Teachers Association are some of the Organizations in which Prof. Parameswaran has participated actively. Prof. M.Parameswaran has served as Vice President of the Translation Forum for more than one term.

He is an active member of Calicut University Teachers Association (CUTA). He has held various responsibilities in the Teachers Association, namely Joint Secretary, Secretary, Vice-President and President. Arangu (The stage), Tapasya, Bharatheeya Vichara Kendram and Swadeshi Science Movement are only a few organizations in which Prof. Parameswaran has actively participated by holding key Positions.

PARTICIPATION IN PROFESSIONAL ORGANIZATIONS

Prof. Parameswaran has never neglected the Professional Organizations for his social commitment. He is a member of national bodies like ILA, IASLIC and IATLIS and International Organizations like International Society for Knowledge Organization (ISKO). He has continued for about a decade as the Regional President of Kerala Library Association (KLA).

PART I :
DIGITIZATION AND ELECTRONIC LIBRARIES

1

The Five Laws in Information Society And Virtual Libraries Era

M.P. Satija
G.N.D. University
Amritsar - 143005

ORIGIN OF THE LAWS

Ranganathan was highly impressed and influenced by the library services to each and every citizen of the U.K.given by its library system.[1] But despite the devoted teachers with best minds having wide and varied experience. Ranganathan found library science teaching a bundle of tricks in the School of Librarianship and Archives, University College, London during 1924-1925. His inquisitive and analytical mind inured on philosophy and mathematics could not submit itself to what he considered unworthy practices and rules that were taught to be remembered by the rule of the thumb - take it as such or leave it. After a great deal of pondering and further experience of library work, he realised the lack of normative principles to guide and explain the myriads of library practices then prevailing. The prescription lay in formulation of normative principles to cure the hodgepodge situation. By the late 19th century the scientific methods had already been successfully applied to what later became social sciences. Professor Pierce Butler

(1886-1953) and his colleagues at Library School of the University of Chicago had already advocated the use of scientific methods to library management. Having diagnosed the malady, Ranganathan set out to discover and formulate the normative laws governing libraries. This, a stupendous task, required lot of intensive experience, insight, vision and a catalyst of intuition. Intuition helps the large number of empirical precepts to boil down to few fundamental laws[2]. Ranganathan with perseverance and keeping the problem in the subconscious mind analytically observed all the practical details to distil them into laws. This dramatic story of the origin and formulation of laws has been told and retold by Ranganathan.[3,4]

Thereafter, Ranganathan set out to elucidate the newly discovered laws and deduce their general implications. Conformity of the deductions with the existing practices confirmed their validity. Subsequently, these were fully developed and published in a book in 1931 with the title: *The Five Laws of Library Science* (Chennai: Madras Library Association. xxxii. 458p). The book was an instant success despite the doubts of some sceptics on the scientific nature of our work. The second edition was brought out in 1957 when he had gained immense experience of teaching and observation of documentation work in R & D centres in India, Europe and USA. The second edition also contained a chapter on the nature of science and scientific methods to convince others that library service lay in this domain. It reached more hands than the earlier edition. There was even an unfulfilled demand for an American edition of the book in American English. Nevertheless, it got him deservedly famous. To quote Pauline Cochrane "Dr. Ranganathan had done nothing more than publish the Five Laws of Library Science, he would have to be seriously considered for the Library Hall of Fame".[5]

The laws have stood the test of time as these became more and more acceptable as the time passed by. The popularity continued even after Ranganathan's death as evident from comments on them in different languages of the world. e.g., in Chinese.[6] To say that they are mere slogans is to be ignorant of the nature and structure of scientific laws.[7] These laws have not been dictated from above.

These are not statements of opinions or mere ideals of a missionary. These are shared definitions of ideal conduct. These laws have been precipitated and sifted from actual practices in all categories of libraries. Ranganathan had an uncanny gift to do this.

Peter Achinstein, a philosopher of science, lays down the following lingual characteristics of a stated law.[8]

* Laws are simple, precise, and few in number.
* Laws are essentially general in nature
* Their subject is general
* Syntactically they are general, as they generally begin with "All". "Every", or "No".
* A law expresses a generally which can be used to express other regularities.

Simplicity does not mean shallowness, but it is in unravelling the complex structure of universe in that discipline, and stating that in simple linear equation. Simplicity lies in the smallness of numbers of parameters and their varied interrelations,

How strikingly and easily the Five Laws qualify Achinstein test is too obvious. From philosophical and epistemological standpoints they fully hold the status of the laws. These are quite simple in appearance as the basic laws always are and should be. These laws are not anything invented or imposed but have been discovered and formulated. Struck by their simplicity many votaries wondered as to why these too obvious looking laws could not be formulated earlier!.

Their acceptance as normative laws has been acknowledged by numerous library scientists and practitioners. With time not only these have attracted more adheres and advocates, but they continue to be valid in changing library environment. Laws inhere modernity and have self-renewing power of applications. The laws are subejct to the Quarnic principle of *ijihad* - a principle of reinterpretation.[9] In his time Ranganathan had shown them to be equally applicable to documentation work[10]. In the succeeding ear of intensive and pro-active service of micro-documents by information centres his disciples and others have demonstrated the validity of laws by simply changing the parameter "book" to "information". The laws have logic-deductive structure. They evince to hold latently, or as obvious corollaries, every practice current or future. They attest the dictum that a true theory is a repertoire of practice. The laws have proved fountainhead of his path breaking and voluminous work. They further attest Francis Bacon's conviction in the *Novum Organum* that "axioms rightly discovered . . . will draw after them trains and troops of work". They have prognostic value and portend towards the future trends as elucidated by FW Lancaster.[11] These laws provided fundamental statements of goals that information services should strive for, and they are as relevant today as they were . . . years ago." The Five laws hold the reins of every bit of theory applicable to information services. It requires a moderately inventive mind to deduce from them new principles from time to time. All the ultra-modern services of information centres could be deduced from or validated by the Five Laws. Automated libraries have witnessed their applications more tangibly. But every invention is grounded in social milieu of its time. Is not the information society environment with virtual libraries a radically different one?

INFORMATION SOCIETY

It is phase of human civilization come into being due to long evolution in information and communication. Ushered by the information revolution the information society has heralded a new era in human civilisation. It has brought in wide and far reaching changes: a new economy new modes and technology of communication, new life and work styles and new modes of education. It has been facilitated by democracy and free flow of information. Not only the outlook seems different, there is clear shift in economic and social values. A social revolution has taken place. Information Technology (IT) has emerged as the most powerful agent of social change and economic transformation. The IT has made constantly swelling volumes of knowledge even accessible to the masses. New forms of telecommunications transit cornucopia of information round the world in a split second and diffuse it with an amazing speed. The Internet has brought more knowledge in circulation than ever before. And is still growing rapidly.

Information society is witnessing the power of information and knowledge at its best. Today the information is most valuable and sought after commodity and resource. It is prime mover of the society. Production, distribution and consumption of information has multiplied to astronomical figures. Knowledge now an international public good and its benefits extend to all those who can access it irrespective of political boundaries. Organisation of the economic relations has been transformed. Investment in its generation gives much higher returns than in production of industrial goods.[12] Recent economic theories indicate that growth of knowledge can generate endless potential for economy.[13] Knowledge growth is brought out by institutions of higher education and research through R & D. Libraries help generate more knowledge by disseminating it. Investments in knowledge creation and dissemination is becoming an engine of economic growth. Sophisticated and systematic theoretical knowledge aides advances in every social sphere.

Economy, social mores and politics have been affected visibly. Social laws, values and attitudes are changing. Fast flow of information is radically changing social relations and have brought in new educational technology especially for distance learning. Education is out reachers the deprived. The government world over are acquiring new roles while jettisoning some old jobs. The MNCs are acquiring para-governmental roles. The governments, as we define today, will not survive the change to manage society effectively. Free and fast flow of information, easy and inexpensive means of transportation, fall of dividing lines have shrunk the world into a global village where everybody and place is connected and wired. It is the death of distance. Political structure need redesigning. This in turn has resulted in the emergence of world economy, cosmopolitan culture and international movements. New techniques in genetics and molecular biology have transformed the quality of life throwing both formidable geographical, cultural, ethical and legal issues. In fact a whole range of political issues have cropped up. Feminine, human rights, green peace movements, even international terrorism, and rampant cyber crimes are product of the information revolution. Today's wars are info-wars in many senses of the term. Social and cultural mobility brought in by globalisation has been well stated by S.T. Hettige.[14]

Today, the market forces play a significant part in the distribution of life chances in society. Almost unrestricted flow of information, media images and cultural goods into the country has facilitated the spread of new life styles and consumption patterns. As a result consumption based life styles and social identifies today openly compete with conventional life styles and identifies based on social positions occupied by individuals. In the new environments, the dress. hair styles, personal possessions, consumer tastes, hobbies, etc may be even more important than the actual occupational roles individual occupy.

This shift requires the enactment of new cyber laws on the part of the governments and legislators. Indeed it has created same social and human problems which require new laws and attitudes to solve them.[27]

Knowledge society is an ever learning society. Alvin Toffler has aptly said that the illiterates of the 21st century will not be those who cannot read and write, but those who cannot learn, unlearn and relearn. Eric Hoffer has emphasized the same value with a warning: "In a time of drastic change, it is the learners who survive: the learned find themselves fully equipped to live in a world that no longer exists". Its citizens have to constantly acquire new set of skills. Need of the long lessons were never so self evident and pressing.

Alvin Toffler in a long drawn empirical and analytical study of the social and economic trends distils are following characteristics of the information society[16]:

a. Knowledge creation and transfer leads to creation to wealth.

b. Industrial production has become cyclic, customised and demassified with the use of IT.

c. Knowledge is a superior substitute for the conventional factors of production, such as land, labour, raw materials and capital.

d. Electronic information, being eminently fluid, has become a fine medium of exchange.

e. Managers, researchers and information professionals are the new heroes of the information society.

f. Producer and the consumer fuse into a "prosumer".

g. This global and wired society allows local production with global technology.

NEW FEATURES AND ROLES OF LIBRARY AND INFORMATION CENTRES

Libraries and information centres are the warehouses of the most valuable goods of the information society. Information production is in astronomical quantities leading to information overload in many cases. There are nearly a billion of PCs in use today. See how the internet is taking everybody in its fold. Its 195 million users in 1999 has grown to half a billion now, with many additions everyday. Every third house in advance countries owns a PC. There are 800 million web pages; and 5.50,00 books published every year. There are 7,50,000 information related companies around the world with a market exceeding one trillion US dollars.

Organic and inorganic materials have different physical and chemical properties under extremely high or low pressure or temperature. Systems, be they social or biological, have to be managed differently in abnormal environs. Is not this phenomena applicable to information, which is a pattern of mass-energy? Electronic information and libraries have the following distinct features[17]:

a. Highly compact storage

b. Ease of reproduction, multiplication, editions and manipulation.

c. Contents can be easily detached from is container/media, and put into other media without trace of previous.

d. Ease of transmission, communication and storage.

e. Hypertext and non-linear format allows a text to be fragmented and organised in a new mode.

f. Seamless integration of print and electronic media; and then of audio, video, text and animation in multimedia.

g. Sophisticated and multiprong searches through keywords, freetext Boolean operators, class numbers, thesauri and their permutations and combinations.

h. Wall less libraries are leading to a vision of multimedia global virtual library (MGVL) inaugurating an ear of "death of distance".

i. Remote and wireless access transcends barriers of time and place.

j. Convergene of technologies; see the cell phone is getting more multifunctional and powerful than the PC. Now we are beginning to see bio-digital convergence.

k. Cost of technologies is decreasing while its power is increasing.

Power and nature of new media have a visible impact on the shape, wares, functioning and service of libraries. We are called upon to organise. CDs and websites just as books and other documents. Traditional acquisition policies and methods are no more practical. Library and information use pattern has changed in face of information networks, wall-less libraries, powerful library systems, OPACs and convergence of technologies.

This technology is not static or stale. Metamorphic changes are still in the offing. Apex outcome of the new environment is virtual library.

VIRTUAL LIBRARY

A library is a growing social institution, as described by the 5th Law. The major stages in its evolution are:

* **Pre-paper library :** of clay tablets, papyrus, tree leaves, parchment, etc. etc.

* **Traditional Library :** of manuscripts, incunabula and printed books and documents on paper.

* **Hybrid Library :** Individual and stand alone library of print, micro and electronic documents served mostly through automation.

* **Virtual Library :** Networked digital library configured in the cyber space from the collection of scattered physical libraries.

At the outset it may be made clear that it has nothing to do with virtual reality, nor it is antithetical to the traditional or physical library. This library is a vision of technology with great potential for the future. Even the term has been challenged.[18] It is a computer based telecommunication linked practical library which provides services as any other library. As the name suggests it does not exist as any single housed collection, but is a medium to access information scattered in various physical collections. It has to be configured and structured individually. Being a hypermedia, it provides much more services which a paper based library cannot. Therefore, it is rightly seen that "decades from now...the physical library will be less visible to the public than the virtual library..."[19]. Digital and virtual libraries hold a special promise for the developing countries. Their priorities include poverty alleviation, unemployment, public health, safe drinking water, disaster management, environment protection and human rights and civil liberties. Information and awareness on these issues can now more easily be given than ever before Digital technology provides the system developers a golden opportunity to develop a non-commercial mechanism to build and disseminate information for social development.[20]

Ranganathan's laws were sufficient and quite valid in the previrtual libraries days. Social environment is changing drastically. To quote Toffler, "Something new is arising on the planet and it does not fit into the assumptions and paradigms left over from the

Second Wave"[21]. But systems have differently or get defunct in extreme environment or in paradigm shift. Ranganathan himself had visualized that normative laws are valid till the boundary conditions laid down by social needs remain the same. Two Finnish librareans Kuronen and Pekkarinen have given the example that Newtonian physics is valid only with small masses and velocity. In the space travel era these laws are subsumed by the theory of relativity. Take a social example, huge information with fast communication have changed the face of national and international money markets. "The amount of money transacted in international money market is at least hundred times greater than that in real economy". A similar situation occurs when the information-which is instant power- flows globally and is delivered or accessed at the speed of light. The five laws though still valid do not seem sufficient. These Finnish authors with arguments have proposed two new laws in their various writings. [22, 23, 24]. These are:

6th Law: Every reader his library.

7th Law: Every writer his contribution to the library.

Here, the reader means a searcher, and library means the virtual variety.

First Law: Information is for use. It signifies availability of information and removal of barriers in its use. Information being a prime mover of the information society is the most valuable commodity and an economic asset. Information and knowledge industry employs more than the 65% of the labour force in advance economies. It has devised methods and policies for the acquisition and free flow of information overcoming the barrier of time and space. Information marketing and Knowledge Management square well with this law. The superhighway of information at the moment is the highest manifestation of the 1st law. Inter and intra-national digital divide is a matter of serious concern for all of us. Next comes the formulation of information policies-which India still does not have to our great national disadvantage and embarrassment. We do not have any policy to harness, utilise and control our greatest asset and resource. As a national we are somewhat flouting this law. Libraries need to play a role in the development of national information infrastructure.

Second Law : Information is for all and sundry. Virtual library is an individual oriented library. Further to availability it ensures accessibility of information. Information is a social commodity which needs a producer and consumer. Different channels of information TV, cable TV, DHT TV, cell phones, networks especially the Internet, intranets, LAN ensure information for all in a democratic way. In face of information overload, it is mandatory to customize information to suit individual needs. Information literacy programmes, IFLA's UAP are a step in this direction. E-books, navigation systems, and digitisation programmes support this law. This law recommends users studies and education programmes. Search engines, subject gateways, e-mails, bulletin boards ensure information for all. Virtual library provides simultaneous access to numerous documents through intelligent agents. IT has come as a great boon for physically or mentally challenged, and geographically isolated and socially disadvantaged.

Third Law: Every byte of information its user. Second and third laws are based on democracy and service, respectively, Third Law, which supplements the first two laws, ensures usability of information. Information is effective when it is used. There are two users of information: a) Computers, b) Human Beings. With use it multiplies and produces knowledge which in turn produces wealth. In the market it is a commodity strictly governed by the demand-supply law. Economic value of information ensures its effective use. No information will be generated for which there is no demand. All the present research on user studies is to ensure the generation of that information for which there are likely anticipated users. Marketing of information products for services is in fulfilment of this law. Libraries have to be proactive in their services to promote the use of existing information.

Fourth law: Save the time of the netizens is to ensure timely information. Time is the most scarce, exhaustible and unreplenishable resource. All the information storage and communication technology is geared to save time. As the information grows exponentially, so quickly it becomes obsolete. So timely supply of information makes the differences in this competitive world. To save the time of the staff the policies are outsourcing, becoming a member of a network, consortia or a bibliographic utility like OCLC, OPACs offer a single interface to numerous databases with seamless integration of print and electronic sources save time of the user..CCF, MARC21, Metadata and various Markup Languages help standardization. Technology convergence is a great time saver. New tools and techniques are required to organise electronic knowledge for its timely delivery and organised packages.

Fifth law: Library is a trinity of users, staff and collection. This law has a holistic approach. Information is growing with a tremendous rate. Information from the very beginning has the property of growing, multiplying and improving qualitatively. The information revolution, we are witnessing, is the highest manifestation of this law. Knowledge grows as the society grows and vice versa. Growth of knowledge and social change are intertwined-and cannot be seen separately. Growth is diversity in time. In that way it is linked with the 4th law. FW Lancaster's famous thesis of paperless libraries ensues from this law.[25] Not only new information and subjects are emerging, new media and communication services too are growing. Content Management (CM) is the technique developed to combat with ever changing information on the web and intranets. The virtual library is at the apex of this growth.[26]

INADEQUACY OF THE LAWS

But the laws are bit inadequate in face of high speed and flow of huge quantities of information, changing modes of it organisation storage, access and communication. Ease of reproduction and remote access require new proprietary (IPR) laws. The two new laws proposed by the Finnish colleagues deserve serious consideration for their wide and insightful dimensions of the information society. The dwell on the new cooperative and interactive relations between the users and the documents of the virtual library.

Sixth Law: Every reader his library. It is a supplement of the second law that is every reader his book. The new technology allows a searcher to navigate through and configure his set of information scattered in the cyber space. It recognizes reader's right and liberty to an individual library: librarians are obliged to recognize individual searcher as the centre of the new library and to empower them accordingly.

Seventh law: Every writer his contribution to the library. The era of irrespressible information with free flow provides means to each author to a virtual library. It demands reader's participation in building and managing the library. It is in turn deals with the individual's freedom of expression-a right more practically exercisable than in print media. This law guarantees in practice the freedom of opinion and expression. In the age of telecommunications expression usually takes the electronic form. The line between expression and publishing is blurring specially using markup languages. It in fact strengths democracy.

If accepted, detailed implications of these laws need to be further worked out.

It is obvious that information science, more than the library science, has made the value of the laws quite tangible and their application more apparent. This shows Ranganathan's rationality of approach and his far vision. The Laws might as well find their tangible validation in the knowledge and wisdom society of the future.

REFERENCES

1. Yogeswar, Ranganathan, *S.R. Ranaganathan, pragmatic philosopher,* Mumbai: Bharti Vidhya Bhavan, 2001, pp.38-58.
2. Ranganathan, S.R. *The five laws of library science,* 2nd ed. Mumbai: Asia, 1963, p.362.
3. Ranganathan, S.R. "*Library science and its development*".

In: *Souvenir,* State Book Festival in Ambala State Library, 1966, pp.5-8.

4. Ranganathan, S.R. *Prologomena to library classification,* 3rd ed./ed. by M.A. Gopinath, Mumbai: Asia, 1967, Chap DB, pp.115-122.
5. Cochrane, Pauline "Dr. S.R. Ranganathan" *Lib. res & tech. serv.* 14 (4) Fall 1979: 582-584.
6. Liu, J. "The 5 laws of library science in China today". *Jl of inf. comm. & lib. sci.* 4 (3) 1998: 68-73 (Describes in Chinese language the implications of Ranganathan's laws in China).
7. Sen, B.K. "Five laws of library science?" *Iaslic bulletin* 47 (3) Sept. 2002: 121-140.
8. Achinstein, Peter. *Law and explanation: an essay in philosophy of science.* Oxford: OUP, 1971, pp.5-14.
9. Satija, M.P. *S.R. Ranganathan and the method of science.* New Delhi: Aditya, 1992, pp.98-103.
10. Ranganathan S.R. "Documentation" In : *Social science research and libraries/ed.* by Girja Kumar. Mumbai: Asia, 1960, p.116.
11. Lancaster, F.W. *If you want to evaluate your library....* London: LA, 1988, p.8.
12. World Bank. *The Task Force on Higher Education and Society. Higher education in developing countries: peril and promose.* Washington, D.C.: The Bank, 2000, p.35.
13. Gill, Sucha Singh. In: The Tribune (Chandigarh), dated 14 Dec. 2002, p.12.
14. Hettige, S.T. *Globalisation, social change and youth.* Colombo: German Cultural Institute, 1998, p.8.
15. Girja Kumar. Professor S. Dasgupta Memorial Lecture (5th: 2002: *Delhi Library Association*), p.9.
16. Toffler, Alvin, *Powershift: knowledge, wealth and violence at the edge of the 21st century.* New York: Bantam Books, 1991, pp.232-234.

17. Satija, M.P. "Digital information and services". Introductory address given as Director Thematic sessions. National Laslic Seminar (20: 2002: *Patiala*).

18. Brerude, R.M. "Virtual or actual: the term library is enough" *Bull of Med lib. Assn.* 87 (1) 1995: 85-87.

19. Martel, Charles. "Going, going, gone" *Jl acd. libship.* 25 (3), May 1999: 224-25.

20. Witten, Ian *et al.*, "The promise of digital libraries in developing countries". *The electronic library.* 20(1), 2002: 7-13.

21. Toffler, Alvin. "Tommorrow's economy" *India Today* 28 (11) March 11-17, 2003, p.28.

22. Kuronen, Timo and Pekkarinen, Paivi. "Ranganathan's five laws of library science revisited: the challenge of the virtual library" *Herald of lib. sc.* 35(1/2) Jan/April 1996:3-17.

23. Kuronen, Timo and Pekkarinen, Paivi. "Ranganathan's revisited: a review article" *Jl of libship & inf. sci.* 31(1) March 1999: 45-48.

24. Pekkarinen, Paivi. "On 'new' Ranganathan laws for structuring the content of the virtual library" In: International Study Conference on Classification Research (*6th: 1997: London*), pp.144-146.

25. Lancester, F.W. "Library is a growing organism". In: *Ranganathan's philosophy/ ed.* by T.S. Rajagopalan. New Delhi: Vikas, 1986, pp.51-53.

26. Gorman, Michael, *Our enduring values: librarianship in the 21st century*. Chicago: ALA, 2000, p.18-19.

27. Sharma, S.L. "Globalisation and socio-cultural discontents". *Social Sciences Research Jl*, 10(3), 2002: 69-84.

2

Professional Education for Digital Librarianship

Prof. C.A. Augustine
Former Head
Department of Library and Information Science
University of Kerala, Thiruvananthapuram

INTRODUCTION

While writing in July 2000 for the Prof. K.A. Isaac Festschrift volume (Devarajan, 2000) the author discussed the 'digital revolution syndrome'. By 'digital revolution' he meant the contemporary developments in fields of electronics and communication that opened up enormous possibilities for recording, storing, transmitting and accessing intelligible information in a variety of digital forms, like texts, still images, moving images, sounds and/or any of their combinations. The word 'syndrome', was borrowed from medical field where it denoted "concurrence of symptoms, characteristics, patterns of behaviour, happenings, feelings, options, actions and the like pointing towards the incidence of some desease and the anxieties and fears arising there from". The expression 'digital revolution syndrome' was aimed at pointing towards the unnecessary anxieties and fears born on this rapid spread of digital information networks among those who have been handling until now mainly other forms of recorded communication, like people engaged in the fields of library, archive and documentation. Today, only after about four years from then, while writing for the Prof. M. Parameswaran Festschrift volume those anxieties and apprehensions of people have almost come true, so to say that it is no more a syndrome than a disease which is fast spreading in the library and information profession. The seriousness of this disease varies according to local environments. The impact was felt either as a virtual surrender of the concerned minds to the new situation in total disregard to their past practices and achievements, or as a state of disillusionment and frustration arising from incompatibility and incompetence of persons, and all traumas in that connection. What can be done to restore the health of our profession by ways of prevention and cure. This ought to be a subject of direct concern for library schools and professional organizations in a country like India who was emotionally immature to accept such drastic changes in information communication and knowledge.

SENTIMENTS FOR THE OLD

Library schools in India, by and large, are confounded by some confusion. Much enamoured of new concepts and technologies with their prospects in library and information system (LIS) management they are, at the same time, unwilling to part with the traditional methods and practices. This may be partly due to their deep sentiments centering round the great Indian luminary, Dr. S.R. Ranganathan, whose contributions in systematizing the discipline of librarianship and elevating it to the status of a science have been very much fundamental and unique. Many seniors in Indian library profession consider this legacy as a matter of great pride and carry the same even to international library fronts. In this perspective it comes natural that leaders of the profession involved in curriculum planning and revision in library schools are obsessed to the old and resisting drastic changes towards the new. Such decisions often make our course programmes hotchpotches without due conformity to the needs of the contemporary profession or any international standards.

IMBALANCE IN LIBRARY MODERNIZATION

The confusion confounding Indian library schools is partly also due to the fact that libraries and information centers in India are not growing alike with respect to modernization. Many of our libraries are old fashioned and they still continue with the traditional methods of library operations and services. Almost all of our public and academic libraries fall in this category. In university and college libraries the induction of the new information and communication technology (ICT) has been done only as an appendage for prestige. ICT has not yet duly integrated into the library operations and services or have replaced fully the traditional techniques and methods. In the case of the special libraries, especially the science / industrial / research libraries the degree of modernization varies from a wholly manually operated library to an almost fully computerized library situation. Our public libraries are almost wholly book lending libraries with reading rooms.

NEED FOR A TWO STREAM LIBRARY EDUCATION

The main difficulty with library schools in India is that they are not in a position to design and conduct specialized courses for different types and levels of libraries and the diverse positions. The present practice is to conduct generalist courses intended to produce librarians for all libraries, and in that process they fail to produce the required expertise for different library positions of modern times. It is high time that our LIS courses are designed and conducted in response to the market need for different positions, separately. A dichotomy into Library Management courses and Information Management courses looks a reasonable proposition. In accordance with this division, LIS positions have to be viewed as belonging to two separate cadres and the qualifications and experience for positions in each cadre/stream need to be prescribed differently. A new classification of LIS positions has to be evolved with their portfolios and qualifications. Course programmes have to be designed and conducted specifically for each of these jobs.

LIS TOP MANAGEMENT

At present, library hands with the prescribed minimum qualifications join at the lowest position and go up the ladder through automatic promotions according to seniority-cum-merit. This is so almost in all public sector institutions with statutory tenure of service. One danger inherent in this system is that when the senior most person comes up to the top management position where sophisticated library/information operations and services have to be planned, implemented or managed he/she becomes a square peg in a round hole. In many cases we come across incompetent hands heading LIS institutions with great potential for development and taking them to ruins. What we are lacking in is the right professional leadership. The fact that six out of the seven university libraries in Kerala have been without the due leadership of university librarians for a very long time now, explains why the academic libraries in the State could not go ahead with the modernization targeted by the nation.

The twofold qualifications and competence required of top management positions in LIS are namely in management techniques and in ICT applications. The old practice of library positions getting equated with teaching /academic positions in all respects does not gain much ground in the modern context. Chief librarians unlike their teacher counter parts have to do more with management of men, materials and money than with anything else.

IMPORTANCE OF ICT

The new challenges for LIS profession are born out of the unprecedented opportunities opened up by the recent developments in ICT. The challenge of ICT generally is well described by a UN High Level Panel Report (UN, 2000). It reads:

"The world is undergoing a revolution in information and communication technologies (ICT) that has momentous implications for the current and future economic and social situation of all the countries of the world.

In March 2000, an estimated 276 million persons worldwide were users of the Internet, with a growth rate of roughly 150,000 persons per day, 220 million devices were accessing the World Wide Web and almost 200,000 devices were added each day. Web pages totalled 1.5 billion with almost 2 million pages being added each day. E-commerce, or business conducted over Internet, totalled $45 billion as recently as 1998 and an estimate in January 2000 projected it could explode to over $7 trillion as early as 2004.

These are astonishing figures, unprecedented by any measure, but they reflect activity by less than 5 per cent of the world's population. The gross disparity in the spread of the Internet and thus the economic and social benefits derived from it is a matter of profound concern. There are more hosts in New York than in continental Africa; more hosts in Finland than in Latin America and the Caribbean; and notwithstanding the remarkable progress in the application of ICT in India, many of its villages still lack a working telephone.

The formidable and urgent challenge before national Governments and the development community is to bridge this divide and connect the remainder of the world's population whose livelihoods can be enhanced through ICT. As each day passes, the task becomes much more difficult. To give just one example, exploding e-commerce ties individuals, firms, and countries closer and closer together, while those who do not try to catch the "Internet Express" run the risk of being further and further marginalized. Developing countries have great potential to compete successfully in the new global market, but unless they embrace the ICT revolution promptly and actively, they will face new barriers and the risk of not just being marginalized but completely bypassed" (Report of the High-Level Panel on Information and Communication Technology. New York, 17-20 April 2000).

The estimates given above, having been made in 2000, by the same rate of growth per year might have grown much larger by now. Thus, as on March 2004, there might be 495 million users, 512 million devices and 4.4 billion web pages. The points made in the above passage are almost equally relevant to the development of LIS in India since ICT is a proven instrument for information management. One should not wonder if at all future library managers are drawn from ICT experts in total disregard of LIS background. Such a situation must be avoided at all costs in the interest of the LIS profession. This should be the focal point of all curriculum design and development efforts in library schools of India.

EDUCATION OF DIGITAL AGE LIBRARIANS

Many hold the strong view that the basic concepts and methods of traditional librarianship are equally relevant and applicable in digital librarianship also. This view cannot be totally disputed, especially in view of the philosophic and scientific base that traditional librarianship could establish and maintain. But in the cases of the digital librarianship there are also many other things one should know and master. This knowledge relates to mainly two areas: collection development of digital resources, and services with digital resources. It is the purpose of this paper to deal generally with the first area, namely, the digital resources collection development.

DIGITAL RESOURCES COLLECTION DEVELOPMENT

What constitute 'digital resources'? 'Digital' is a generic description of anything held in electronic format. At a closer look one may find a distinction between 'digital' and 'electronic', but for the purpose of this paper, the two terms are used inter changeably.

By definition, therefore, 'digital resources' means "any electronic product that delivers a collection of data, be it text, numerical, geographical or time based, as a commercially available title". They may include full text bases, electronic journals, image collections, other multimedia products, and of course, collections of numerical data, delivered on CD-ROM, on tape, via the internet, and so on" (Stuart De Lee, 2002).

Another significant term with more or less the same connotation is 'e-information' which has been defined by the International Coalition of Library Consortia (1998) as follows: "a broad term that encompasses abstracting and indexing services, electronic journals and other full text materials, the offerings of information aggregators, article delivery services, etc. E-information can be accessed via remote networks from information providers, or locally mounted by a consortium or one of its member libraries."

SOME PECULIARITIES

There are differences in dealing with digital resources from print resources in the matter of collection development. Although the basic steps involved in collection building may be the same in both cases, digital resources present special problems and warrant strategic approaches. Some of these peculiarities are listed below:

(a) Digital resources are marketed very often directly to individuals bypassing the librarian and the collection development policy of the institution.

(b) Digital resources, except the freely accessible internet sites, are mostly high cost items. Their price fluctuations are also unpredictable. Both these features can upset the normal budgeting decisions.

(c) Digital resources being widely advertised among targeted individuals it becomes difficult for the librarian to withstand the pressure put on him by them and to decide after duly evaluating the quality of the product against its cost implications. There may be also hidden costs behind them in the form of new hardware and/or software.

(d) In the case of e-journals very often the subscriptions or price tags are tied together with their print versions.

(e) Providing online access to the required digital resources may imply membership in networking, user names and passwords, remote access, integration with existing catalogues, platform dependencies, etc.

(f) Digital resources enable monitoring their use easier than print materials and therefore decisions regarding their onward subscriptions or retention on the server can be taken appropriately.

THE DIGITAL RESOURCES LANDSCAPE

Collection development in digital resources has to deal with three different categories of items produced by digital publishers (Lancaster,1995):

(a) texts available in electronic form where the electronic version is the exact equivalent of a paper version already available;

(b) texts available only in electronic form with the print on paper displayed electronically but with various 'value added features' like search and data manipulation capabilities; and

(c) completely new publications having the state of the art capabilities of electronics, like hypertext, hyper media, and other multimedia features

(d) There is a large variety of digital resources available for consideration of any collection builder. Those who are new to the field should be provided with an overview of the products and the problems they will have to encounter. The Distributed National Electronic Resource (DNER) of UK has mapped out the electronic resources landscape as follows:

* Journals,
* Images,
* Moving images and audio,
* Geospatial data,
* e-Books,
* Learning materials,
* Discovery tools, and
* Research data

The above listed categories may not be mutually exclusive, meaning thereby that one and the same item may come under more than one category. Some resources have only the data whereas others may have the data combined with interface; there can be remote services or local provision of services; and there can be items that are services as well as that are products. The following, perhaps, is a more or less understandable picture of the electronic resources landscape:

Abstracting and indexing services and other bibliographic sources (like OPAC, citation index, Table of Contents, etc.), Numerical Collections and textbase, e-Journals, e-Books, Multimedia products, and News services.

Each of the above listed items may have some particular nuances and present peculiar problems that may usually emerge when deciding to acquire.

ASSESSMENT OF DIGITAL ITEMS

Besides awareness about the range of products and their peculiarities the collection builder must have opportunity for their trials and evaluation so that the priority in procurement of each product could be fixed. An initial assessment of each item is necessary on the basis of the basic criteria, like cost, content and capability. The capability to deliver the product satisfactorily to the end user includes the technical capability in terms of networks, servers, client machines, authentication systems, and so on. It is desirable to have this evaluation done by involving a panel of experts representing subject specialists, technology people, end users, interface people, and administrative personnel.

12. Licensing issues

Negotiating the license is another important task in collection building. Licenses are subject to negotiation based on the bargaining power of the institution. The contract to be signed at the time of purchase will detail the responsibilities and obligations of the provider and the buyer. There are several things the digital librarian ought to know and ensure. The license should guarantee a satisfactory quality of service for the subscriber, and it should be clear as to what is allowed and what is not allowed by both parties. All terms and conditions should be clearly spelt out including hidden charge, if any, retrospective costs, etc. The license should clearly state how long the subscriber is tied to the deal, and what options are open for cancelling the subscription, if needed, and for renewal of the license in future.

Perhaps the most crucial part of license negotiation, but at the same time the most difficult to finalize, is the price structure in which there is always scope for a bargain. There are several models of pricing in force. In essence, the choice lies between a one-off fee (i.e. outright buying of the ownership of the product for use locally) and a recurrent fee (i.e. a lease license or subsrciption). The latter covers the cost of up-gradation also. Some may offer even a combination of both the models.

DELIVERY OF THE RESOURCES

Releasing the digital materials as quickly as possible for use is of top priority. But, when mounted on the local server, they may present problems of incompatibility of networks, software, hardware, etc. These problems have to be overcome. The digital materials have to be integrated into some system by which the readers can easily find and access them. Most institutions that build up digital collections tend to provide a central catalogue which also acts as a means of direct access. There are two approaches to cataloguing digital products. One is a gateway and the other is integration with existing catalogues. The former aggregates the electronic resources from the main collection and present them side by side with the print collection in the library catalogue A gateway is simply the index of all the electronic resources available. This goes against the proposition that electronic resource collection should also be seen as a part of, and not separate from, traditional collection development. Traditional systems such as MARC are being used to catalogue electronic resources. We might envisage a scenario whereby the user searching the OPAC will locate electronic as well as print resources.

DATA ARCHIVING

Along with delivering the electronic resources for use there ought to be the archiving of every new item. When dealing with large quantities of data a high storage and secure back up service is very much advisable.

INTERNET RESOURCES

The ease of dissemination of information via the internet has resulted in an unimaginable quantity and variety of sources of potential interest to any internet user. But the problems faced by users are very serious. The most serious is the Information Overload. There is too much information to sift through and utilize in any meaningful way. Another problem is the doubtful quality of information accessed. Any one, anywhere with access to the internet, can now become an author and their own publisher. Therefore, without the constraints imposed by the publishing trade, huge volumes of junk are being produced. Because of this much of the information available via the internet are potentially useless. They may even be inaccurate and misleading. Thus, while the internet can often prove to be a valuable source of information, it can also be a sheer waste of time as it gives information which is often useless, outdated or difficult to authenticate.

The situation warrants that there is need for somebody who can help serious end users in searching for quality information and in filtering through materials and assessing their quality once they have been found. This is the ideal role of the digital librarian. For fulfilling this role he needs to be educated:

- in using search facilities that can maximize the quality of information retrieved;
- in assessing the quality of an information source;
- in evaluating particular types of sources; and
- in using checklists, kitemarks, and other quality indicators (Cooke, 2001).

Search facilities can be broadly grouped as (a) search engines, (b) gateways and virtual libraries, (c) subject catalogues and directory services, and (d) other search tools. Search facilities falling under each of these categories have their advantages and disadvantages when put to specific purposes.

The quality of internet information has to be assessed according to its source, in terms of its coverage, authority and reputation, accuracy, currency and maintenance, accessibility, presentation and arrangement of information, ease of use, etc. Several different types of checklists and rating tools are being used in evaluating the quality of internet information. Some of these tools have only questionable validity. Kite marks and seals of approval are used, and they take the form of badge or logo displayed on internet resources. These are certifications of third party approval of information based on a particular set of standards. For example, the two badges awarded by Quality Search Engine are used to indicate sites are 'QSE certified Child Safe'. The 'CIN Seal of Approval' badge used to indicate sites containing no pornography or any type of questionable content. The 'Internet Seal of Approval' log indicates that an organization has met rigorous standards of quality, honesty, and customer services, and works had to establish high standards of integrity for Internet Commerce. Among kite marks or seals of approval, of special interest are those developed in the area of health and medical information in the internet. The HoN Code of the Health on the Net Foundation launched in 1996 and the logo issued by them is being observed as a check against dubious Web sites (Cooke, 2001).

CONSERVATION OF INTERNET RESOURCES

Internet being a source of tremendous downpour of information, both good and bad, digital librarian can access, validate and archive whatever that are found to be useful for the institutions and its end users. There are now techniques like Data Mining, and Data Warehousing in use among LIS professionals. Their wider application will lead to creation of new subject catalogues, and directories as well as gateways and virtual libraries with the authentication or certification of their parent institutions.

DIGITAL IMAGING TECHNIQUES AND PROCEDURES

In building up digital collections, next to acquiring published digital resources and archiving internet resources, comes the relevance of digital conversion of locally available non-digital resources. A library or its parent institution may have a commitment in which the conservation of the old and rare documents in various physical formats will become desirable or even unavoidable. For example, the digital conversion of various traditional knowledge sources, both in print and manuscripts, in local languages, various cultural artifacts, folk arts and literature, etc. may become crucial to an institution identified with history, culture, indigenous medicine, etc.

The digital librarian ought to be having adequate exposure to the state-of-the-art techniques and procedures in digital imaging. Such exposure is invariable whether the work of digitization is to be got done through outsourcing or through in-house operation.

ORGANIZING MULTIMEDIA RESOURCES

The multimedia resources pose many problems and challenges for information storage and retrieval. 'Multimedia, according to the more modern definition, is the integrated storage, retrieval and display of words, numbers, images and sounds by a computer system' (Burke, 1999). The component media which may include 'items or 'objects' like text, graphics, animation, speech, music and video are to be managed in a multimedia database where the ability to retrieve an individual item or groups of items with specific characteristics is a key function. Full multimedia systems are dependent on digital technology, and this will be the trend in systems of the future, although at the present there are also multimedia systems which have some components stored on analogue media such as videotape, analogue video disks, non-digital cassette tapes, etc. The development of the mass storage systems using CD-ROMs, and the explosive growth of the internet-based information sources have pressed in the knowledge of information storage and retrieval using multimedia as an essential perquisite for a digital librarians.

CONCLUSION

The author has tried to bring out a case for a full-fledged

and specialized education and training for librarians in digital libraries. It is practically impossible for our library schools to produce professional manpower required for both the traditional non-digital libraries and the modern digital libraries. To attempt to do so will be doing injustice to both the needs. What is suggested here is a two-streamed library education, one with emphasis on Library Management and the other with emphasis on Information Management. It is with the latter that digital librarianship must be identified. The main areas of expertise that should go into the collection development aspect in the education of digital librarians are discussed in this paper.

BIBLIOGRAPHY AND REFERENCES

Association of Research Libraries (USA) (1997), Principles for licensing electronic resources www.arl.org/scomm/licsensing/princliples.html

Atherton, N. (2001), Electronic content via the internet: access and exploitation, Managing Information, 65: Jan-Feb.

Augustine, C.A. (2000), 'Digital revolution syndrome' in Devarajan, D. Ed. New Challenges in librarianship, Ess Ess Publishers.

Burke, Mary A. (1999), Organization of multimedia resources; principles and practice of information retrieval, Gower Publishing.

Cooke, Alison (2001), A guide to finding quality information on the internet; selection and evaluation strategies, edn.2, Library Association Publishing.

Devarajan, D. Ed.(2000), New challenges in librarianship, Ess Ess Publishers.

Dickinson, G.K. (1994), Selection and evaluation of electronic resources, Libraries Unlimited Inc.

Emory University General Libraries, Collection development policy: electronic formats http://academic.uofs.edu/organization/codes/emory.html

Flaxbart, D. (2001), Collection development in the internet age:

an introduction, Issues in Science and Technology Librarianship, Spring.

George, V.L. (2000), Selecting and managing electronic resources; a how-to-do-it manual for librarians, Neal-Schuman Publishers.

Haar, J (1990), 'Choosing CD-ROM products', College and Rsearch Libraries News, 51 (9), 839-41).

Hanka, R. and Fuka, K. (2000), 'Information overload and 'just-in-time' knowledge', The Electronic Library 18(4), 279-84.

Holleman, C. (2002), 'Electronic resources: are basic criteria for the selection of material changing?' Library Trends, 48(4), 694-710.

International Coalition of Library Consortia (1998), Statement of current perspective and preferred practice for the selection and purchase of electronic information.www.library.yale.edu/consortia/statement.html

ISBD(ER): International Standard Bibliographic Description for Electronic Resources http://ifla.inist.fr/VII/s13/pubs/isbd.html

Kidd, T. and Rees-Jones, L. Eds. (2000), The serials management handbook; a practical guide to print and electronic serials management, Library Association Publishing.

Kovacs, D. (2000), Building electronic library collections: the essential guide to selection criteria and core subject collections, Neal-Schuman Publishers.

Lancaster, F.W.(1995), 'The evolution of electronic publishing' Library Trends, 43 (4), 518-27.

Laurence, H. and Miller, W. (2000), Academic research on the internet; options for scholars and librarians, Haworth; Information Press.

Lee, Stuart D. (2000), Digital imaging: a practical handbook, Library Association Publishing.

Lee, Stuart D. (2002), Building an electronic resource collection; a practical guide, Library Association Publishing.

Lee, S.H. Ed. (1999), Collection development in the electronic environment; shifting priorities, Haworth Information Press.

Metz, P. (2000), 'Principles of selection for electronic resources', Library Trends, 48(4), 711-29.

Meyers, B (1996), 'Electronic publishing: a brief history and some current activities', IP News, Fall.

Pedley, P. (2000), 'Electronic journals', Managing Information, 61: Jan-Feb.

Stein, S.D. (1999), Learning, Teaching and Researching on the Internet: a practical guide for social scientists, Longman.

United Nations (2000), Report of the UN High- Level Panel on Information and Communication Technology.

Weihs, J.R. (1991), The integrated library: encouraging access to multimedia materials, edn.2, Orysx Press.

Weitz, J, (2000), Cataloguing electronic resources: OCLC-MARC coding guidelines www.oclc.org/oclc/cataloging/type.html

Yin Zhang (2001), 'Scholarly use of internet-based electronic resources', Journal of the American Society for Information Science and Technology, 52(8).

3

Impact of Information Technology on Libraries

Rajashekhar D. Kumbar

Librarian

Jansons School of Business

Karumathampatti,

Coimbatore – 641 659

INTRODUCTION

We are passing through an era of rapid technological and socio-economical changes. The aura of such changes makes us believe that we are living in an information society. The technological revolution during the last five decades has made tremendous impact on the way, how information is processed, stored, retrieved and disseminated. Believe it or not, admit it or not, the growth and development of Information Technology (IT) are one of the most significant achievements of the present century. Access to IT is limited- few people have seen these, even fewer used these, and fewest yet understood these. The IT by now is recognized all over the world as an instrument of progress. IT is considered being as one of the current key factor in shaping the present societies and to formulate policies for future.

Innovations and developments in communication technology,

networking and computer-based information systems and services have paved the way for the distribution of information from the producer of information to the consumer of information in a very fast and effective way. Minimizing the cost of information at the generation, storing and supply levels IT play an important role in the design of information systems, process of communication, information seeking behaviour of the users of the information. Information is the basic ingredient that contributes significantly for the continuous growth of research and development (R&D) activities. India being a developing country, much of its development, particularly in Science & Technology depends upon the availability, accessibility and dissemination of right information to the right users at right time, pin pointedly, expeditiously and exhaustively.

INFORMATION TECHNOLOGY

IT is generic term used to denote all activities connected with computer based processing, storage and transfer of information. The term IT represents ensemble of technologies which are ability to store, process and disseminate the information. IT is a catchall term used to describe products and services created by rapid changes in computer in communication technologies and their fusion together. IT is the new science of collecting, processing, storing and transmitting electronically the information which is the life-blood of complex industrial societies and it is growing in importance. The benefits of computers can only be realized through modern communication networks, which of course can only be build with the help of computers. They are totally inter-dependent in fact we may say that the two have become almost inseparable in the present ever- growing information society. The information technologies have revolutionized or in facts completely transformed the concept of a library. Library is no longer a storehouse of information. The optimum utilization of the library resources could only be achieved by integrating library databases in a network connecting all the constituent units of the organization.

NEED FOR INFORMATION TECHNOLOGY

Information recorded is static unless, it is used. The use of information makes it kinetic and generates more knowledge. Thus, science and technology rests firmly on foundation laid by the information generated in the past, effectiveness of future and efficiency of present information transfer. Further, the need for technology arises partly due to the concept of multimedia. The conventional printed book is taking up other form such as microfilm, microform, sound record, and computer tapes, Which require special equipment for their processing and partly to meet the requirement of fast and accurate information and its transfer, over long distances. Paperless information centers are fast emerging with advancement of technology the benefits like fast and easy access to information, lesser storage space offered by electronics and optical media have attracted the attention of library management.

THE DEVELOPMENT IN INFORMATION TECHNOLOGY

There are three distinct strands namely computers, microelectronics and communication technology in the development of IT. Today there has been a convergence of these technologies by using different sophisticated equipment to carry out all the tasks. It becomes difficult to think at present that those were quite separate operations in the past. However, looking at the historical background of IT, we need to treat basically in three different aspects, namely-

a. Development of technology for recording and storing data,

b. Development of technology for analysis and process of data, and

c. Development of communication technology.

All these three aspects have gone through well-defined stages of development which correspond to man's over all technological development. These stages include manual, mechanical, electronic and electromechanical methods.

Technological Development in Recording and Storage of Data

The storage media used at various times in history has determined the development in storing and recording. They include clay tablets, paper, punched cards, electronic media etc. The present development in IT has sprung up on the paper medium. It is an ideal medium for recording large quantities of information. Information is recorded on the paper with the help of manual, mechanical, electromechanical and electronic methods. Information can be arranged in a systematic order on a paper, but it occupies more space and not able to record audio form of information, machine can not read the information easily preserved on paper. The next major development in recording and storing is the punched card. During the early 19th century data are stored and recorded by holes punched in cards and such recorded data are to be read by electromechanical machines. Thus a new storage media during the 19th century was conceived and developed like microfilm, microfiche, and microcard. These storage media are machine readable, small in size but with more storing capacity and consume less space. To achieve these advantages magnetic storage media developed which are known as floppy disks, hard disk and magnetic tape. Thus another new technology i.e. CD- ROM was developed for storage of data during 1980s. CD-ROM is the abbreviation of Compact Disk Read-only Memory. It is a high capacity optical storage device of 12-cm diameter which can store up to 650 MB of information. It provides high capacity at a comparatively low cost and single manufactures standard for sound recording and computer data storage. But it is a read-only medium and data can not be rewritten on them for updating purpose. Currently developed Digital Versatile Disk or Digital Video Disk (DVD) is a new optical storage technology having a large capacity CD with advanced multimedia support with at least seven times the storage capacity of CD-ROM and can be manufactured with about the same price. DVD technology consists of five different formats -DVD Video, DVD-Audio, DVD- ROM; DVD-R, DVD-RAM. DVD-RAM drives allow rewriting DVD-RAM disks many times. Thus storage and recording technology has developed from the clay tablets to the DVD technology in terms of increasing storage capacity, easier portability, long-life span and reduction in size and cost.

Technological Development in the Analysis and Process of Data

The task of analyzing data includes both calculating and comparing. A primitive form of abacus was used in ancient Greece and Egypt, and consisted rows of beads laid out in grooven or threaded on wires. Numbers were represented by pushing beads to the results of the side of the wires. It performed only addition, subtraction and multification. These mathematical operations were possible when the value of number falls between zero to ten. Sir Charles Babbage, who designed the first computer in the year 1833, used an early type of punched card to enter and store the data. Mechanical and electromechanical devices are not able to perform ballistic calculations and take more time for ordinary calculations. This gave rise to the development of electronic digital computer. Modern electronic digital computer systems have gone through five generations of evolution. The first generation of computers was designed in the late 1940s and early 1950s. Use of binary notation (i.e. 0 and 1) as machine language, use of vacuum tubes for the central processor construction and magnetic core devices for stored programs are some of the important features of the machines in the first generations of computers. IBM650, ENIAC, MARK-I, EDSAC, UNIVAC and EDVAC belong to the first generation computers. These computers were very costly in terms of production as well as maintenance. The second-generation computers came in to being in the early 1960s with the advent of transistor technology. Transistors are semiconductor devices that are functionally equivalent to vacuum tubes but smaller in size, consume much less power and are far more reliable compared to the vacuum tubes. The Third generation computers were developed using integrated circuits (ICs) in the early 1970s. The new technologies further reduced the size of computer and power consumption of computers and also improved the reliability. The development of high level language also provided better human machine interface. The Fourth generation computers came into existence during early 1980s with high technology like small-scale integration (SSI), medium scale integration (MSI), large-scale integration (LSI) and very large scale integration (VLSL). The development of VLSI led to the emergence of microprocessor, which constitutes the entire central processing unit [CPU] on a single chip. Computers built with microprocessors are known as microcomputers. Two major manufacturers of microprocessor emerged in the field: Motorola Inc and Intel Corporation. IBM adopted Intel series of microprocessor for their personal computers (PCs). The latest chip from Intel Corporation is known as 'Pentium'. On the basis of microprocessor number, the PCs are named like PC/XT, PC/AT, Pentium, Pentium II, Pentium III, Pentium IV and the like. PCs and Super computers come under fourth generation. These computers have large storage capacity, memory, speed, accuracy and diligence. The fifth generation of computers came in to being in the early 1990s with desire to handle sophisticated non-numeric applications such as pattern or speech recognition, knowledge processing etc. It includes Inference Engines, Knowledge bases, Natural language Inference, Photonic devices and computing in optical domain.

Technological Development of Communication Technology

One can preserve, store and process the information through storage and processing technology but the dissemination of information can be only through communication technology. The power and importance of information can enhance with the help of communication technology. The development of communication technology related to development of all these technologies which are communicating and disseminating the information. Telecommunication means communication at a distance based upon the transmission of electromagnetic signals. The development in communication technology is based on the following aspects:

* Messenger and Portal services
* Mechanical and Electromechanical system

* Telephone and related system
* Digital telecommunication system

FACETS OF INFORMATION TECHNOLOGY

IT is a comprehensive term used for all the activities connected with computer based processing, storage and transfer of information. It involves computers, electronic media, satellite, and telecommunication and mass storage devices. IT does not confine only to hardware and software but it also covers the techniques and methods used for collection, storage, processing and dissemination of information. The IT can be grouped in the following areas: Communication technology, Networking technology, Reprographic and Micrographic technologies, Storage technology, Barcode technology and Multimedia, etc.

Communication Technology

Telecommunications technology refers to the transmission of data as represented by electronic signals and to the hardware, software and procedures that make it possible. The emerging trends in telecommunication play a pivotal role in dissemination of information. Data communication refers to the means and methods where by data is transferred between the processing locations. The link permits a direct interactive bond between the people at the workstations and central processing system.

Networking Technology

The conglomerations of computers, databases and telecommunication have led to the creation of information network. Since no library is self - sufficient, libraries are coming together to share their resources and services by using modern telecommunication facilities. The networks facilitate access to information at great speed, high reliability and reduced cost. Some of the successful networks in the world are OCLC, INIS, AGRIS, MEDLARS, INFLIBNET, ERNET, SERNET, MALIBNET, DELNET, etc.

LAN: Local Area Network is a network linking computers

and other devices with in a limited geographical area, usually not more than a kilo-meter or two from the central service (for e.g. Campus-wide network in organisations)

WAN: Wide Area Network is a network linking several organisations at regional, national and international level (e.g. NICNET, INFLIBNET)

MAN: Metropolitan Area Network is a network linking more than one organigation may be at Metropolitan City level. (e.g. DELNET, CALIBNET, etc.)

Internet

Internet is the networking of computer networks around the world which facilitates transfer or hiring of information among all the computer users connected to these networks. It is a worldwide communication system, which links together thousands of computers and global interconnection of network of networks. The concept of Internet working of networks exists in earlier days also. According to the Internet Society, it consist today more than 30,000 networks in 96 countries. World Wide Web (WWW) made the Internet usage more popular among the users. Internet has made it possible to reach any people or access any information on the cyberspace. Starting with basic tools like E-mail, FTP (File Transfer Protocol) and Telenet the Internet has progressed to provide user-friendly tools like Gopher, WAIS (Wide Area Information Server) and WWW for information publishing and access.

FEATURES OF INFORMATION TECHNOLOGY

The convergence of electronics, computers and communication technologies formed the basis for an advanced information society. The main features of IT have a direct impact on information society as follows:

1. Cheaper data storage e.g. optical storage media that increased the storage capacity of the libraries.
2. Digitization of resources - text, graphic photographic speech,

sound etc. that provides quick transmission of any type of data.

3. Better data transfer between different systems and media, which have promoted the resource sharing among the libraries.
4. Improved telecommunications, such as ISDN with greatly increased capacity for data transmission, which facilitated introduction of new services such as E-Mail, Fax etc.
5. Increased reliability of hardware and software, which has increased the performance efficiency.
6. User friendly systems developed to enhance the interface between technology and users of the library.

AREAS OF APPLICATION OF INFORMATION TECHNOLOGY IN LIBRARIES

The applications of IT in different library activities are briefly described below:

Acquisition

The computers have eased the burden of acquisition system of the libraries with the help of computer reordering, checking of duplicate orders and follow up action can be taken care automatically. A vender list may be prepared in database form. Books awaiting selection can also be entered in a computer database. A list of books under selection can be generated and circulated among selection committee members by E-mail. If the library has a website these can be hosted on the website. User's opinion can also be taken through the website. Selection committee members can electronically convey their advice. Users can directly send their suggestion for acquiring particular books or subscribing to certain Journals. Purchase order can also be generated through computer. Bills can be obtained electronically. Payments can also be made electronically making use of electronic commerce facilities.

Classification

In classification activity electronic media can be of great

help. Classification schedules are now available on CD-ROM and on line. (Www.purl.org/oclc/fp) Some software can be generated which help in on-screen classification. Such software can even be saddled with artificial intelligence. Barcode strips can be generated containing accession number and book number.

Cataloguing

The application of IT in the area of cataloguing can be made in following ways:

1. The information of the accessioned books ways can be converted to the catalogue data.
2. The catalogue can be queried on screen.
3. Arrangement of catalogue cards can be classified as well as alphabetical sequences.
4. Computerised catalogue makes possible import/export of bibliographic data in both standard exchange format (MARC) and non-standard format (Non MARC) and automates the stock verification process.
5. To verify the technical term automatically through thesaurus.
6. Printing of the holding and other bibliographical record easily for documentation services.
7. Bibliographical information/catalogue can be made available on the Internet. Online Public Access Catalogue (OPAC) becoming quite popular.

Serial Control

IT helps in periodical subscription and subsequent monitoring of the receipt of individual issues. It helps in maintaining record of budget sanctioned and expenditure on various categories of periodical. Computer has made it possible for the automated reminder generation of missing issues of the periodicals.

Reference Services

Reference services can also be operated electronically.

E-mail can give a request for a reference service. Catalogue, database, CD-ROM journal, abstracting journals can all be queried for providing reference service. Reports can be prepared by using various automation packages and sent electronically to the user. "Digital reference services have made a solid beginning in the libraries. However, it appears that using the Internet as a medium for the reference process is still in its infancy" User education and referral services provided through IT equipment are very effective and quick.

Document Supply

Document supply can be variously automated using IT. A document can be located through a union catalogue on CD-ROM or even an on-line database. The document can then the obtained as an image form from the point of availability by file transfer and sent to the user as a file, which the user can download. This electronic document delivery will speed up the process of document delivery tremendously.

CAS (Current Awareness Services)

Anticipatory current awareness services can be given by keeping in mind the focus of the library. The CAS of an automated library can do the following: - review the select publication immediately upon receipt, select the items of relevance to the program of the R & D under taken by institutions, notify the items to the departments to whom they are related or to the scientists who are working on those topics. IT helps to increase the quality of this service with the help of Internet connection. the web based electronic bulletin board facility and direct to user syndrome through network connection.

SDI (Selective Dissemination of Information)

The selective dissemination of information (SDI) consists of scanning key words (research profile of individual users) in the current literature, filtering of information, and transmitting the retrieved information to the users on their desks. The construction of profiles according to the standardised terms is an intellectual Job. It can form a foundation for routine SDI service. A constant monitoring mechanism of service is evolved out of useful feedback and constructive comments. Based on a user profile, on line database can be queried, searches can be conducted through the Internet, electronic journals can be looked up, then a report can be prepared and delivery can be done to the users.

IMPACT OF INFORMATION TECHNOLOGY

Information is a vital resource and valuable input for societal development. The information revolution makes development more speedy than ever before. Now the avenues in new information technologies and plummeting computing coasts are sticking distance and eroding borders and time. The rapid development of information and IT has tremendously increased our capacity to process information and accelerated growth in the information intensive sector. The impact of IT arises from its attributes such as enabling technology, which can be applied in a wide range of different circumstances, the capacity of the technology increasing at an exponential rate and the cost of the technology falling rapidly. These attributes of IT will trigger a new wave of economic growth stimulating the development of information society. It is indeed the avenues of IT that should be utilised to the possible extent in libraries and information centres to make use of the information speedily, effectively, efficiently and with precision. The impact of new technologies is seen in almost every human activity. The change in the pattern of collection, storage and dissemination of information are some of the major challenges in any library. The basic concept in the use of new technology is to free the librarian and information officer from the routine jobs connected with the library operation in acquisition, classification, cataloguing, circulation control, serial control, etc. which can be entrusted to computer. New storage technologies enabled information to be stored in far less space and in a more retrievable format. Modern databases management systems (DBMS) enabled information to be accessed much more quickly, more accurately, more comprehensively and provide analytical tools to give management more pertinent data. Communication technologies are help to communicate information to the user more quickly and more efficiently. The technology of reprography made a big impact on the document delivery system. Most of the research libraries have reprographic machines and provide photocopy of document on demand. The microforms will have a great impact on libraries and the world of books will be replaced by the microforms. Using reprography and micrographic techniques, we can condense the bulky archives and newspapers and solve the storage problems. They also serve the purpose of preservation. They help in resource sharing and save the time of users. IT has not changed the mission (to provide right information for user community), but the IT has assisted the methods of executing it, by giving information and documents at the desk of patrons. Mission is not technology dependent but technology helps to achieve the mission by providing more comprehensives and extended services to patrons in a more flexible manner. IT has changed the boundaries of the libraries these facets have significant impact on libraries as a modern library is smaller in size but bigger in respect of image or value of libraries information storage and retrieval.

CONCLUSION

There is no doubt that the information environment is becoming increasingly digital and the IT has a wide- ranging impact on the library and information centres. IT will shape the future information world and is considered to be a new wealth creator by offering immense opportunities for the libraries. As the technology is changing at vary fast rate, there is still scope for the librarians and others involved in library activities to develop more skill and have matching human resources to keep pace with this changing IT environment.

REFERENCES

1. Devarajan,G.(1999).Information Technology in

Libraries.NewDelhi : Ess Ess Publication ; 1-3.

2. Agrwal, S.P. (1982). Times to Lunch National Information System for Social Science. Library Herald. 20 (2-4) ; 164.
3. Bakewell, K.G.B. (1977). The Special Library. In Annual of Library Economy. Ed. by R. Northwood Lock. London: Cure Bingley ; 14.
4. Ahmed, S.M. Javed & Munshi, Md -Nasir-Uddin (1995-96). Using IBM PC in Libraries: Some buying Tips. Library Herald. 30(3-4) ; 90-8.
5. Akthar, Mubeen A. (1998). Library Automation. Indian Journal Information Library and Society.11(1-2) ; 93-100.
6. Carter, Roger. (1987). The Information Technology Handbook. London: Heinemann Professional Publisher ; 29-39.
7. Anand, C.M. & Sen, B.N. (1991). Manpower Development for Computer Application to Library and Information Activities: Role of INSDOC. IASLIC Bulletin.36 (4) ; 137-69.
8. Ball, A.J.S. (1980). Videotext Network. Computer. 13 (2) ; 8.
9. Cochrane, Pauline A. (1992). Information Technology in Libraries and Ranganathan Five Laws of Library Science. Libri. 42 (3) ; 235-41
10. ALA Glossary of Library and Information Science. (1983). Ed.by Heartskill Young. Chicago: ALA ; 212.
11. Bashir, Ahmad; Khan G.M. & Wani G.M. (1996). Emerging Information Technology. Lucknow Libraries. 28(1-4) ; 14-24.
12. Ahuja, J.P.S. (1992). Building a Micro Computer based Local Area Network for Libraries: From Concept to Percept. Locknow Librarian. 24 (1) ; 2.

4

COMPUTERISATION OF LIBRARY OPERATIONS: RECENT TRENDS

G.Dhanasegaran
Deputy Librarian,
Dr.T.P.M.Library
M.K.University
Madurai – 625 021.

RECENT TRENDS OF INFORMATION STORAGE AND RETRIEVAL

The present age is regarded as the age of information. Information has become a commodity in the context of Information explosion. We are living in the information society. Library/ information centre is the light house for information dissemination where the users can explore the vast resources of information.

The number of users is growing rapidly. To meet the needs of the users the collections of the library are also increasing day by day. So there is a need of more space for storing information.

In the present electronic age, all sorts of information and their resources are available both in print and electronic form. This is causing information over loaded which shall have to be managed properly for effective and purposeful utilization of available resources.

Library personnel also faces trouble to provide specific information to the reader with in a short time. In this situation, it is essential to fitter this huge information and provide only those, which is pin-pointedly relevant and required by the user.

Due to enormous capacity of data storage, processing and retrieval of information, the Indian Libraries and Information centres have attracted towards the use of Information Technology for computerisation of library activities and services in order to extend computer based library and information services to the end users.

The New Education policy, 1986 recommended that Information Technology should be used in libraries for providing effective library and information services to the academic community.

New trends in information Technology have changed the images of the library and information processing world wide. Users are also becoming IT literate day by day.

COMPUTERISATION OF LIBRARY OPERATIONS

It is the process of computerising the library functions using the modern technology like application of computers, telecommunications, computer software, microforms of storage media, human interface etc, and other micro information technology which helps in information storage and retrieval process. This covers usually house keeping operations such as acquisition, serial control, cataloguing circulation, references and administrative work.

Compterisation of library operations is the technologies used for collection, processing, storage, retrieval, dissemination and transmission of information at local, regional and international level.

NEED FOR COMPUTERISATION

The information storage and retrieval problem has become progressively more serious in recent years especially in the areas of science and Technology where the volume of data and information is increasing at an unprecedented, nearly exponential rate. Therefore, computerisation is the only answer to organize and disseminate the tremendous flow of information in a systematic way.

Computer aided system is more convenient, more flexible and more comprehensive and in the long run more economical. Following are the need for computerisation of library operations.

1. To improve library and information services for end users.
2. To help in providing enormous capacity of data storage and retrieval.
3. To improve efficiency of work.
4. To reduce the repetitive work and save time of library professionals in routine house keeping operations and library services.
5. To bring accuracy and speed of work.
6. To provide prompt library services.
7. To increase efficiency in technical processing.
8. To improve efficiency of library administration and management.
9. Financial savings due to computerisation.
10. To help in bibliographic control and updating of databases.

PLANNING FOR COMPUTERISATION

Library computerisation plan may be chalked out through the Project Management Team which consists of Librarian, Technical Expert and consultant. The major activities that may be planned can be broadly categorized as :

Budgeting

a. Cost of library software
b. Cost of Hardware including components of networking UPS etc
c. Cost of other software
d. Consultancy charges for consultants
e. Labour charges for site preparation
f. Integration and Testing expenses

g. Expenses of data analysis, data conservation and bibliographical data entry

h. Training expenses

i. Other contingencies

Site Preparation Plan

a. Space for SERVER Machine

b. Space for Client Machine

c. Separate space for UPS/Batteries /Generator

d. Plan to fix Network cable, Hubs and Other equipments

e. Adequate space to computer systems to support user search facility ie OPAC.

f. Other plan for furniture and fixture should be carried out.

g. Time frame to start and finish the implementation process

h. Plan to monitor the progress of implementation.

Implementation Team Training

Library computerisation helps the in-house staff to get training in the process of implementation of the Library software. Library should select right employees who have the right attitude ie willing to change, learn new things, not afraid of technology and good functional knowledge.

End-user-Training

Library personnel will be given sufficient training on how to use the system. The personnel are identified with their skill levels, divided in to groups and then trained on the new system. The end-user training is much more important.

Maintenance and upgradation

Maintenance of Library computerisation may be broadly divided into four major categories.

1. Library database and software maintenance

2. Network maintenance
3. Hardware and other equipments maintenance
4. Human Resource maintenance

In the case of up-gradation, one if its methods used is up-gradation of the software modules. Other method of up-gradation involves the complete change in the hardware, software and networking environments. Therefore, to get the advantages of the current trends of Hardware and software the library should be up-graded entirely with the latest Hardware and software Configuration.

STEPS INVOLVED IN COMPUTERISATION

The first step regarding the computerisation of library and information services is to decide for computerisation. The next step is to perform a system analysis. After finalisation of activities to be computerised, the detail examination of each activity should be carried out which are as follows:

1. To identify the data elements
2. To calculate the total storage capacity required
3. To ensure that the software is able to handle the size, number of fields and records.
4. To identify the various activities to be computerised
5. To identify those data elements which are common to several functions.

Library house keeping jobs are supposed to be computerised based on priority may vary from library to Library. Every library needs to create data base of the whole library initially because without which computerisation of other house keeping jobs cannot be completed.

Computerisation of a library is divided into following five phases.

1. Preparation of bibliographic data bases
2. Computerisation of library house keeping operations
3. Networking and acquisition of materials in digital form

4. Digitisation of theses, dissertations, project works and rare books
5. Digitisation of books and serials.

USES OF COMPUTERISATION

The main objective of computerisation of library operations is basically to integrate all library activities towards ensuring an easy and accurate retrieval of information. Computerisation has helped libraries in improving library activities and accelerating their working. It saves the effort, time and manpower of libraries. It saves the time of the users, staff and increases productivity and reliability. The indirect benefits include better image, improved user good will, user satisfaction and so on.

Computerisation can play a vital role for efficient library operations and services because it ensures the following:

1. Improvement of control over collection
2. Effective control over the entire library operation
3. Improvement of the existing services and introducing new services
4. Sharing of resources among various libraries in a region effectively
5. Avoiding duplication of work and
6. Using the services of the existing staff effectively.

DIFFERENT AREAS OF COMPUTERISATION OF LIBRARY OPERATIONS

The process of computerisation starts with the background study regarding the objectives and major functions being used in the different sections of the library. The key areas of computerisation will be identified. It is always good to do a cost – benefit analysis. The library can conduct a feasibility study by a team of in – house –executives. Following are the areas of computerisation of library operations.

1. Acquisition
2. Cataloguing
3. Circulation
4. Serial control
5. On-line Public Access Catalogue
6. C.D- ROM database searches
7. Office automation
8. Information Retrieval and its Dissemination.

Acquisition

An acquisition system should cover the entire range of activities from the time of making proposal to acquire an item until it is finally paid for and accessioned. It should also provide the support for automatically picking of data for letter generation, printing, signing and posting. The purchase item should be grouped and can be retrieved in many ways. This system should maintain payments information to follow –up the purchase easily.

An acquisition system should cover the scope for

1. Proposal for acquisition
2. Inquiry to book sellers
3. Purchase orders
4. Books on approval Memos
5. Purchase bills
6. Payment details of purchase bills
7. Credit notes
8. Detailed information about vendors
9. Multiple currencies and conversion Rates and so on

Cataloguing

A cataloguing system should have the features to catalogue any type of material such as books, serials and non-book materials. Data entry for card should be menu driven. Rules of punctuation should be programmed to give consistent and accurate cards. The card should be available in standard (5" x 3") size. It should support unlimited number of added entries. Some other features of Cataloguing system should be.

1. Authority control on author/Publisher/name /key word
2. Accession details of items
3. Cardex for bound volumes of journals
4. Bibliographic details of serials
5. Accession Register
6. Catalogues and labels printing

Circulation

Circulation system should be based on lending rules. This system should provide support on the following:

1. Membership information/Registration card with Member's photograph and ID
2. Loans and Reservations data
3. Circulation status
4. Issues, Returns, Reissues
5. Issue/Return facility with Barcode
6. Reservations
7. Rules for fine computation for overdue items
8. Inter library loan monitoring system
9. Letter generation for collection of reserved items, overdue loan notices, nodue certificate, membership renewal, reminder etc.

Serial Control

Serial control system should help to achieve an effective utilization of periodicals budget. It should allow for tracking receipt of issues, filing claims for issues not received, preparing binding orders etc. Some of the features that should be supported by serial control system are :

1. Information of Publisher/Agent
2. Periodicity and Delivery mode
3. List of journals
4. New Subscription/Renewal of Subscription
5. Reminders
6. Binding orders
7. Request/Acknowledgment for Gift/Exchange
8. Payment Forwarding note
9. Accessioning of bound volumes.

OPAC and WEB-Aware OPAC

On line Public Access Catalogue should offer powerful on-line search facilities to search through Library catalogues. OPAC should index all relevant words in the description of item to conduct the search. A good OPAC module should provide the query support for Boolean operators such as AND, OR, NOT as well as wild card matching.

Web aware OPAC module of the library software should have the capability to put entire library information on the Internet/ Intranet. It should also support features of catalogue browsing, Circulation details, word/phrase search, view card etc. Retrieval of data should be simple.

Information Retrieval and its Dissemination

A computer based information storage and Retrieval system consists of the following two phases.

1. Storage, feeding and storage of information in the computer
2. Retrieval –search-selection and answering the query. These facilitate retrospective search. It provides periodically current awareness service.

CURRENT TRENDS IN THE COMPUTERISATION OF LIBRARY OPERATIONS

Due to information explosion there is a tremendous growth in the resources of the Library. Libraries are now heavily involved in the structuring process. Libraries are undergoing a rapid change to cope up with the demands of rapidly changing information requirements of its users. Libraries are growing and developing day by day and they are being forced to adopt computerisation and digitization. In course of time the new professionals with high technology skills will replace the traditional librarianship in the years to come.

In view of enormous capacity of data storage, quick processing, access, retrieval and dissemination of information, Library and Information centres in India have started using multi-media digital computers with latest software/hardware (configuration) with communication devices of modem and teleconferencing device, digital web camera etc., for information storage, processing, retrieval and dissemination of information, creation of databases, and house keeping of library operations.

It is hoped that with the introduction of modern technology in the form of computerisation, network and internet facilities, the libraries will be able to provide better services to the users at a lower cost in the near future.

REFERENCES

1. Balakrishnan, S and Paliwal, P.K, *Ed.* Automated Library Serials.– New Delhi: Anmol Publications, 2001. PP.1-252.
2. Chopra, H.S, *Ed.* Library Information Technology in modern Era. – New Delhi: Common Wealth Publishers, 1999. PP.1-195.
3. Clayton, Marlene. Managing Library automation – USA: Gower Publishing Co., 1987.PP.1 – 239.
4. Devarajan, G and Rahelamma, A.V, *Ed.* Library Computerisation in India – New Delhi: Ess Ess Publications, 1990. PP.1-159.

5. Krishnan Gopal. Modern Library Automation.– Delhi: Authors Press, 1999. P.1-264

6. Murthy, T.A.V, *Ed.* First convention Planner – 2003. Automation of Libraries in North Eastern Region: Trends, Issues and challenges.- Ahmedabad: Information and Library Network centre, 2003. PP.1-384.

7. Pandey, S.K, *Ed.* Organisation of Library automation. – New Delhi: Anmol Publications, 2000. PP.1-305.

8. Rajiv Adhikari. Library Serials Automation.– Delhi: Raja Publications, 2000. PP.1-279.

9. Raman Nair, R. Computer application to Library and Information services.– New Delhi: Ess Ess Publications, 1992. PP.1-279.

10. Singh, S.K. Library Technical Services : Millennium approach.- Delhi: Author's Press, 2000. PP.145-198.

5

Application of IT in University Libraries in Kerala: A User Point of View

Dineshan Koovakkai
Professional Assistant
University Library
University of Calicut
e-mail: dineshkoovakkai@yahoo.co.in

Dr. Jalaja V.
Reader, Department of Library and Information Science,
University of Calicut

INTRODUCTION

The advancement in technology has facilitated the dissemination of information in larger amount and in greater speed. Computers and communication technologies have great potential for providing the information services in a more effective way. Libraries which have the ultimate aim of satisfying the customers are using the advanced technologies in processing, storing and disseminating information.

University libraries which are meant to serve the academic community are expected to provide up to date information with greater speed in order to satisfy the needs of the academics. Information Communication Technologies (ICTs) are being increasingly used in University libraries in Kerala also with the aim of providing better user satisfaction. As such, the library services are automated in most of the University libraries in Kerala. They have the internet connectivity as well for the users to get the vast amount of information available all over the world. However, the users of the university libraries in Kerala are not getting the full benefits of IT application to libraries.

AREAS OF IT APPLICATION IN LIBRARIES

It has been generally accepted that IT can be applied in the library house keeping operations and in providing information services. IT can be applied to the library housekeeping operations such as acquisition, cataloguing, circulation control, serial control etc. Areas of IT application of acquisition system include duplicate checking, on-line ordering, claiming, bill processing, accounting etc. In cataloguing, the data regarding the documents entered in the computer in the acquisition section can very well be manipulated for producing different types of catalogues. The computer will automatically provide access to the data elements already fed into the computer in the acquisition section. The card catalogue can also be produced using printers. In circulation control, IT can be used in creating databases of the users, check in and check out processes, reservation, fine collection etc. serial control is one of the most complex areas where computers can be used. The processes that can be automated in serial control include ordering, receiving, indexing, claiming, accounting, check in and check out etc.

Information services that can be provided in libraries using IT include : providing facilities for information retrieval using OPACs, CD-ROM, Internet and services like Current Awareness Service, Selective Dissemination of Information, on-line search services, reference service, Document Delivery Service, resource sharing etc.

WHAT DO THE USERS GET FROM IT APPLICATION?

Informal interviews with the users of university libraries in Kerala reveal that they are neither aware nor interested in the automation of the in-house operations of the libraries. It is a fact that the automation of the activities of the acquisition section such as duplicate checking, ordering, bill processing etc. are out of the purview of the interest of the general users. Like wise, the automated cataloguing, serial control etc. also are not much of interest to the users. The users are generally interested only in the operations which have direct impact on them. As such the services/facilities provided to the users using IT alone are important to the user point of view. The services/facilities generally provided by the university libraries in Kerala are automated issue and return of documents, OPAC, Internet, CD-ROM search facilities, on-line search facilities etc.

Automated Issue and Return of Documents

Most of the university libraries in Kerala use various software packages such as LIBSYS, SOUL etc. for issue and return of documents. Bar code technology also is used to make the process speedy and error free. The ultimate aim of the automated charging and discharging of documents is to save the time of the users. However, considering the Indian situation where everything requires documentary evidence and fear of failure in the computer system, manual system of charging and discharging (using borrower's tickets) also is simultaneously followed in most of the automated university libraries in Kerala. This causes inconvenience to the users. Instead of saving the time of the user, this system causes wastage of time and effort. Thus, the users are not actually benefited from the automation. However, the computerised issue of documents helps the users to know the copy status of the documents (whether they are issued and if issued, to whom). The due date for the return of the documents can also be found out easily.

On-line Public Access Catalogue (OPAC)

On-line Public Access Catalogue (OPAC) is actually the most important aspect of library automation when viewed from the part of the user. The catalogue which is available on-line and can be searched through the computer terminals is known as OPAC. It allows multi-dimensional searches providing as many access points as the data elements. Though the search options in OPACs depend largely on the capacity of the software used, generally most systems allow searches through the access points such as author, title, subject, class number, key word, combination etc. Among these, key word and combination searches are unique to computerised catalogues. Through these, the user can search for documents using a word or combination of words in the title or content/abstract. The combination search provides option to search for documents using Boolean logic (AND, OR, NOT). Term truncation is another advantage of this search. Through term truncation, users can search on parts of words by putting an arbitrary symbol such as question mark (?) after the part of the word. The computer will select all possible alternatives in place of the arbitrary symbol. Right truncation, left truncation and middle truncation are possible.

Internet

The internet is a network of networks which links the generators and users of information. A large amount of information required by the academics is available on internet in the form of e-journals, e-books, statistical sources, databases etc. For publishing the research out put of the academics and for knowing the current developments and events in their fields of interest, internet is the fastest medium today. E-mail facility provides much scope for the academics to contact experts in their field and to send their papers to journals and conferences. Hence, it is the responsibility of the university libraries to provide access to the internet facility to the academic community.

Most of the university libraries in Kerala provide internet facility to their users. However, payment is required for using this facility. Those who are unable to pay will be deprived of this facility in the university libraries in Kerala. In some University libraries, the access to internet is limited to a class of users.

CD-ROM Search Facility

As a high capacity optical storage device, Compact Disk-Read Only Memory (CD-ROM) plays a vital role in storing textual, graphic and other information. Many of the abstracts, statistical information, full text etc. are now available on CD-ROMs. Retrieval of information stored in CD-ROMs is easier than retrieving information from printed sources. The academics, especially, the researchers need this resource for the easy retrieval of the required information. However, the CD-ROM search facility is not so extensive in university libraries in Kerala. The stock as well as the searching facilities of CD-ROMs is poor in most of the university libraries in Kerala.

On-Line Search Facility

On-line databases contain millions of records covering many years. The on-line vendors provide on-line search facility for many of the databases. The on-line search facility, is however, not so strong in university libraries in Kerala. With the advent of UGC-Infonet consortium, university libraries are on the path of providing access to various resources like e-journals and electronic databases on-line.

INFORMATION SERVICES

Many of the information services that an automated library can provide are not actually available to the users of the university libraries in Kerala. As stated earlier, the services like Current Awareness Service, Selective Dissemination of Information, reference service, Document Delivery Services, resource sharing etc. can very well be provided using IT with greater speed and accuracy. However, most of the university libraries are not providing these services to their users using IT. Hence, the users of the university libraries are missing the chances of getting the right information at the right time. It is because of the under utilization of the prospects of available IT facilities in these libraries.

THE PROBLEM OF DIGITAL DIVIDE

The increase in the amount of digital information consequent on the application of IT in University libraries causes denial of opportunity of accessing such information to a group of users who are not able to use the modern technologies. It is a general feature that IT based resources are provided at a cost. Those who are unable to pay for them will be deprived of the opportunities of accessing the ever-changing information at the right time.

CONCLUSION

IT has its impact on libraries all over the world. University libraries in Kerala are still in the stage of infancy in the application of IT in the provision of information services except to an extent the specialized universities like CUSAT. Though most of the university libraries have automated their library in house operations and connected to the net, the provision of information services has not reached the expected level. The users who are not interested in the automation of the in house operations are looking for speedy access to all types of information. The computerisation of library operations is now incapable of saving the time of the users. CD-ROM and on-line search facilities have not developed to the fuller extent. Internet facility provided only to a few (Those who are able to pay) also causes problems. The non-availability of these facilities for various reasons creates the problem of digital divide as well.

REFERENCES

1. Baby, M.D. (1998). Use of information technology in information handling in libraries. *KELPRO Bulletin* 2(1), 9-12.
2. Dineshan Koovakkai & Jalaja, V.(2003). Re-engineering

human resource in libraries for handling electronic information. In Sharma, Pandey S.K. ed. *Electronic Information Environment and Library Services: a contemporary Paradigm.* Delhi: Indian Library Association.

3. Jalaja, V & Dineshan Koovakkai. (2000). Document searching through OPAC. *University News* 38 (50), 14-19.
4. Jalaja, V & Dineshan Koovakkai. (2004). The problem of digital divide among the academic community. *University News* 42(3), 8-9.
5. Malaisamy, T.K. (1998). Information technology in library management and education. *IASLIC Bulletin* 43(1), 27-31.
6. Ramakrishna Reddy, K. & Sudarshan, B. (1997). Computerised document circulation. *IASLIC Bulletin* 42(2), 73-80.
7. Singh, Om Shashi Shekhar. (2003). Internet and libraries in digital environment. *ILA Bulletin* 38 (3), 40-42.

6

Impact of Electronic Journals in Higher Education

P. Mounissamy
Assistant Librarian
National Institute of Technology
Tiruchirappalli, Tamil Nadu
e-mail: moun@nitt.edu.in

INTRODUCTION

It will no longer be necessary to browse through a paper journal contents page hoping to find an article of interest. Instead readers will be able to register their areas of interest and the electronic publishing system will deliver articles which match those requirements to the reader's desk top (Wiles, 1997).

This general idea already works in principle. The concept of shifting from ownership and storage to accessibility and availability of documents is given more important. Higher Education institutes are establishing Electronic Learning Resources Center to ensure cost effective way of article provision. It has had significant impaction on the way, the academic community uses, stores, and preserves information. An effort is made to understand how this technology is affecting the library and user by conducting a survey at National Institute of Technology, Tiruchirappalli in June 2003.

ELECTRONIC JOURNALS

The first electronic journal appeared during 1970s. They were not available to a larger number of users; this is one of the reasons why they were not widespread (Tenopir, 2000). Today, most of the electronic journals appear as parallel version of its print counterparts. Major publishers publish electronic journals and offer them as special services or databases e.g. Science Direct, SpringerLINK. Electronic journals could be accessed through gopher, ftp, telnet, e-mail or discussion lists, but today they are mainly accessed through web. Electronic journals are identified as an important component of future library systems.

DEFINTIONS OF ELECTRTONIC JOURNALS

Electronic journal is a periodical literature or serials publication available in digital format that is made available as an individual title via an electronic medium, typically the World Wide Web. E-journal for all practical purposes may thus be defined as those journals which are available in electronic media; some may be available on CD-ROM; a few may be available only on online; some may be available both in electronic media and in print (Ravichandra Rao, 2002).

FEATURES OF ELECTRONIC JOURNALS

Because of multidimensional features of the electronic information sources compared with print sources users and libraries have started subscribing to and using electronic sources. The positive features of electronic journals as compared with print journals are as follows:

1. Allows remote access;
2. Can be used simultaneously by more than one user;
3. Provide timely access;
4. Supports different searching capabilities;
5. Accommodate unique features
6. Save physical storage space;

7. Can support multimedia information;
8. Do not require physical processing
9. Can be environmentally valuable;
10. Can be saved digitally.

ELECTRONIC JOURNALS AT THE NIT

Electronic databases, namely, IEL Online, ACM Digital Library, ASME Journals, ASCE Journals, ASTP, Springer Verlag, and ScienceDirect are accessible by the National institutes of Technology, Trichirappalli under consortia subscription by INDEST, MHRD, Govt. of India.

CONDITIONS OF USE FOR ELECTRONIC JOURNALS:

All the available electronic journals at NITT are governed by license agreement, which restrict to NITT students, faculty or staff members. It is the responsibility of the individual users to ensure that these resources are used for personal and or educational non-commercial purposes only without systematic downloading, distributing, and printing entire journal issues. Breaches of agreement with publishers could result in the suspension of access to the resources for the entire institute.

IMPACT STUDY

Impact of electronic journal in the library and Librarian is concerned with space, utility and cost effective analysis, publicity and feed back and so on. Impact of electronic journals is directly concerned with the user satisfaction in terms with how well the library's services and resources meet user needs. Particularly, in the Web based learning resources, the evaluation of online database, users rating, their satisfaction with software functionality, interface maneuverability, network speed and reliability, or some other aspect of usability are most important aspects to be studied to highlight the impact of the new technology.

SIGNIFICANCE OF THE STUDY

Electronic resources and information services are being provided to meet the users expectation. Without conducting a study of users attitudes towards electronic resources, librarians have no way of knowing whether the faculty find expensive online databases easy to learn and effectively use. The study offers a way to identify obstacles that faculty might encounter while attempting to perform routine academic and research assignments.

SCOPE OF THE STUDY

This study confines itself to the impact of electronic journals in the National Institutes of Technology, Tiruchirappalli, though there are number of colleges. This study includes electronic journals, faculty and students who use electronic journals.

AIM AND OBJECTIVES OF THE STUDY

The study is concerned with the following aim and objectives

1. To find out how NITT academics perceived and use electronic journals for their research and teaching assignments.
2. To learn about user attitudes regarding the current and future impact of technology on their use of the Library.
3. To gain insight into their awareness of issues related to archiving
4. To find out the frequency of usage of the electronic journals.
5. To find out the access point of the electronic journals.
6. To know the quantum of electronic journals in a month.
7. To identify the initiator who introduced accessing electronic journals to the respondents.
8. To rank the various key advantages of electronic journals.
9. To bring out the problem faced by the respondents while accessing electronic journal.
10. To find out the major electronic journals accessed to the maximum extent.

METHODOLOGY

The National Institute of Technology, Tiruchirappalli was used for the study purpose. Since, the universe is large, simple random sampling was adopted as mode of study. Questionnaires were distributed to students and faculty of NITT to get the data. Statistical tools such as percentage Chi-Square, "t" Test, and ONE WAY ANOVA were used.

The researcher got permission from the authorities of the NITT to conduct the study. The researcher also explained them the nature and purpose of the study and conducted a pretest with few faculty and students and found satisfactory and then questionnaire was administered to test the sample.

The researcher approached each of the faculty and students having INTERNET access in the institute and explained them the purpose and contents of the questionnaire as well as the research study and then the questionnaire was given and collected after two hours. The data were collected in January 2004 and analyzed using SPSS software package.

FINDINGS

1. Over 60% of the respondents say they are comfortable using electronic resources, they believe that a variety of electronic resources are important to their research, and they consider electronic databases to be invaluable.
2. Physics Department students and staff respondents were more.
3. 84.1% respondents were males.
4. 63.6% of the respondents belong to 18-25 age group.
5. 25% of the respondents access electronic journals daily. 45.4% access once in a week. 14.8% access electronic journals once in a month and 14.8% access as and when they feel like it.
6. Majority of the respondents were initiated to access the electronic journals by articles, announcement and Institute Newsletter.

7. Out of 100 total respondents 58% of the respondents experienced many problems while browsing the electronic journals.
8. The problem was inadequate Internet connection, downloading problem and screen format, eg. Pdf
9. Most respondents accept electronic journals for their project and research activities.
10. IEL online has been accessed by majority of the users.

Rank sequence of advantages of electronic journals are as follows:

1. Access from different location
2. Timeless availability
3. Available before print version
4. Simultaneous usage
5. Full Text
6. Easy accessibility as compared to print version
7. Access from desktop
8. Downloading facilities
9. Easy interaction
10. Authors can be contacted through e-mail
11. Archival facilities.
12. At NITT, few staff has terminals on their desk and rest of the staff and all the students have to go the CSG, INTERNET LABORATORY of the Campus.
13. Users are happy to scan an article on the screen, but they want to read it in depth, they want a print copy. The recent trends in mounting electronic journals in adobe's PDF format also discourage screen reading and encourage print. Such journals are not easy to manipulate and read on screen.

IMPACT ON LIBRARY

Digital formats of information improve library and lower

down the subscription cost under consortia subscription. Space is the most important requirement for print media format where as networks, computer hardware, software, and system staff is required to provide access to electronic journals. The chief impact of print journals on infrastructure is managing the physical space for growth of the collection over time. The transition to electronic journals essentially eliminates space concerns. Since there is provision for archival access, keeping back volumes and physical processing, and maintenance staff are not required.

As the Electronic information service is available throughout the campus, users need not come to library for accessing the journals. This encourages the users to make use of the electronic journals. Digital librarian, the information provider, is replacing the traditional role of librarian.

SUGGESTIONS AND RECOMMENDATIONS

1. The frequency with which user access the system depends on the distance they are from the nearest terminal. Increased availability of computers to students may also will have more changes in academic working patterns.
2. Direct links to electronic databases may be considered to ensure effective use of electronic databases.
3. Month-wise usage report for electronic journals could be measured using log on file system besides requesting the publishers concerned. It would provide as basis for comparative study and provide evidence to support future budget request or increase the level of bibliographic instruction.
4. Library and Information professionals have to create more awareness functions to market their new electronic journals services.
5. Networking with thought leaders, influential persons in other departments and engaging them to spread the word about the electronic journals services may be considered.

6. Periodical new services/Product trails for specific user groups are to be introduced.

7. Permanent archival provision may be considered to have access to back runs.

CONCLUSION

It is crystal clear from the result that the younger generation is accepting digital reading culture. The advantages and disadvantages reported by the respondents are almost identical as listed in earlier studies. The low-level problems, especially delays in gaining access and impediments to moving about within and between journals are major de-motivating factors in the use of electronic journals.

Some of the problems faced by the users are within the control of the publishers and can be alleviated by the publishers. Length on screen reading, when an article has to be read in depth remains unpopular. Double column layouts are particularly troublesome for users. The adobat Acrobat software used by several commercial publishers does not yet adequately support user-friendly journals usage. It is slow to deliver articles. Use of electronic journals is going to require a considerable training exercise, especially if publishers keep changing what they are doing.

Factors, which are not under the control of the publishers of electronic journals such as Network, delay, increasing traffic and inadequate band width etc. are to be taken care by the subscribing institute.

REFERENCES

1. Higher education libraries. New Library world, 99(1144), 1998 pp. 243-247 Ashcroft, L and Langdon, C. Electronic journals in
2. Fecko , M.B, (1997). Electronic Resources: Access and issues, Bower Saur, London, ISBN 1-85739-065-2
3. Indian National Digital Library in Science and Technology

(INDEST) Consortium, MHRD, Government of India, Brochure ,Jan 2003

4. Jennifer Lagier, Measuring Usage and Usability of Online Databases at Hartnell College , P.hD thesis, Southeastern University, 2003

5. Tenopir, C. (1999). Factors that influence online database use, ACRL Ninth NationalConference Papers, April 8-11, 1999, Detroit, MI. Retrieved January 22, 2002 from the World Wide Web: http://www.ala.org/acrl/tenopir.pdf

6. Tenopir, C. (2001). Database and online system usage. Library Journal, 126(16), 41-45. Retrieved February 8, 2002 from WilsonWeb on-line database: http://vweb.hwwilsonweb.com

7. Tenopir, C. and Read, E. (2000). Patterns of database use in academic libraries. College & Research Libraries, 61(3), 234-46. Retrieved October 1, 2001 fromWilsonWeb: http://vweb.hwwilsonweb.com

8. Tomney, H.; Burton, P. F. Electronic journals : a study of usage and attitudes among academics, Journal of information science, 24, 6 (1998), 419-429.

9. P. Mounissamy, An Evaluation of usage and usability of electronic journals, M.Phil. thesis, 2002, Algappa University, Tamil Nadu.

7

Digitization of Project Reports: An Experience With GSDL

Dr. N.S. Harinarayana
Lecturer, Department of Library and Information Science
University of Mysore
Mysore

Sunil M.V.
Librarian
SDM Institute of Management Development
Mysore

Namratha G.R.
Student, II Year MLISc
Department of Library and Information Science
University of Mysore
Mysore

INTRODUCTION

The explosion of interest in research and practice of digital libraries has spanned the boundaries of computing, networking and information science. A digital library has dissolved the barriers to 'information equity' and acting as an information highway for the knowledge to every citizen of the country. A digital library is "an organization that provides the resources, including the specialized staff, to select, structure, offer intellectual access to, interpret, distribute, preserve the integrity of, and ensure the persistence over time of collections of digital works so that they are readily and economically available for use by a defined community or set of communities" (Digital library federation). As per Fox "A digital library is a distributed technology environment which dramatically reduces barriers to the creation, dissemination, manipulation, storage, integration, and reuse of information by individuals and groups"

The main functions of a digital library, as well as of a conventional library may be summarized as 1) Collection; 2) Organization and representation; 3) Access and retrieval.

- Collection does not mean acquisition of information or documents, but includes techniques that allow to detect those information sources that are useful to a user.
- Organization and representation require that the information resource are classified and indexed according to criteria relevant to the potentiality of users.
- Access and retrieval involve the design and organization of materials in order to retrieve effective information items, when the user requires them.

Building digital libraries is one of the most important grand challenge problems faced by the information professionals. The question that is being asked by professionals is how to build an effective digital library? A quick perusal of the literature concerned suggest, that various projects are on to build a small to medium size digital libraries. To name a few, Texas A&M University, Illinois Wesleyan University, Alabama Library Association V.V. Giri National Labour Institute, Association of Indian Labour Historians, etc.,

One of the problems of the digital library building is the software. Fortunately there are a few good open source software around such as GSDL, D Space, e print, Fedora, etc., We have selected GSDL for the obvious reasons such as, it is a Window based software; local expertise is available; a few proven projects are based on GSDL and so on.

GREENSTONE

Greenstone digital library software is a comprehensive, open-source system for the construction and presentation of information collection. GSDL is developed at the university of waikato and distributed in cooperation with UNESCO and Human Info NGO, issued under the terms of GNU General Public License. It is used to tackle the issues of digitalization and providing the facilities ranging from multilingual information retrieval to distributed computing protocols, interoperability to search engine technology, metadata standards to multiformat document parsing, multimedia to multiple operating systems, web browsers to plug-and-play DVD's. Collections built with Greenstone offer effective full-text searching and metadata-based browsing facilities that are attractive and easy to use. Moreover, they are easily maintainable and can be augmented and rebuilt entirely automatically. The system is extensible; software "plugins" accommodate different document and metadata types. GSDL is compatible with formats like .doc, .pdf, and other much in use formats.

Here are the some of the versions of GSDL

Versions	Released Date
2.41a	NA
2.41	NA
2.40	2nd July 2003
2.35	25th May 2001
2.31	28th Feb 2001
2.30	3rd Jan 2001
2.27	5th Nov 2000
2.26	9th Oct 2000
2.25	3rd Sep 2000

We have adopted 2.40 version. The latest version 2.41a includes new plugin for processing CDS/ISIS databases, the ability to export multiple collections to CD-ROM and many other bug fixes and improvements.

We can build the collection in GSDL by using

1. Collector
2. DOS Command
3. GLI (Greenstone Librarian Interface)

Greenstone software is the 7th recipient of biennial NAMUR award. The award is given in recognition of GSDL contribution in rising awareness internationally of the social implication of information and communication technologies.

GREENSTONE LIBRARIAN INTERFACE

Greenstone Librarian Interface (GLI), a graphical tool to assist us with building digital libraries using Greenstone. The GLI gives us access to Greenstone's functionality from an easy-to-use, 'point and click' interface. To use this tool we will need a suitable Java Run-time Environment (version 1.4.0 and beyond), Perl and Greenstone.

TASK

This paper explains the task of digitalization of 60 project reports, which is the intellectual effort of the students in Major Companies to solve the particular managerial task. This digitization and presentation of the project reports is designed to facilitate the user in easy to access via web, self-installable CD and through the library database.

The task doesn't limit its boundaries to digitalization of project work it has extended to accessing the information regarding the student and his contact details. It also enumerates the company information by providing hyper link to the company website.

PROCEDURE FOLLOWED

In this paper we review some techniques followed to digitize the reports which were in MS Word.

Analysis of the Text

Copies of the project were collected from the students in MS word format, after clearing the copyright issue with the companies on which projects were done. For uniformity of display, we converted the whole text into "Arial" and font size to "12"

Characterizing Images of Text

The images in the text has to be analyzed and the .doc file is saved as .html to have the figures as Images (.gif/.png/.jpg/.tif). The image files so obtained are linked to the .html file with the string <IMG src=" .gif">.

Enriching the Display

Meta-data was added to the web-pages, for further contact about the project or its author. The same acts as an alumni database for the institute.

```
<marquee height=5% width=100%
scrollamount=3%scrolldelay=2BGcolor = "lavender">
<font face =”Arial”>
<b>
<Font color = blue>
Name of the College
</b>
</font>
</marquee><br>
<br><br>
<center><TABLE>
 <TR><!— Row 1 —>
<TD><IMG SRC=”file image of the student”width=125
height=175></td>
<TD></td>
<TD></td>
<TD></td>
<TD></td>
<TD></td>
<TD></td>
<TD>Name      Name of
the Student
<br><br>e-mail       e-mail
id
<br><br>Area       Area of
Specialization
<br><br>Batch       Year
/Batch
<br><br>Company    Company Name
<br><br>URL of the Company    <a href = /
a>Company URL
```

```
<br></TD>
</TR>
</TABLE>
</center>
<br><br>
<hr width=100% color=red#rrggbb>
<br><br>
```

This string is inserted at the beginning of the text at .html.

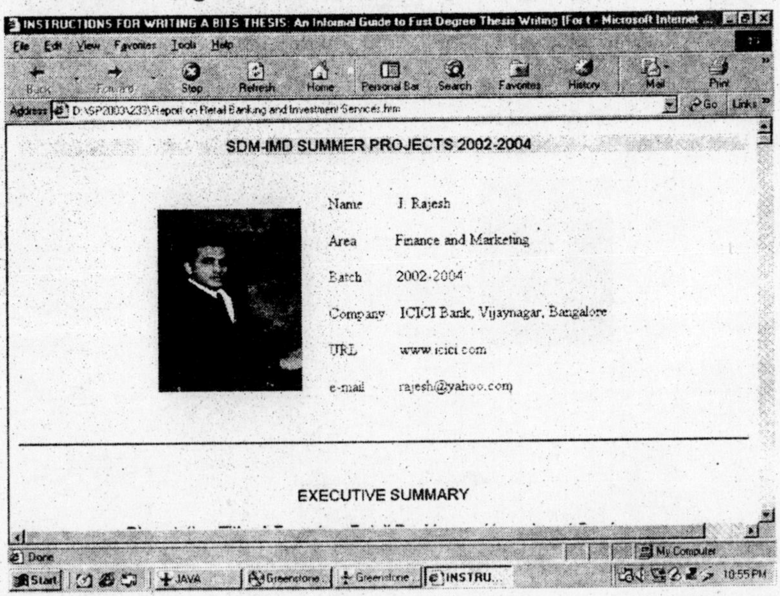

Importing the .html to GSDL and Indexing

The completely formatted and aligned .html file and the supported image files are placed in a folder and imported to GSDL using Librarian Interface. The file imported is enriched by feeding the data regarding the project in ENRICH screen in LI. The CLASSIFIERS and HIERARCHY is selected and framed in the DESIGN screen of LI. The CREATE command finalizes the importing and building of the file into DL.

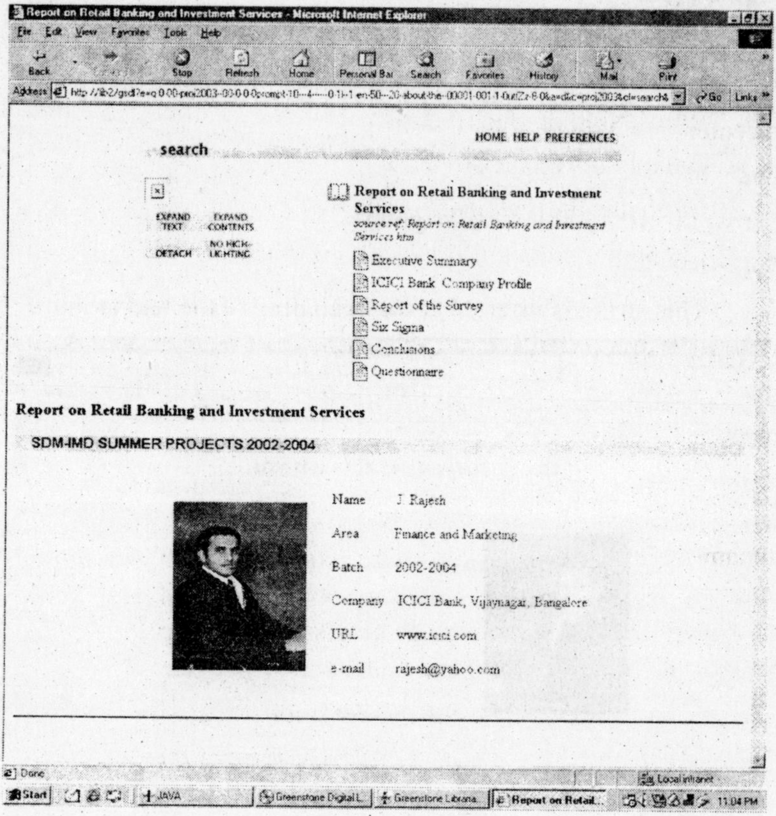

Accessibility

The digital library of summer projects so developed is made available through

* web – linking to the institute website; archiving in the GSDL site
* CD – converting into self-installable CD
* LAN – placing in the Local Area Network and made it available to the key users of the library.

Results of the Experiment

So far we are able to integrate and solved the following problems,

* Conversion of .doc to .html
* Linking the images to .html
* Enriching the document with related additional information
* Maintaining the uniformity in display
* Providing the accessability through different modes

CONCLUSION

Development of digital library technologies is becoming more and more significant in view of its myriad applications: education, health care, preservation of heritage, science and economy, as well as the quality of life on the whole. Converting and enriching of the documents can offer an added value in building intelligent digital libraries. This task has led us to have new additional tasks in the field of digitization. Knowing the things about digitization reminds the famous quote by Sir Alfred Tennyson in Ulysses:

* All experience in an arch where thro'
* Gleams that untravell'd world, whose margin fade
* Forever and forever, when I move.

REFERENCES

1. Watanabe, Vasuhiko and Nagao, Makoto (1997) "construction of retrieval system for pictorial book of Flora". 13th conference of IEEE.962-967.
2. Witten, Ian. H, (2001) "How to build a digital library using open-source software",4th International conference of Asian digital libraries, ICADL 2001 Tutorials, 109-200.
3. www.greenstone.org
4. Witten, Ian, H. (2003) "Customizing digital library interfaces with Greenstone", TCDL Bulletin, Summer 2003. www.ieee-tcdl.org/Bulletin/current/witten.html

5. Witten, Ian, H. (2003) "Examples of Practical digital libraries: Collections built Internationally using greenstone", d-Lib Magazine, March 2003 http://www.dlib.org/dlib/march03/witten/03witten.html

8

THE DIGITAL DIVIDE OR SOCIETAL DIVIDE?

Prof. (Dr.). G. Devarajan

Head, Dept. of Library & Information Science

& Director, College Development Council

University of Kerala

Thiruvananthapuram-34

INTRODUCTION

Information is a vital and regenerative resource. It is a basic component of societal development. The information and communication technology (ICT) is relied upon heavily by the information centres in order to satisfy the varied information needs of the user community. In all spheres of information activities of mankind there is a significant investment in the Internet as an enterprise and with wide utility to support teaching, scholarship and administrative matters. The application of new technology has accelerated and widened the existing information gap between the developed countries and developing countries. The information gap between the rich and poor is growing within a country or even region itself. This leads to "digital divide" between the information "haves" and "have-nots".

BRIDGING THE DIGITAL DIVIDE

The avenues of information and communication technology have helped in the democritisation of information. But more than 80% of people in the world have never even heard a dial tone, let alone surfed the web. In fact the gap between information "haves" and "have-nots" is widening. As far as developing countries are concerned the stratification of information rich and information poor is going to be a big social problem. Various countries and organizations are making attempts to bridge the information gap.

BRIDGING THE DIGITAL DIVIDE-INDIA

National and state-level agencies in India are making attempts to bridge the digital divide. In 2000, the Government of India in collaboration with an information technology corporation started a project, known as the "Hole in the wall" experiment, to provide computer access to the city's street children. An outdoor five-station computer kiosk was set up in one of the poorest slums of New Delhi. Though the computers themselves were inside a booth, the monitors protruded through holes in the walls, as did specially designed joysticks and buttons that substituted for the computer mouse. Keyboards were not provided. The computers were connected to the Internet through dial-up access. A volunteer inside the booth helped to keep the computers and Internet connections running. No teacher or instructor was provided, in line with the concept called 'minimally invasive education'. The idea was to allow the children unfettered 24-hour access, and to learn at their own pace and speed. According to reports, children who flocked to the site taught themselves basic computer operations. They worked out how to click and drag objects; select different menus; cut, copy, and paste; get on the Internet; and change the background "wallpaper". A number of projects are being undertaken in various states in India to bridge the Digital divide. The AKSHAYA is a project in Kerala inaugurated by the president of India, Dr. A.P.J. Abdul Kalam on 18th November 2002. The project envisages the establishment of 9,000 community information centres across the State as part of a campaign to bridge the digital divide. These centres are to be established through private initiative, with the objective of having one centre within two km. of each household. The project would commence in Malappuram and Thiruvananthapuram in January 2003 and the entire state is proposed to be covered by May 2004. As part of the project, one person from each family will be trained to enable him to use the computer for day-to-day communication and information needs.

A shot in the arm for n-Logue is the mandate from the Tamilnadu government to network and put in place the infrastructure required in ten districts. Tamilnadu's Rural Access to services through Internet (RASI) project has already got 70 villages in each of the two districts –Madurai and Cuddalore -networked and running.. And nearly 5-10 villages are getting networked every month in these districts. RASI project seems to be different from other government projects that start with a bang and die even before inaugurations come to an end. It has attracted attention from corporate bodies, educational institutions, hospitals and private telecom companies.

Akin to a PCO booth, the telephone cum Internet access point for a villager will be housed in a kiosk named "Chiraag". It uses Prof. Jhunjhunwala's corDECT technology to provide the last mile wireless connection. The kiosk is equipped with a PC with CD-ROM and multimedia, web camera, printer, corDECT wall set, speaker microphone and power backup for four hours. The language barrier has been taken care by providing local language software. Networking rural India with telephone and the Internet is becoming a reality with "Chiraag".

IMPLICATIONS AND ISSUES

Digital divide is marked not only by physical access to computers and connectivity, but also by access to the additional resources that allow people to use technology well. In the real sense of the term "digital divide" it gives overriding importance to the physical availability of computers and connectivity, rather than to issues of content, language, education, literacy, or community and social resources. A problem with the digital divide concept is in its implication of a bipolar societal split. As Cisler argues, there is not a binary division between information "haves" and "have-nots" but rather a gradation based on different degrees of access to information technology. As Henry Jenkins argues, "the rhetoric of the digital divide holds open this division between civilized tool users and uncivilized non users. As well meaning as it is as a policy initiative, it can be marginalizing and patronising in its own terms". He also opined that the notion of a digital divide implies a chain of causality i.e. lack of access to computers and the Internet harm life chances. While this point is undoubtedly true, the reverse is equally true; those who have already marginalized will have fewer opportunities to access and use computers and the Internet. In fact, technology and society are intertwined and co-constitutive, and this complex in interrelationship makes any assumption of causality problematic. The digital divide framework provides a poor road map for using technology to promote social development since it overemphasizes the importance of the physical presence of computers and connectivity to the exclusion of other factors that allow people to use ICT for meaningful ends.

CONCLUSION

The division of information rich and the information poor is more serious and dangerous than economic stratification of rich and poor. A critique of the notion of a digital divide is necessary to fully inform and unleash efforts to use technology to promote social inclusion. A framework of technology for social inclusion allows reorienting the focus from that of gaps to be overcome by provision of equipment to that of social development to be enhanced through the effective integration of information and communication technology into communities and institutions. This kind of integration can only be achieved by attention to the wide range of physical, digital, human, and social resources that meaningful access to information and communication technology entails. A society that is free from digital divide and societal divide would pave ways for holistic development of a nation and global society.

REFERENCES

1. Aichholzer,George and Schmutzer,Rupeer . *The Digital Divide in Austria.* Vienna: Institute of Technology Assessment,2001.
2. Carvin,Andy . "Mind the gap: The digital divide as the civil rights issue of the new millennium," *Multimedia Schools,* 7(1)2000
3. DiMaggio,Paul J and Hargittai,Ezster . "From the 'digital divide' to 'digital inequality': Studying Internet use as penetration increases," *Working Paper 19, Center for Arts and Cultural Policy Studies, Woodrow Wilson School.* Princeton, N.J.: Center for Arts and Cultural Policy Studies, Woodrow Wilson School, Princeton University,2001.
4. Lievrouw,AL . "The information environment and universal service," *Information Society,* volume 16, pp. 155-159.2000.
5. Mitra, S . "Minimally invasive education for mass computer literacy," *CSI Communications* (June), pp. 12-16.1999.
6. Patterson,R and Wilson, E. "New IT and social inequality: Resetting the research and policy agenda," *Information Society,* volume 16, number 1, pp. 77-86.2000.
7. Warschauer, Mark. *Electronic Literacies: Language, Culture, and Power in Online Education.* Mahwah, N.J.: Lawrence Erlbaum Associates.2000.

9

New Ages in Preservation - is Digital Preservation Different?

J.P.S.Kumaravel
Information Scientist
Dr.T.P.M.Library
Madurai Kamaraj University, Madurai – 625 021
E-mail: jpskumar@yahoo.com

INTRODUCTION

Digital libraries, whose history spans more than a decade are surely among the most important and influential institutions to emerge in recent times, Their mission is to dissolve barriers to 'information equity'; Digital libraries seek to bring the highways of knowledge to everyone. The explosion of interest in research and practice of digital libraries has spanned the boundaries of computing, networking, and information systems and sciences.

Digital libraries are complex information systems. Their design, development, management and use require application of scientific, technological, methodological, economic, legal and other innovations. Digital library technologies are rapidly developing and are still evolving. The grand challenges of Digital libraries research and development centers on interoperability-the ability to access.

ADVANTAGES OF DIGITAL ACCESS

Digital imaging technology offers distinctive advantages to institutions with impressive collections of scholarly resources. Information content can be delivered directly to the reader without human intervention. Information content in digital form can be retrieved by readers remotely, although such delivery may tax the capabilities of even the most sophisticated projection equipment and networks. Digital image quality is extraordinary and is improving constantly. It is now possible to represent almost any type of traditional research material with such visual quality that reference to the original materials is unnecessary for most, if not all, purposes.

The power of full-text searching and sophisticated, cross-collection indexing affords readers the opportunity to make new uses of traditional research resources. Newly developed system interfaces (the look and feel of the computer screen) combined with new ways to deliver manageable portions of large image data files promise to revolutionize the ways in which research materials are used for teaching and learning. It is no wonder that there is a nearly overwhelming rush to jump on the digital bandwagon.

PRESERVATION IN THE DIGITAL WORLD

The essence of traditional preservation management is resource allocation. People, money, and materials must be acquired, organized, and put to work to prevent deterioration or renew the usability of selected groups of materials. Preservation largely is concerned with the evidence embedded in a nearly endless variety of forms and formats. Things are preserved so that they can be used for all kinds of purposes, scholarly and otherwise.

People with the responsibility of preservation have determined that some small portion of the vast sea of information, structured as collections of documents, books, collections, and other things, has research value as evidence well beyond the time and way intended by those who created or published it (Buckland, 1991). This distinction between the value of the information content (usually text and illustration) and the value of the evidence embedded in the artifact is at the heart of a decision-making process that is itself central to the effective management of both traditional and digital library materials.

In the digital world, preservation is the creation of digital products worth maintaining over time with the following presumptions.

* Preservation is a reality and not merely a metaphor for or symbol of access.
* The time to be concerned about the long-term persistence of digital products is when a system is designed and before digital conversion has begun.
* A digital product has its own identity and exists within a market economy. It is not necessary to sell or license a digital product for the product to have an identity within a community of end-users.
* The work to design and create a digital product adds value to the information contained in the documents that serve as sources. The value added to a digital product must ultimately result in a product that is an essential and vital capital resource to the institution that has chosen to create it in the first place.
* The persistence of digital products requires careful attention to the maintenance of content (the bits and bytes) functionality (how the bits work in a system).
* Preservation in the digital world is not absolute, but depends instead on the continuing transformative impact of the digital product on the information work of end-users.

Digital preservation raises challenges of a fundamentally different nature which are added to the problems of preserving traditional format materials. Digital preservation means the planning, resource allocation, and application of preservation methods and technologies necessary to ensure that digital information of continuing value remains accessible and usable. Digital preservation encompasses material that begins its life in digital form as well as material that is converted from traditional to digital formats.

CHALLENGES IN PRESERVING DIGITAL MEDIA

Recording media for digital materials are vulnerable to deterioration and catastrophic loss, and even under ideal conditions they are short lived relative to traditional format materials. The question of preserving or archiving digital information is not a new one and has been explored at a variety of levels over the last five decades. The main challenges in preservation of digital information are

* Technological obsolescence
* Migration over from one form to another due to change in Hardware/Software platforms
* Legal and organizational issues
* Deep Infrastructure for storing and accessing digital information
* Defining the conceptual framework
* Information Integrity

Technological Obsolescence

More insidious and challenging than media deterioration is the problem of obsolescence in retrieval and playback technologies. Early attention to the difficulties in preserving digital information focused on the longevity of the physical media on which the information is stored. Even under the best storage conditions, however, digital media can be fragile and have limited shelf life. The rate of change in technology is 3 to 5 years. Any new devices, processes and software that are replacing the products and methods used to record, store, and retrieve digital information last for 2- to 5-years. Even the most fragile media may well outlive the continued availability of readers for those media.

Efforts to preserve physical media thus provide only a short-term, partial solution to the general problem of preserving digital information. Indeed, technological obsolescence represents a far greater threat to information in digital form than the inherent physical fragility of many digital media.

Records created in digital form in the first instance and those converted retrospectively from paper or microfilm to digital form are equally vulnerable to technological obsolescence. Another challenge is the absence of established standards, protocols, and proven methods for preserving digital information. With few exceptions, digital library research has focussed on architectures and systems for information organization and retrieval, presentation and visualization, and administration of intellectual property rights.

The critical role of digital libraries and archives in ensuring the future accessibility of information with enduring value has taken a back seat to enhancing access to current and actively used materials. As a consequence, digital preservation remains largely experimental and replete with the risks associated with untested methods; and digital preservation requirements have not been factored into the architecture, resource allocation, or planning for digital libraries.

Migration from one Platform to Another

Digital information today is produced in highly varying degrees of dependence on particular hardware and software. Moreover, it is costly and difficult for vendors to assure that their products are either "backwardly compatible" with previous versions or that they can interoperate with competing products. Refreshing thus cannot serve as a general solution for preserving digital information and this conclusion has prompted discussion of other kinds of solutions.

Refreshing digital information by copying it from medium to medium and the possibility of maintaining a complex set of emulators describe two distinct points on a continuum of approaches to preserving digital information. However, neither refreshing nor emulation sufficiently describes the full range of options needed and available for digital preservation. Instead, a better and more general concept to describe these options is migration.

Migration is the periodic transfer of digital materials from one hardware/software configuration to another, or from one generation of computer technology to a subsequent generation. The purpose of migration is to preserve the integrity of digital objects and to retain the ability for clients to retrieve, display, and otherwise use them in the face of constantly changing technology.

Legal and Organisational Issues

Addressing and resolving the legal and practical questions of migrating intellectual property in digital form necessarily involves the creators and owners of intellectual property, managers of digital archives, representatives of the public interest, and actual and potential users of intellectual property.

Deep Infrastructure for Storing and Accessing Digital Information

The process of building deep infrastructure involves multiple and interrelated factors. One of the biggest unknowns is the full impact on traditional information handling functions of distributed computing over electronic networks. The effort to meet the cultural imperative of digital preservation requires a complex iteration and reiteration of exploration, development and solution.

The limited life of magnetic and optical media pose a significant problem, although this is not the primary limiting factor for digital preservation. Recent research on the longevity of magnetic media indicate a useful life span of 10 to 30 years if they are handled and stored properly. Some optical disk technologies promise life spans of up to 100 years. Most authorities argue that enhanced media longevity is of little value because current media outlast the software and devices needed to retrieve recorded information. Optical media are susceptible to damage from high humidity, rapid and extreme temperature fluctuations, and contamination from airborne particulate matter. To prevent these problems, it is imperative to store magnetic and optical media under strict environmental controls that are not always available, affordable, or convenient.

Even modest improvements which produce storage media with larger per unit storage capacities and greater tolerance to variations in temperature and humidity will lower preservation costs by lessening the need for strict environmental controls, reducing the frequency with which digital media must be "refreshed" through recopying, and decreasing the number of storage units that must be handled.

Defining the Conceptual Framework

In order to lay out the conceptual framework for digital preservation it is essential to start with an analysis of the digital landscape, focusing on features, including stakeholder interest, that affect the integrity of digital information objects and which determine the ability of digital archives to preserve such objects over the long term. The principles that responsibility for archiving rests initially with the creator or owner of the information and that digital archives may invoke a fail-safe mechanism to protect culturally valuable information. The analysis should explore in detail the roles and responsibilities associated with the critical functions of managing:

* the operating environment of digital archives;
* strategies for migration of digital information; and
* costs and financial matters.

Information Integrity

In the digital environment, the features that determine information integrity and deserve special attention for archival purposes include the following: content, fixity, reference, provenance, and context.. The notion of content is a complex idea that operates at several different levels of abstraction. To preserve the integrity of objects in their charge, digital archives must decide at which level, or levels, of abstraction they are defining information content.

At the lowest level of abstraction, all digital information objects consist of simple bitstreams of 0s and 1s. One can distinguish objects from one another merely by distinguishing the configuration of bits. Preserving the integrity of an information object in this sense means preserving the bit configuration that uniquely defines the object.

At the highest level of abstraction, digital archives define content in a way that transcends the limits of the hardware and software systems needed for reading and interpreting the bits of an information object and for rendering it for use in a specific format and structural representation; that is, they define content in terms of the knowledge or ideas the object contains.

CONCLUSION

The preservation community has at its disposal a variety of tactics for digital preservation that appear to work effectively for certain types of materials in certain restricted environments, but we have not yet developed solutions that are scalable to the general problem of digital preservation. The methods used will vary depending upon the complexity of the original data objects, the extent to which the functionality for computation, display, indexing, and authentication must be maintained, and the requirements of current or anticipated users. But any solution must be scalable from the laboratory, prototype, or pilot project to the wide range of individuals and institutions who have a need to make digital materials last longer than the current generation of technology permits.

REFERENCES

1. Conway, Paul "Digitizing Preservation: Paper and Microfilm Go Electronic." Library Journal , 1994 (February 1), Vol. 119, p.42-45.
2. Garrett, John R., et. al."Toward an Electronic Copyright Management System." Journal of the American Society for Information Science 1993, Vol.44(8) p.468-473.
3. Levy, David M. and Catherine C. Marshall. "Going Digital: A Look at Assumptions Underlying Digital Libraries,"

Communications of the ACM, 1995, Vol. 58, No. 4. p.77-84.

4. Graham, Peter S. "Requirements for the Digital Research Library" , College and Research Libraries, July 1995, Vol. 56(4). P.331-339.

5. Task Force on Archiving of Digital Information. "Preserving Digital Information," Report of the Task Force, commissioned by the Commission on Preservation and Access and The Research Libraries Group, Version 1.0, August 24, 1995.

10

IT Literature in Library and Information Science Journals: An Informetrics Study

Dr. P.M. Naushad Ali
Lecturer, Department of Library Science
A.M.U Aligarh-202 002
Email:pmnali@hotmail.com

Atiya Masood
Ex-Student, Department of Library Science
A.M.U Aligarh-202 002

INTRODUCTION

Periodicals are the purveyors of latest Information. Library science periodicals are an essential component of the holdings of a library, which supports research, and other academic activities of a library school. Information technology has become a part of library environment today as almost every subject field is scrambling to find ways to harness the power of information technology. It has added a great value to the library and information services. Research into new developments and trends in such diverse areas such as communications and Information Technology, Internet, CD-ROM and Digital Libraries etc. necessitate the use of professional research journals. A great deal of the information required in this context will generally never appear in book form. Moreover, there is always demand for such periodicals which contain more literature on Information technology, in this circumstance, every year need arises to drop certain title to subscribe new titles to meet information needs of researchers. Much of the success of any library aiming to serve the interests of researchers will depend up on the policy adopted towards the selection and retention of periodicals. A periodical subscription means a recurrent commitment of library funds because the librarians do not generally conduct informetrics studies to ascertain contents and change the subscription policy of the periodicals. The decision-making regarding the dropping of certain periodicals becomes logical as well as easy, through a study.

Bibliometric studies turn out to be the science of measurement relating to the quantity (number) of document; whereas informetric studies cover the metric studies relating not only to the document but also to concepts discussed in the documents, therefore bibliometric studies are considered as a subset of informetric studies.

Informetrics may be defined as application of statistics to the information science or information content. Changes in the structure and dimension of information industry have reflected on information sources and thus impact on the selection of journals. The main purpose of this informetrics study is to identify and select a portion of significant, reliable and relevant journals and contributors on IT based literature in Library and Information Science.

OBJECTIVES OF THE STUDY

The major objectives of the study are as follows:

1. To prepare a ranked list of journals on the subject IT in library and information science
2. To study the authorship pattern on IT literature in LIS journals.
3. To find out geographical and subject scattering of literature.
4. To identify the productivity of authors in this field.
5. To observe chronological distribution of journals.

6. To know the language(s) in which most of the literature on the subject has been Published
7. To know the most used bibliographic form of document.

HYPOTHESES

1. There is a significant difference regarding geographical scattering of articles on IT in library & information science
2. English language is the most used language by the contributors of article in the field of IT.
3. Journal article will be the most used bibliographic form of documents.
4. Influence of single research may be seen in authorship pattern of IT literature on Library and Information Science.

METHODOLOGY OF THE STUDY

The first step is to select the source document from which data is to be collected. For this purpose, the data has been collected from Library and Information Science Abstract (LISA), which is published from U.K, is most authoritative and comprehensive source material on the subject. 3815 references on the topic Information Technology and related fields have been collected on the 5"x3" catalogue cards from the volumes of Library and Information Science Abstract(LISA) from 1997-2000. Each reference consisted of information about the name of author(s), title, source journal, place, form and text language were noted on cards. In other words, a short bibliography was compiled on the cards.

ANALYSIS OF DATA

After preparation of entries, the next step was to analyze the data, which was collected from the source document. The total data collected on separate cards were arranged and rearranged in order to conduct the following studies.

Journal Wise Distribution

In the collected data, all the 3815 references were published in 746 periodicals, which have been ranked up to 31st position. However, Table 1 lists only 22 periodicals, in which the frequency of occurrence of items is up to 22. Table 1 shows that the first rank was occupied by the journal title ***Computers In Libraries (U.S.A)***, which accounts for 4.11% of the total references. Next five positions are occupied by journals ***Library Hi-Tech*** (U.S.A-3.77%), ***Link-Up*** (U.S.A—2.67%), ***Computer Networks*** (U.S.A—2.65%), ***Information World Review*** (U.K—2.38%) and ***Information Today*** (U.S.A—2.33%) respectively.

Table 1. Journal Wise Distribution

S. No	*Rank*	*Name of Journals*	*Country*	*Frequency*	*%*
1	1	Computers in libraries	U.S.A.	157	4.11
2	2	Library-Hi-Tech	U.S.A	125	3.27
3	3	Link-Up (U.S.A.)	U.S.A.	102	2.67
4	4	Computer Networks	U.S.A.	101	2.64
5	5	Information Word Review	U.K.	91	2.38
6	6	Information Today	U.S.A.	89	2.33
7	7	Searchers	Canada	73	1.91
8	8	Online	Switzerland	53	1.38
9	9	Net	Netherland	52	1.36
10	10	Vine	U.K.	44	1.15
11	11	Managing Information	U.S.A.	40	1.04
12	12	Library Hi-Tech News	U.S.A.	39	1.02
13	13	The Electronic Library	U.S.A.	36	0.94
14	14	Internet World	U.K.	28	0.73
15	14	Data Base	U.S.A.	28	0.73
16	14	Bulletin of Medical Library Association	U.SA.	28	0.73
17	15	College and Research Library News	U.S.A.	28	0.73
18	15	Bibliotheek Blad	Netherland	22	0.57
19	15	Ariadne	Netherland	22	0.57
20	15	Artificial Intelligence	Netherland	22	0.57
21	15	Reference Librarian	U.S.A.	22	0.57
22	15	Synopsis	U.S.A.	22	0.57

The present ranking list can be used for the libraries in taking policy decisions regarding the subscription list of periodicals to meet information requirements of library professionals and researchers.

Ranking of Authors

Table 2 deals with the ranking of authors with numbers of their contributions. One of the objectives of this study is to find out authors whose contributions are significant in the field of IT. For this purpose, a ranking list of eminent authors has been given in table 2 in order of their frequency of occurrence. The first four eminent authors in the field are:

1. Jacso, P (32 items)
2. Calenge, B (29 items)
3. Kelly, B (22 items)
4. Machovec, G.S (21 items)

Table 2. Author Wise Distribution

S.No.	*Rank*	*Name of Authors*	*Frequency*
1	1	Jasco, P	32
2	2	Calenge,B	29
3	3	Kelly,B	22
4	4	Machovec,G.S	21
5	5	Mackearney,M	20
6	5	Abell,A	20
7	6	Caladine,R	19
8	7	Hamitton, F.J	18
9	8	Ebben,M	17
10	9	Desmarais,N	15
11	9	Lansdale,R.E	15
12	9	Mc.Croskey, J.C	15

13	10	Sherman, C	14
14	10	Young, R.M	14
15	10	Adam,L	14
16	10	Forelbery,H	14
17	10	Hassio,A	14
18	10	Schicke,P	14

Country Wise Distribution

The country wise analysis (Table-3 and Fig.1) shows the countries producing most of the literature on the subject. The countries have been ranked on the basis of frequency of occurrence of items. The analysis has revealed that 1294 of articles were published from U.S.A, followed by U.K. and German which produced 21.96% and 7.39% research articles respectively (see Fig.1) .

The analysis not only shows the most potent countries of research on application of IT in Library and Information science but also indicate the wide coverage of LISA, as the publications from as many as 36 countries of the world, have been listed.

Table 3. Country Wise Distribution

S. No.	*Rank*	*Country*	*Frequency*	*Frequency Percentage*
1	1	U.S.A.	1294	33.91
2	2	U.K.	838	21.96
3	3	German	282	7.39
4	4	France	226	5.92
5	5	Japan	127	3.32
6	6	India	98	2.56
7	7	Netherland	96	2.51
8	8	Hong Kong	82	2.14
9	9	Russia	64	1.67
10	9	China	64	1.67

11	10	Canada	61	1.59
12	11	Switzerland	60	1.57
13	12	South Africa	58	1.58
14	13	Italy	56	1.46
15	14	Spain	52	1.36
16	15	Hungry	49	1.28
17	16	Australia	46	1.20
18	17	Malaysia	39	1.02
19	18	Burundi	28	0.73
20	19	Scotland	23	0.60

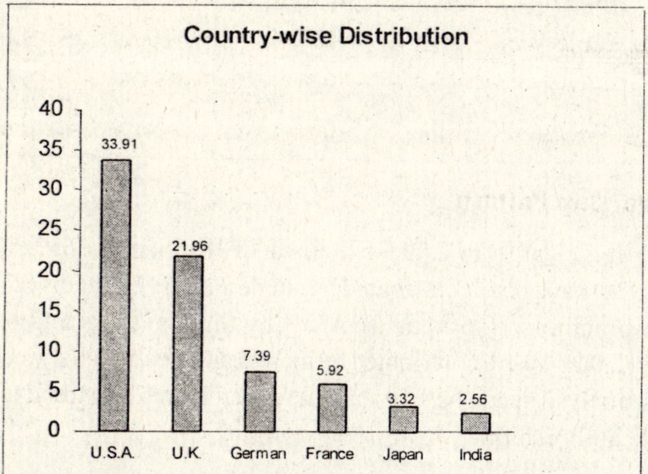

Figure 1

Subject Wise Distribution

Table- 4 deals with the ranking of subject heading of 3815 items divided into 8 subject headings taken from Library and Information Science Abstract (LISA). Analysis shows that 821 items,(21.52%) published under the heading 'library technology', is followed by 'Internet' with 738(19.34%). 'CD-ROM Database' with 628 items (16.46%) and 'Communication and Information Technology' 502 (13.15%) items.

Table 4. Subject Wise Distribution:

Subject Area	*Frequency Occurrence*	*Frequency Percentage*	*Cumulative Frequency*
Library Technology	821	21.52	21.52
Internet	738	19.34	40.86
CD-ROM	638	16.46	57.37
Communications and Information Technology	502	13.15	70.48
Electronic Publishing	423	11.08	81.57
World Wide Web	406	10.64	92.21
Digital Library	192	5.03	97.24
Expert System	105	2.75	99.99

Authorship Pattern

It is clear from Table–5 that, out of 3815 items, 2559 citations (67.07%) have been contributed by single author, 932 items (24.42%) by two authors, 246 items (6.45%) by three authors and only 78 items (2.04%) were contributed by more than three authors. According to the analysis it can be said that there is an increasing trend towards single authorship.

Table 5. Authorship Pattern

Authorship Pattern	*No. of Contribution*	*Frequency Percentage*	*Cumulative Frequency Percentage*
Single	2559	67.07	67.07
Two	932	24.42	91.47
Three	246	6.45	97.94
More than three	78	2.04	99.98

Language Wise Distribution

Language plays a significant role in the exchange of scientific information. Information about the most dominant language is very much useful for the librarian in the acquisition of periodicals and provision of translation service to the user.

Deduction can be drawn from Table –6 and Fig-2 that, the total of 3815 items were published in nine different languages. English was found to be the most dominant language as 3139 items constituting 82.28% of the total were reported to be published in that language. Russian (4.79%), French (4.014%) and Italian (3.22%) occupy 2nd, 3rd and 4th positions respectively.

Table 6. Language Wise Distribution

S.No. Rank	*Name of Language*	*Frequency Occurrence*	*Frequency Percentage*	*Cumulative Frequency*
1.	English	3139	82.28	82.28
2.	Russian	183	4.79	87.07
3.	French	158	4.14	91.21
4.	Italian	123	3.22	94.43
5.	German	73	1.91	96.34
6.	Chinese	69	1.81	98.15
7.	Japanese	49	1.28	99.43
8.	Bulgarian	12	0.31	99.74
9.	Turkish	9	0.23	99.97

Language-wise Distribution

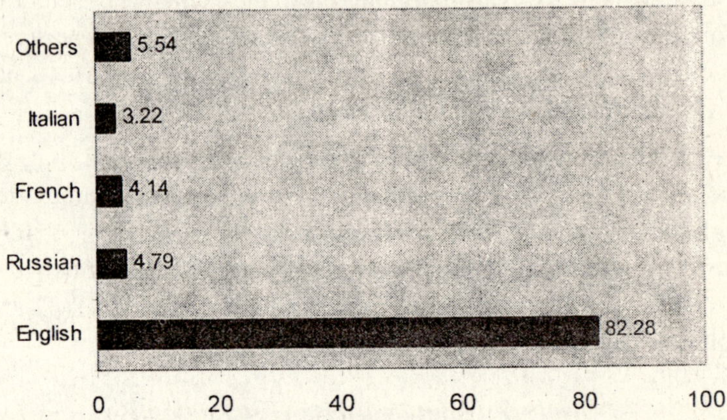

Figure 2

Bibliographic Form of the Literature

Table –7 presents the data of different bibliographic forms used in the total number (3815) of reference analyzed. 93.11% of items (3552) were in the form of journal articles, whereas 4.37% and 2.51% were conference proceedings (167) and bulletins (96) respectively. Most of the studies on IT have been communicated through scientific journals.

Table 7. Bibliographic Form of the Literature

S.No.	*Bibliographic Form*	*No. of Citations*	*Percentage*
1.	Journals	3552	93.11
2.	Conference Proceeding	167	4.37
3.	Bulletin	96	2.51
	Total	3815	99.99

CONCLUSION

From the study it is found that the journal title '*Computers in Libraries*' published from USA is the most productive journal, reporting 157 items i.e. 4.11% of the total, followed by '*Library hi-tech* ' also published from USA with 125 items i.e. 3.77% of the total publications. Author wise analysis has been done to know the contributors who produced most of the documents. It was found that 2559 items were produced by single author and 932 items are contributed by double authors, 246 items are contributed by three authors and only 78 items were contributed by more than three authors. The first three ranked authors are i. Jacso, P (32 items) ii. Calenge , B (29 items) and iii. Kelley (22 items). USA is the most productive country with 1294 (33.91%) items followed by Germany with 833 (21.26%) and France with 282 (7.39%) items respectively. Language wise analysis shows that English is one of the languages which is used very frequently by as many contributions as 3139 (82.28%) documents on the subject 'IT' was published in English. It is followed by Russian and French with 183 (4.79%) and 158 (4.14%) items respectively.

From the findings, it can be concluded that this study is very much useful to the researchers and librarians, for the preparation of subject bibliographies and to know the countries which are leaders in the field. It will be equally important for the documetalists to understand most productive journals and authors, country wise and language wise scatter of literature, in preparation of documentation list on IT based literature in library and Information Science.

PART II :

COPYRIGHT AND IPR ISSUES IN THE DIGITAL ENVIRONMENT

11

COPYRIGHT IN THE DIGITAL ENVIRONMENT

Dr. P.Venkata Ramana
Assistant Librarian
JNTU School of Planning & Architecture
Maheever Marg, Masab Tank, Hyderabad-500 028

INTRODUCTION

The recent rapid revolutionary developments in Information and Communication Technology (ICT), dramatic growth in networking, boom in Internet/WWW and knowledge explosion are transforming the whole world into a global knowledge society. In a knowledge-based economy, knowledge products have become vital resource for the growth and development of every field of human activity. The creation and ownership of knowledge products is gaining immense importance in knowledge economy.

Intellectual property contributes significantly to the socio, economic, cultural, scientific and technological development of a society. Since technologies in all fields of human activities are developing exponentially, the field of intellectual property is also expanding rapidly. Intellectual property rights (IPR) have attracted global attention in recent times due to globalisation, liberalisation and commercialization of trade and commerce.

INTELLECTUAL PROPERTY RIGHTS

The enormous developments in various fields of arts, science, technology, industry, trade, and commerce during the last decade are mainly due to the research and development output resulting from the systematic, consistent and creative efforts of writers, artists, programmers, entertainers, scientists and technologists all over the world. All these new creations of the human intellectual efforts are known as intellectual property. Intellectual property comprises all those things that come from the human intellect, whether they are ideas, inventions, words, music, theatre or art. This would include books, periodicals, pamphlets, archives, databases, internet resources, computer software, inventions etc., Broadcasting, cable casting, telecasting rights are some of the new branches of intellectual property.

Intellectual property represents the fruit of an individual creativity. The objective of intellectual property is to encourage creativity, ideas and inventions for achieving, social, cultural, economic, scientific and technological development of the society. It helps to protect, reward and enjoy the economic or other fruits of their labours. The owner of intellectual property has certain rights, which prevent others from making use of that property without permission. These rights are called intellectual property rights (IPR), protected by IPR law. According to the law, if anybody does make use of or copy that idea or invention without permission, it is an infringement of law and can be sued for the damage caused.

TYPES OF INTELLECTUAL PROPERTY RIGHTS

Trade Related Intellectual Properties (TRIPs) Agreement covers the following nine categories of intellectual properties.

1. Copyright and related rights.
2. Trademarks including service marks.
3. Undisclosed information including trade secrets
4. Industrial designs
5. Geographical indications including appellations of origin.

6. Layout designs of integrated circuits
7. Patents
8. Patenting of Micro-organisms.
9. Protection of plant breeder's rights.

As there are many types of intellectual property, there are varied differences with respect to the formalities, procedures, policies, evaluation tests, term periods, strengths of protection, penalties for infringement, enforcement rights and remedies against infringement for each type of intellectual property.

COPYRIGHT IN THE DIGITAL ENVIRONMENT

Copyright is one of the most important types of intellectual property. Copyright in digital environment has raised numerous legal issues and practical problems that concern to library managers, information scientists, archivists, authors, publishers and information users. The importance of copyright has grown enormously in recent times due to rapid revolutionary developments in the field of computer, communication, networking, publishing and entertainment technology. Today protection of copyright has become much more complex and serious in digital environment as the digital works can be copied-, reproduced and distributed/communicated easily, quickly, and inexpensively with modern technological devices like photocopies, scanners, tapes, cassettes, video recorders-, CD/DVD writers etc.,

Copyright means the exclusive right to do or authorize others to do certain acts in respect of the work. It is the right to copy or reproduce the work in which copyright subsists. It protects the results of an author, artist or other creator's intellectual skill, judgement and labour or capital expended in the creation of original piece of work. It prevents others from copying, hiring out, performing and broadcasting, amending or deforming the work.

Copyright in a work is automatic and subsists as soon as the work comes into existence provided it is original. No formalities like registration and required to acquire copyright. The term of the copyright is the life of the author of the work plus 60 years with certain exceptions. In 1988, the US made changes in the Copyright Law known as Sonny Bone Copyright Terms Extension Act. According to this Act, exclusive right to the work of authors and inventors is available for 70 years after their death.

Copyright has been emerged as an increasingly important instrument in regulating international flow of information ideas and knowledge products. It attempts to satisfy both the wish of information to have simple and easy access to scholarly information and the wish of creators/owners to protect their commercial or other interests.

CLASSES OF COPYRIGHT WORKS

To keep pace with the dynamic environment, a number of changes have been made in the Copyright Act of 1957 by the Amendment Act of 1994, which came into force from may 1995, Copyright Law provides protection for the following classes of works.

1. **Literary work** refers to written or printed matter. The definition of literary work was amended to include computer programs, tables and compilations including computer databases.
2. **Dramatic Work** includes any piece of recitation, choreographic work or entertainment in dumb show, the scenic arrangements or acting form, which is fixed in writing or otherwise but does not include a cinematograph film.
3. **Musical Work** means a painting, a sculpture, a drawing (including a diagram, map, chart or plan), an engraving or a photograph. Whether or not any such work possesses artistic craftsmanship.
4. **Artistic work** means a painting, a sculpture, a drawing (including a diagram, map, chart or plan), an engraving or a photograph. Whether or not any such work possesses artistic craftsmanship.

5. **Cinematograph film** means any work of visual recording on any medium produced through a process from which a moving image may be produced by any means and includes a sound recording accompanying such visual recording.

6. **Sound Recording** means a recording of sounds from which such sounds may be produced regardless of the medium on which such recording is made or the method by which the sounds are produced.

OBJECTIVE OF COPYRIGHT LAW

The main objective of copyright law is to encourage authors, composers, Artists, etc., to create original works by rewarding them with the exclusive right for a limited period to exploit the work for monetary gain. It protects the owner of the copyright work from an unlawful reproduction or exploitation of his work by others. The economic exploitation is done by entrepreneurs like publishers, film producers or sound recording producers to whom the owner of the copyright licenses the particular rights for a monetary consideration. People who economically exploit the copyright are the greater beneficiaries of the copyright law than the creators of works of copyright.

According to US Constitution, the objective of copyright protection is to promote the progress of science and useful arts, by securing for limited times to authors and inventors the exclusive right to their respective writings and discoveries.

DIGITAL WORKS

Digital works comprise computer programs, software, e-publications, databases (CD/DVD and online) multimedia, Internet and network resources etc., Copyright law has been changed over the years to keep pace with new development to include other knowledge products such as computer programs/software, databases, network resources etc.

With the widespread use of modern information & communication technolog., many information products like data.

reports and research papers are being created in digital form. The digital information products can easily be copied, reproduced and distributed generally through the various Net-based services such as the web, e-mail, FTP files etc., All these digital products are covered by the copyright laws.

Databases are available in CDROMs/DVDs, networks or online which can be easily accessibly by remote users anytime and anywhere. Development of databases involves huge amount of human and financial resources. Modern technologies enable to copy full or substantial part of the database easily at a fraction of the costs involved in developing the same. The database creators wanted to restrict unauthorized copying from these databases in order to get returns on their investments. The copyright protection available to literacy, artistic and dramatic work is also applicable to the databases as they are treated as 'literary works' in copyright Act amended in 1994.

FAIR USE IN THE DIGITAL ENVIRONMENT

The copyright Act provides exceptions to certain users, which shall not constitute an infringement of copyright. The copyright work can be used for certain specified purposes without copyright infringement. The objective of these exceptions is to enable the reproduction of the work for certain public purposes such as private study and research, criticism, comment, reviewing, news reporting etc., which is not an infringement of copyright. These are the defenses against infringement action, as the use of the copyright work for such purposes does not damage the legitimate interests of the copyright owner.

In determining whether the use made of work in any particular case is a fair use, the factors to be considered shall include:

1. The purpose and character of the use, including whether such use is of a commercial nature or is for non profit educational purposes.
2. The nature of the copyright work.

3. The amount and substantiality of the portion used in relation to the copyrighted work as a whole; and
4. The effect of the use upon the potential market or value of the copyrighted work.

A huge debate is raging world wide on the issue of 'Fair use' of copyright of electronic works in digital environment. A group of Chief Executives of the California State University (CSU), the State University of New York (SUNY), and the City University of New York (CUNY), in an effort to protect the Educational system from the onslaught of overzealous Copyright protectors, made the following statement.

"The fundamental mission of higher education is to advance and disseminate knowledge. This mission is realized through the use of various information formats, learning environments, and modes of delivery without unreasonable copyright restrictions".

INFRINGEMENT OF COPYRIGHT

Under copyright rules, if someone copies, distributes or displays a copyrighted work publicly without the authority of the copyright owner, it is an infringement of copyright. Even innocent infringements are subject to penalties. Copyright law also holds that helping someone else to violate copyright rights is an infringement called contributory infringement.

Internet being a public domain has copyright protection. If any one copies indiscriminately any content on the Internet and use it, not for fair use purposes but for commercial benefit, it would become an infringement of copyright.

Digital piracy in software movie, music, video films, games etc, has become a global phenomenon and moved into more dangerous levels. The Annual Global Software Piracy study organised by the Business Software Alliance indicates a rise in piracy rate from 37% in 2000 to 40% 2001. The industry is worried about the estimated loss of $11 billion in 2001 (ET 6.9.02). According to recent survey carried out by the A.P. Film chamber, the Indian Film industry looses about Rs.300 crores annually to piracy. Book publishing industry is loosing about 4.5 billion pounds sales at global level due to piracy.

Many countries have laws to prevent piracy, which are mostly on paper and not so effective in practice. For effective implementation of piracy laws, the role of law enforcement agencies and judiciary is most crucial. Piracy can be controlled only when it is seriously taken by the Governments law enforcement agencies and the judiciary.

DIGITAL RIGHTS MANAGEMENT (DRM) TECHNOLOGY

Copyright issue has become the most serious concern for writers, publishers, end users and libraries in the digital environment as the digital works can be easily copied- distributed and used unauthorized by numerous users. Producers of digital works are making serious efforts to control the unauthorized use of digital products through licensing agreements Cryptography, digital watermarks and digital signatures and DRM Technology.

Digital Rights Management is a set of technologies that content owners can use to protect their copyrights and stay in closer contact with their customers. In most cases it is a system that encrypts digital media content and limits access to only those people who have acquired a proper license to play the content. DRM helps content providers to protect their content and maintain control over distribution, by creating licenses for each digital media file.

Microsoft's Windows Media Rights Manager is a secure technology that helps to protect the rights of content owners, while enabling consumers to obtain digital content easily and legitimately. IBM has introduced the Electronic Media Management System (EMMS), which offers the freedom to innovate in the digital world by providing sophisticated and advanced technologies that help secure digital content of any kind.

Strong and more powerful Digital rights management technology needed to be developed to keep pace with the vast improvements in the new digital technologies.

THE DIGITAL MILLENNIUM COPYRIGHT ACT (DMCA)

The Digital Millennium Copyright Act (DMCA) is a complex Act passed in USA which deals with copyright and digital technology. It is the most comprehensive reform of copyright law. It takes copyright principles into the digital information age and establishes complicated rules.

The DMCA raised numerous legal and practical issues for the library community. It contains many new statutory elements. The key issues and the most important statutory provisions of DMCA include the following:

* Technological protection Measures (TPMS)
* Copyright Management information (CMI)
* Fair use in the digital millennium
* Maintenance of the public domain
* Library preservation & exemption update
* Online service provider limitation on liability
* Study on Distance education and digital technologies
* Database legislation
* The sonny Bono copyright term extension Act

INTERNATIONAL TREATIES

The success of Copyright Laws depends largely on the full participation and co-operation from the different countries of the world. There is a strong need to develop international consensus towards creating conducive environment to bring harmonization in the copyright laws and make them universally applicable and acceptable by all countries for free transborder flow of information/ technology in a digital world.

The following are the major international treaties that are contributing to the cause of protecting copyrights of authors, inventors, producers etc.,

1. The Berne Convention for the protection of Literary and Artistic Works (adopted in 1886 & Revised in 1971)
2. The Universal Copyright convention.

3. The Agreement on Trade Related IPR (Trips Agreement, 1995)
4. The WPO Copyright Treaty (WCT, 2002).

The WIPO Copyright Treaty (WCT) aims to bring International Copyright Law in line with the digital age. It offers more comprehensive protection for creators and creative enterprises in the digital environment. The purpose behind the treaty is to ensure the quality and authenticity of digital content and to enable creators, performers and concerning industries to reap the financial rewards of their talent, creativity and investment. It protects literary and artistic works, a broad category that includes books, computer programmes, music, art and movies.

CONCLUSION

Digital technologies along with immense opportunities have also posed new challenges and created more complex problems to copyright protection in digital environment. Electronic copyright is one subject that is attracting a worldwide attention in recent times due to the wide spread usage of Internet and WWW. The creators of books insist on absolute protection of their original material while users demand easy access to the material without any restrictions. There is a clear need to develop an equitable and workable solution that protects the interests of the copyright owners and also serves the needs of information users. Copyright Law has to balance the rights of both the owners and the users. Many developed countries are reviewing the existing copyright laws and enacting new laws with provisions of serious punishment for copyright violations in order to overcome the problems posed by the digital technologies. Severity of penalties for copyright violations will discourage widespread piracy.

REFERENCES

1. Chaterjee, Sudipta; Basak, Amita and Bandyopadhyay, Electronic copyright and the Librarian, IASLIC Bulletin 47 (27), 2002. p.97-113.

2. The Copyright Act with amendments 1994, Government of India, 1994.
3. Duggal, Pavan. Breaking new ground in Net Copyright Laws. Economic Times, 3.3.2002.p.9.
4. Fairuse of copyright in Education-An analysis, Naavi, Com.
5. Gupta, V.K. and Pongannaya. Legal protection for Databases. In R.Vengan *et al* (eds). CALIBER 2000: Information Services in a Networked Environment in India. February 16-18, 2000, p.4.31-4.45.
6. Lakshmana Moorthy, A and Karisiddappa, C.R. Copyright in Networked Environment in R.Vengan *et al* (eds) CALIBER 2000: Information Services in Networked Environment in India. February 16-18, 2000. p.4.18-4.30.
7. Lutzker, Arnold P. Primer on the Digital Millennium: what the Digital Millennium Copyright Act and the Copyright term extension Act mean for the Library Community, p.1-27. (wttp://www.arl..org/info/frm/copy/primer. html)
8. Narayanan,P. Intellectual Property Law. Calcutta, Eastern Law House, 1997. 561p.
9. Oppenheim, Charles, Copyright in the Electronic age. In world Information Report, Paris, UNESCO, 1997, p.349-360.
10. Prabhat Kumar, How to contain software piracy. The Economic Times 6.9.02.
11. Sobha Menon comfat Tactics. The Economic Times. 21.4.2002. p.9.

12

NEED FOR COPYRIGHT REGULATIONS AT GLOBAL LEVEL

M.C.K.Veeran
Assistant Librarian (Sel.Grade)
C.H.M.K.Library, University of Calicut
Calicut University P.O.-673635

T.M.Vasudevan
Lecturer
Department of Library and Information Science
University of Calicut

INTRODUCTION

The creation of multimedia content raises certain fundamental issues regarding copyright and intellectual property. The present copyright laws are totally out of date when considered in a digital networked environment.

The creation of multimedia work needs security on copyright in an economically feasible manner. The law should guarantee that the creators are justly compensated for their works and that the moral integrity of their work is kept intact. The concept of copyright in the electronic environment is therefore legally challenging. As the concept is very complex it has wider social implications.

MANIPULATION OF TEXTS

Electronic impulses can be easily manipulated, modified and erased. These qualities of the electronic database pose challenges to the legal system because the existing copyright laws were developed in a pre-electronic era where we depended on documentary evidence to validate transactions and to confirm contracts. Traditional documents such as letters, journals, articles, photographs, recorded conversations and audio-video types merge into a single stream of in differentiated, electronic impulses creating a new multimedia document, in the electronic environment. The diversity of inputs and outputs makes it difficult to decide which version of the document is the original draft and who is the real author or publisher.

To understand these complexities let us see how are words, texts, sound and images distributed and handled in the digital environment. When texts and images are digitized they acquire the following qualities.

i. Easy to copy

ii. Easy to handle and edit

iii. Easy to transform and reformat from one medium to another

Therefore we can say that the digital images are plastic, i.e., digital works can be easily manipulated, transformed or inserted into other works. Although many authors might prefer their works to remain intact in printed form once the work is digitized the author loses his control over the work. At the same time, we have to acknowledge that facility to manipulate the text is a definite advantage of digital data.

At present we have plenty of data available in the digital environment, which can be manipulated. Then it becomes difficult to determine who is entitled for royalty from such data?. In the case of creative works unfair transformation or manipulation in digital environment can raise legal issues and affect the market value adversely. Publishing agreements do not cover the rights under multimedia contents. Writers often complain that their articles are made available on online services by electronic publishers without authorization for giving royalty to them.. There is growing fear that computers are upsetting relationships among the creators, providers and consumers of art and ideas. Creative people feel helpless to prevent the infinite reproduction of their words, pictures and songs.

Under the present global networking environment we have to think of the Intellectual Property Rights in a broader perspective. Fair use doctrines available in US and Canada give some guidelines in this regard.

FAIR USE/DEALING PRACTICE ON THE INTERNET

Fair use of the copyrighted material considers the following aspects.

* The purpose of the intended use-whether it is for commercial or educational use?
* The nature of the copyrighted material, ie whether it is factual material or created for entertainment?
* The portion used in relation to the copyrighted work as a whole-a sentence, a paragraph or considerable portion from the text.
* Potential harm to the market for the copyrighted work.

The purpose for fair use would be for criticism, comment, news/ reporting or teaching and research. (Multiple copies are required in classrooms for teaching). Fair use dealing in Canada permits people other than copyright owners to reproduce a non-substantial part by others for private study, research, criticism, review and newspaper summary.

VIOLATION OF FAIR USE ON THE INTERNET

Forwarding e-mail messages or a portion of it quoting Usenet and mailing list postings and making private non-commercial copies of texts downloaded from ftp, gopher or web sites are considered as fair use.

The following activities are considered violation of fair use:

i. Scanning in Photographs in GIF formats

ii. Typing in newspaper or magazine articles.

iii. Posting articles or private e-mail written by someone else without their expression.

PROTECTING THE AUTHORS RIGHTS

Several methods of giving protection to the authors in the networked environment are being experimented. One way of remunerating authors and publishers and allow for integrity of networked material is to protect the electronic document by cryptographic means or digital signature method. Cryptography is a technique of converting ordinary text into cipher text (unintelligible) text through encryption. This method is gaining popularity as a method of ensuring security to electronic documents. Cryptography can help access control through password encryption. This protects the confidentiality and integrity of the data. Digital signature is a cryptographic method used by the recipient of a message to verify the identity of the sender and the integrity of the message

NEED FOR INTERNATIONAL LAW

Copyright issues in the digital environment have to be considered in a global perspective. Developed countries like Canada and US have framed regulations on infringement of copyright in the digital environment. However each country framing separate regulations for violation of copyright will not be helped for the digital environment since manipulation of texts through digital environment is a global issue. It has been suggested that a copyright clearing house to issue licenses and clear rights is a necessary adjunct for creating multimedia content on the information highway. Use of digital and multimedia texts downloaded through Internet for purely academic purposes i.e. for study and research should not be considered as copyright infringement. Let me conclude by quoting a sentence from a US court verdict in a case on copyright issue in the digital environment "the primary objective of copyright is not to reward the labor of authors, but to promote the progress of science and useful arts".

CONCLUSION

The present copyright laws are meant to cover printed materials. These are out dated when considered in a digital networked environment, copyright law for electronic resources in the digital networked environment has to be more liberal than similar laws for printed materials. The laws and regulations in this context should be developed at global level, making provisions for fair use of documents.

REFERENCES

1. Branscomb, Anne Wells. "Common Law for the Electronic Frontier". Scientific American, 26(3), (Sept. 1993) : 154-258.
2. Henderson, Carol. "At Stake: Electronic Use of Copyrighted Material". Educom Review, (Jan-Feb. 1995) : 56-57.
3. Marchionini, Gray and Hermann Maurer. "The Roles of Digital Libraries in Teaching and Learning". Communications of the ACM, 38(3), (April 1995) : 67-75.
4. Shade, Leslie Regan. "Copyright in the Digital Networked Environment". McGill University Graduate Program in Communications. 1995. ac 900@freenet Carleton.

13

Copy Right Issues in the Context of Digital Libraries

Meena V.
Research Scholar
Department of Library and Information Science
University of Calicut

INTRODUCTION

Information is a vital resource which is necessary for all kinds of human activity. Today it is the major input which has become the strategic resource for socio-economic development of a country. Information explosion has led to the application of information technology in libraries for various operations like collecting, processing and retrieving information. The modern storage media like CD-ROM, microfilms, microtexts, optical laser discs, floppy discs etc. play important roles in the fastly developing information world.

The proliferation of information generation has necessitated electronic resources to be a part of modern libraries. Electronic information resources contain originally published information in electronic form or information originally published in print form and then made electronically available.

FEATURES OF ELECTRONIC INFORMATION ENVIRONMENT

Electronic information environment has the following features.

* Provide access to very large information collection
* Supporting multimedia content
* Net work accessibility
* User friendly interfaces
* Unique referencing of digital objects
* Reference of various areas of the same time
* Current information services
* Advanced search and retrieval
* Supporting formal and informal learning
* Remote access.

DIGITAL LIBRARIES

The library exists for its clientele and everything that is done in the library is geared to the promotion of service to them. Libraries can play a greater role in identification, listing and classifying information sources and providing systematic approach to accessing the required information. In this manner they could take the rightful place as human agent alongside the search engine in searching the internet.

Internet is the gateway for libraries and information centers to electronic information obtained from different organsiations. Emergence of new technology and communication networks, especially internet helped libraries to become a global society. Library catalogues around the world can be accessed by making use of the world wide web.

The print paper based libraries evolved in to digital libraries due to man's never ending desire to improve his means of communication. Creation of digital resources with the establishment of the digital library is the need of the day.

The advent of modern electronic technologies that ensure quick and effective networking of large number of computers geographically dispersed, brought in logical coherence of distributed databases across the world. The assimilation of such distributed databases and knowledge banks is generally termed as digital library. They are those libraries which have a number of machine readable publications and facilities for remote access to several databases.

The key components of digital libraries are:

* geographically distributed digital information collections
* geographically distributed users
* seamless access provided through several mechanisms

INTELLECTUAL PROPERTY RIGHTS IN DIGITAL ENVIRONMENT

The world wide accessibility of electronic or digitized information sources and the tendency of making duplicate copies from the original document brought new issues relating to intellectual property. Librarians and information scientists are facing many problems regarding copyright issues in their working environment.

Intellectual property right is a general term which covers copyright, patents, registered designs and trade marks. It also covers layout designs of integrated circuits geographical indicators and ante competitive policies in contractual licenses. While considering intellectual property issues in the print era, copyright laws traditionally balanced public good and private interest. This was done by allowing public access to limited number of copies by public libraries and by providing controls to authors/publishers on protection of the intellectual property for a limited period. Apart from this, older technologies protect information because copying required physical handling. The copies were not perfect and the expense involved in copying and distribution was high.

In the digital when we consider the intellectual property right issues, access implies copying. One copy in digital form was sufficient to satisfy millions of readers. Copies could not be distinguished from the original. Moreover the reproduction involved low cost and distribution was instant at negligible cost. Another development in this context is that natural barriers to copyright infringement have been removed and access has become universal.

Encryption is a technical solution which is possible for IPR issues, in the digital age. If the concerned copy is available free of cost, then people will not be ready to buy the item for money. There should be some sort of an arrangement, like licenses to protect individual digital works so that they are not in a position to be copied. Moreover fair use purposes also need to be evaluated. Issues like whether the users are copying the contents for research or study purpose need to be considered.

Digitalization of libraries face new challenges of ensuring access to information and of satisfying the new market pressures of protection of the content provider. In order to safeguard the right of authors and for keeping a balance of interest of public access to information, strengthened copyright protection with fair use provisions are very essential for the present age. It is in this context that introduction of licenses has to be considered.

The information providers of electronic sources need to protect their investments. They are doing so by turning to licenses to define and control the use of their products. Eventhough the copyright act of 1976 includes provision for the educational use of copyrighted materials within a framework that delicately balances the rights of authors, publishers and other copyright owners, there are matters of difficulty with regard to application of the copyright laws in the electronic environment.

PRACTICAL CONSIDERATIONS

There are certain aspects to which considerable amount of thought should be given. Prominent among them is the practical consideration. The institution must clearly define the user group before the information providers as they might put forward certain restrictions. The broadest range of access options could be put forth before the information provider, considering the nature of the resource.

Use of information provided also needs to be considered with regard to its modification or manipulation. Activities which are permissible only should be taken up. The copying provisions need to be reviewed thoroughly so that rights granted under copyright law including fair use, educational needs and library exemptions are not denied. Access should be provided by the Institution within its power of control. Apart from the above aspects more definite and clear rules, if any, are necessary, then the institution should come forward with the same.

Licenses are facts of life in conducting business in the electronic environment. Electronic information resources providers have embraced licenses as legal means to control the use of their products during a time when technology and legislation are still evolving. Being responsible agents of an institution, one should be able to negotiate licenses effectively and efficiently. One should ensure that the user community is informed of its responsibilities under the agreement.

A license may not explicitly mention fair use, educational and library copying rights, or other rights permitted under the copyright Act. Such rights also will be protected but the priority should be users and their needs. After all users are the backbone of the library without which the library does not have any existence at all.

CONCLUSION

In this electronic era the proliferation of information in a variety of form has resulted in the formation of digital libraries which deal with enormous quanitity of data organized in digital media and providing access to such digital information from distant sources. This situation has brought new issues related to intellectual property right which can be solved only on the basis of certain practical consideration. User needs should be considered while solving such issues.

REFERENCES

1. Bark, Dan L. Copyrightable functions and patentable speech communications of the ACM 44.2 (2001): 69-71.
2. Gopikuttan, A. " copyright and libraries", Kerala Library Association Souvenir, 1977, 94-96.
3. Sobhanadevi, A.K. and C.K. Al-Assankutty, "Copyright law: the question of ownership, infringement and fair use in a digital environment". *Organisation of libraries and information centers on 21st century*. Ed. M. Bavakutty, MCK Veeran, T.K. Muhammed Salih, New Delhi, ESSESS Publication, 2001, 61-73.
4. www. Licensing, arl. Org/scomm./licensing/licbooklet, ltml – copy2
5. Isaac, K.A. 'Glimpse of library and Information Science" New Delhi: Ess Ess Publications, 2001, 124-132.
6. Neena singh, "Internet: Importance and usage for library and information professionals" DESIDOC Bulletin of information Technology 21.3 (2001): 17-28.

14

Copyright Issues in Academic Institutions in a Digital Environment

S.Seetharama

(DRTC, Bangalore)

17 Varadarajulu Street,

Chennai – 600 008

INTRODUCTION

The concept of Copyright can be traced to certain fundamental ideas about creativity and possession on the one hand, and to the invention of the printing process which made it possible to produce copies of an original material in large numbers at a low cost. Perhaps, the objective of Copyright is to create exclusive rights to the author, creator, etc over what they have created which would give them name & fame as well as economic / monetary gains. Copyright has relevance to libraries and librarians, as they are custodians of copyright material. While on the one hand they have the responsibility of providing access to their users to information wherever located, they have to take necessary steps to care and protect other people's copyright works. In recent times, with increased use of Information Technology, dissemination of information through electronic means has increased in leaps and bounds. This, in turn, has led to increased awareness of copyright protection as well as copyright infringements by individuals and institutions. One other dimension in the electronic environment has been in regard to formats. Since hardware and software to create digital images / information keeps changing, there is a need in libraries to change from one format to another which raises the question as to whether libraries have the right to change formats because of the ownership of the digital information/ images which have been created. In addition, even viewing electronically is seen by some as a potential infringement of a work because to load the documents onto the screen means making a copy of it and this is not allowed in law. Similarly, transmission electronically of a work or browsing electronically of a work is seen by some as a copyright violation.

Some of these issues have caught the attention of many and are being dealt with seriously by several fora and a clearer picture may emerge in the near future (Cornish, 1997).

COPYRIGHT

Copyright is, as its name suggests, a right to prevent copying of an original work. It comes into being upon the creation of an original artistic, musical, literary or dramatic work. Since copyright is only a right to prevent the copying of the original work, there is no absolute legal monopoly and copyright cannot therefore be used to prevent the independent production of an identical or similar work, without reference to the original work. Copyright rises on a national basis in the country in which the original work is created but may be enforced internationally by virtue of the Berne Convention (1885, Paris revised version 1979), and / or Universal Copyright Convention (1952, Paris revision, 1971). The convention is an attempt by the signatories to afford international protection for copyright works, which originate under the national law of a signatory state.

COPYRIGHT ISSUES WITHIN ACADEMIC INSTITUTIONS

Copyright unlike patents does not appear to have caught the attention of academic institutions since it is not perceived as having major financial and / or legal implications. Basically, copyright issues can be categorized into two types:

* Compliance in relation to third party material (which serve

as inputs),

* Exploitation of materials produced within the institution (i.e. Outputs).

Major proportion of literature on IPR, Copyright and electronic environment emanates from USA, possibly, due to large scale application of ICT in higher academic institutions and the resulting experiences gained. Nevertheless, a large number of articles have been published in UK, Australia and other developed countries. On the other hand, contributions on the subject "Copyright" from developing countries is rather low. One of the reasons is that many Non-western cultures do not have a tradition of IP unlike in the west where copyright and patent laws protect ideas. Perhaps, in developing countries, copyright is observed more in violation than in conformity. In lighter vein, *it appears that* **COPYING IS A RIGHT or** *rather the message is* **"COPY BY RIGHT" or "COPY LEFT AND RIGHT"!**

Compliance

Compliance to copyright is with reference to third party materials - -material of the Web, CD-ROM, and in electronic databases, radio, TV, video, cable, satellite, etc., as well as that in print. In other words, compliance may be described as strict observance of the rights of other copyright holders outside the domain of the academic institution concerned, while copying (i.e., making a single copy for a genuine purpose like teaching and research) a single time is permitted under the Status of Fair Dealing, making many copies is violative of compliance.

Compliance, thus is sought to be achieved by

a) Strict observance of the rights of copyright holders
b) Making individual users aware of copyright and its implications
c) Licensing agreements wherein payments are made to avoid liability for copying.

In spite of the above, compliance is considered a "Grey area" as it is difficult to establish Status of Fair Dealing and how licensing agreements affect the liability of individuals. Further, in instances of violation of copyright law, most of them have been settled out of court though significant costs were involved to the academic institutions (USA / UK) concerned.

In this context, it is worthwhile mentioning that academics regard copyright as a constraint on their duty to disseminate knowledge as it runs counter to a core value of the profession. Another complaint has been that observance of copyright law is different in different countries and that there was an element of unfairness here. In addition, the whole process was inefficient and expensive resulting in few requests for copying.

However, academic institutions in developed countries have suggested / taken certain steps to ensure compliance, which include:

a) Designating a person as Copyright Officer to whom staff and users can address queries on the use of third party material.

b) Creation of a Web site with a guide to copyright and copying - - with emphasis on "Fair Dealing" and issues such as how much and what type of material can be copied "without permission".

c) Ensuring compliance in the creation of teaching material and published research.

d) Considering copyright and its implications as a factor while undertaking projects.

e) Making staff and students aware through well publicised programs of user education / sensitisation.

f) Appointment of "authorised signatory" for signing licensing agreements or assignments.

g) Formulation of a Copyright Policy, which highlights digital material protection, access restrictions and authentication, measures.

While legal precedents in the context of copyright are few, they are conspicuous by their absence in relation to copyright and the Internet. Many cases in USA were settled out of court leaving no legal precedent. It may be said that most of the recent cases involving IPR relate to Patents and includes computer software, which is now patentable.

Exploitation of Outputs

1. Ownership of Outputs

The exploitation of outputs, both of staff & students. The outputs include resulting work of research (reports, articles, lab books, etc) as well as teaching and course materials in media other than in print and work other than text (for example, Web pages, Video clipping, recordings of lectures or live performance of a work of art, such as concert.)

It has been recognised, generally, that the initial owner of copyright in law is the author or creator, irrespective of who commissions or pays for the work. However, an expectation "...is a special rule that subject to contrary agreement, the first owner of copyright in a work created by an employee during the course of his or employment is the employer, not the employee(s)." On the other hand, an Association of University Teachers statement to its members on IPR stated recently "In universities, it should be put beyond question that academics retain ownership of copyright in their writings and other works, so that they may publish them when and where they wish, without control by their institutions," Thus, one can see conflicting and contradicting views being expressed -- so, it is a question of **Management Control Vs Academic Freedom.**

In recent times, with increasing emphasis on Commercialisation of Higher Education, ownership of course material - - electronic or otherwise - - has become a big issue both in USA and UK with some institutions asserting total ownership and control, sharing profits, others giving copyright to administrators not content providers. In other words, course materials have become tradable commodities.

2. *Transfer of Ownership*

Another issue relates to transfer of ownership or licensing. Irrespective of who holds the ownership, it would be useful for the institution to retain the right to continue to use in teaching and research even when it is assigned or licensed to another party. Perhaps, it would be a wise policy for the institution to insist that its staff consult and seek permission before entering into agreement with publishers or any other third party. Further, when the material produced and transferred involves revenue generation. A revenue sharing scheme must be thought of between the institution and the contributors / authors concerned.

SUMMING UP

From the foregoing account, it becomes clear that the issue of Copyright has become critically important largely due to the awareness and recognition by the institutions and contributors / authors concerned on the one had, and financial and legal implications due to commercialisation. As members of the library & Information profession involved in organisation, storage, retrieval and dissemination of information, it is imperative that we recognise the implications of copyright in an electronic / digital environment and assume responsibility to make our clientele aware and thus ensure compliance and exploitation as and when the occasion demands.

In this context, one can arrive at the following conclusions / inferences:

a) While Copyright has become a big and critical issue in the developed countries, it is perhaps, in stage of infancy in developing countries like India.

b) Basically, copyright issues relate to compliance on the one hand and exploitation on the other. This is partly due to large-scale application of ICT, the arrival of Internet on the scene facilitating downloading of information indiscriminately, and financial / legal implications of copyright.

c) In the near future, it would be desirable if not essential for institutions, especially, academic and industrial, to formulate a policy covering all aspects of Copyright and ensure it covers material in or converted to electronic form, highlighting issues, such as, ownership and protection of copyright, compliance and of copyright, third party copyright, revenue sharing, legal implications, transfer of ownership and licensing as well as raising user awareness, copyright with reference to teaching and course materials, research publications, etc.

d) Individual perceptions about ownership among the academic community are different. While older staff believes that they own copyright of their publications, the younger staff believes that the institution will take ownership of all outputs. This brings about the issue of Management Control and Academic Freedom.

e) In the changing teaching environment where distance learning and learning online has become a reality thanks to the application of a range of ICTs, copyright has become a big issue

f) It is necessary that institutions should allocate resources to Copyright Management.

SCENARIOS OF THE FUTURE

The Association of American Universities (AAU) have conjectured / projected four scenarios in the context of Copyright:

a) Enhancing current practices, by educating faculty / users and encouraging them to consider not assigning all their rights to publishers or indeed any at all.

b) Option two saw faculty ownership of copyright as the way forward, although it wondered whether the academic community would be prepared to deal with the necessary paperwork that would result. It considered if contracts could state that authors would not hand over copyright to publishers without prior university permission.

c) The third option is joint ownership by staff and the institution. Here the institution would be expected to give staff considerable support in return for say in what happens to material.

d) The final idea is joint faculty / university consortium ownership. It was noted this option had the highest start-up costs. This is similar to © but copyright is managed by and on behalf of a consortium of institutions and their staff by a specific copyright unit.

BIBILOGRAPHICAL REFERENCES

1. CORNISH (G). Copyright. *In* SCAMMELL (A). Handbook of Special Librarianship and Information work. Edn 7.1997.ASLIB.London.

2. MASHELKAR (RA). Intellectual Property Rights and the Third World. (Journal of IPR. 7; 2002; 308 – 323.)

15

AYURVEDA IN THE CONTEXT OF GLOBALISATION, PATENT AND INTELLECTUAL PROPERTY RIGHT ISSUES

G. Hemachandran Nair
Technical Assistant,
Kerala University Campus Library, Kariavattom
Email: ghnair@yahoo.com

(*Fulbright Exchange Scholar at School of Information Science, at Claremont Graduate University, California in the Fall 2002*)

INTRODUCTION

Ayurveda, the holistic health care system, which originated in Ancient India, is gaining more relevance today than ever before. Ayurveda has been recognised as the most user - friendly and environment - friendly system of medicine. More and more people are turning to natural products due to various factors such as limitation and side - effects of modern synthetic medicine. Several experts are of the view that in the 21st Century, Ayurveda will become the most effective alternate system of medicine, because of its holistic approach, its basic philosophy is the total well being of the individual and the humanity. The influence of Ayurveda among the foreign public began after the Alma Ata declaration of WHO in 1980 which recognised Ayurveda as an alternative system of medicine It has created a major awareness, particularly in the institutional level. This has expanded the scope of Ayurveda rather than merely being an ancient recipe for illness.

An affordable system of health care is the dream of human society. Modern system of medicine has made rapid strides often with magical solutions for problems of health. But it has also made the medical and health services highly expensive and unaffordable to the common man. It is in this context that Indian heritage medical system is becoming a boon to provide a cost-effective alternative (Thara, 2002). It has a significant sociological bearing especially for those who cannot afford expensive health services on account of various socio-economic factors. Thus Ayurveda is destined to become a socially relevant system of medicine.

AYURVEDA IN THE CONTEXT OF GLOBALISATION

The central phenomenon, which will hallmark the turn of the century, will be the globalisation of Ayurveda. It is understood that Ayurveda is a science and art of healing and hence it has to have a global character. In recent years there has been a growing interest in Ayurveda both in its holistic principles and its safe treatment modalities.

The Information technology made the globalization a powerful tool in the hands of developed and information rich countries. The term globalization has been used in a multiplicity of senses. In its most general sense, globalization refers to cross - national flows of goods, investment, production and technology. The Alma Ata declaration of WHO in 1980 has created major awareness about Ayurveda in the Western World. The demand for Ayurveda in foreign countries is multifaceted which actually determines its present status in these countries. This impact is rapidly changing the picture of Ayurveda in India as well as abroad (Patel, 2000).

The Ayurveda and its allied system focus on universal applicability. India being one of the world's 12 mega bio-diverse countries which account for 8 per cent of the recorded species of the world with 45,000 plant species, India is rich in information and genetic materials. India is sitting on gold mine of well-recorded and well-practised knowledge of herbal medicine. So now the Indian Ayurvedic industry wants to do original and developmental research with the help of information technology for new and user-friendly products. Otherwise, the technologically superior transnational corporations will play havoc in the field. It will be detrimental to the traditional Ayurvedic industry.

Globalization is at the center of diverse intellectual and political agendas, raising crucial questions about indigenous systems like Ayurveda. The updating of this ancient wisdom is needed to promote and propagate Ayurveda globally in the 3rd millennium in pace with the development of information technology. The rich biodiversity of India provides lot of opportunities for research and patenting in Ayurveda (Ramachandran, 2002). The process of globalization has already been initiated in Ayurveda. The Gujarat Ayurved University has made outstanding contribution in the globalization of Ayurvedic education by providing Ayurveda education to foreign professionals. The International Organizations like WHO are also deputing the fellows for the purpose of training in Ayurveda in the University. All these developments clearly indicate that Ayurveda education is already globalized (Narayan, 2003).

PATENTS AND INTELLECTUAL PROPERTY RIGHTS IN AYURVEDA

Many people in India feel that Ayurveda should not be allowed to globalize because of the chances of its exploitation by the multinationals at the cost of Indian economy and national interest. With the advent of new patent regime and intellectual property rights, the apprehensions in this regard have further increased. However it seems that because of prevailing legal and economic provisions at international level, the phenomenon of globalization cannot be prevented and moreover India is the preacher of the philosophy of "Vasudhaiva Kudumbakam" for centuries (Singh, 2000).

The idea of open World Trade led to the emergence of General Agreement on Tariffs and Trade (GATT), and the Trade Related Intellectual Property Rights (TRIPs). The greatest concern is the issue of linking the intellectual property with trade in new patent régime creating a situation where the trade will overwhelm the intellectual property. This is against the interest of India. In the context of Ayurveda and similar other assets of traditional national heritage, it is rather unfortunate that like Indian Patent Act 1970, the World Trade Organization too does not make provision of protection of the ancient traditional national heritage of India

Ayurvedic medicine and Indian herbs form one of the most vulnerable sectors in the context of patent regime. A patent is an exclusive right granted to an inventor to make, sell, use and distribute a patented product or products made by a patented process. A number of known herbs and plant drugs of India have been patented by foreigners on the basis of secondary researches. Neem, Haldi, Sunthi, Aswagantha, and Basmati are few among them. Because of the lack of awareness and fallacies in the law, patents are being granted to individuals on the basis of minor secondary researchers ignoring the obvious traditional knowledge. This piracy can be prevented only by major changes in Patent Laws designed to protect the national heritage of a country, which should be considered its Intellectual Property and should not be allowed to be patented in the names of any individual or a country. Ancient traditional knowledge claimed to have originated exclusively from a country should be treated as the National Intellectual Property of the country and that land should be entitled for World Patent with exclusive rights of benefit for that nation (Ramachandran, 2002).

When we consider the Patents and the Indian Systems of Medicine especially Ayurveda, there comes the issue of biodiversity. India is one of the 10 mega biodiversity centers of the world with over 1,15,000 species of plants and animals. According to WHO figures, the primary health care of the developing countries depends on traditional indigenous medicine. This is mainly based on medicinal plants. By the Patents and Intellectual property rights, the traditional knowledge and healing system of underdeveloped countries are cleverly smuggled out by the wealthy developed nations. In recent years intellectual property rights conferred to by awarding patents (or industrial patents), plants breeder rights, copyrights, trademarks and trade secrets to the owner, the amplitude of these rights have been tremendously increased to include biological / living materials which form part of biodiversity of a region (Fowler, 1996).

Globalization or liberalization should have been a gradual process, which would need time for our domestic industry to change, reform and improve itself. Since we are now signatories of GATT and member of WTO, we cannot get away form patent regime. Nor can we escape Intellectual Property Right system. It is therefore necessary that Ayurvedic industry should concentrate on research by resorting modern technology and obtain patents faster. The science of Ayurveda is a goldmine. The rich biodiversity of India provides lot of opportunities for research and patenting. We must also document the unrecorded traditional knowledge and healing systems of tribes and traditional vaidyas. Otherwise they may be hijacked by the powerful multinationals.

BIOPIRACY IN AYURVEDA

Biopiracy means taking biological resources from one country or region to another and using it in the latter's industry, agriculture or other commercial process. A corollary to the loss of indigenous knowledge related to medicinal uses of biodiversity is biopiracy - the piracy and patenting of traditional knowledge. In the earlier decades of last century taking away bio resources from one country to another was not considered illegal and therefore the concept of biopiracy was non-existent. With the growth of knowledge in the field of biological conservation, especially in terms of in situ and ex situ conservation, biopiracy received international recognition. Countries now have started recognising their sovereign rights over the biological material within their boundaries (Agarwal, 1996). Recent developments in the international arena seem to reinforce the process of protecting biological resources of one country from being exploited by another. Biopiracy is now not permissible. An international treaty called the Convention of Biological Diversity (CBD) has converted biological resources from a "common heritage of mankind" to a "national property" and signatory countries are expected to frame laws to this effect (Asif, 1998).

Biodiversity of medicinal plants is the basis of Ayurvedic healing. The appropriation and patenting of Ayurvedic knowledge is another threat to the free flourishing of Ayurveda in the future. The patenting of nimba (Azardirachta indica), haridra(curcuma longa), aswagandha (Withania somifera), maricha (piper nigram), ardraka (zingiber officinale), karavellam (momordica charantia)...... is not just an assault on the collective, cumulative innovations over millennia embodied in Ayurveda.

In the past, the threat Ayurveda faced was from marginilisation through neglect; today's threat comes from marginalisation through its commercial success and popularity. The sudden popularity of Ayurveda poses threat to its integrity as a knowledge system and system of healing(Vandana Shiva, 2003). Patents on traditional Ayurvedic knowledge are doubly wrong- first, traditional knowledge is by its very nature not novel, it is not an invention. It should hence lie beyond the purview of patentability. Secondly, exclusive rights and monopolies go against the spirit of Ayurveda which treats healing as a gift, not a commodity.

REFERENCES

1. Agarwal, Anil (1996) The twin challenges of conserving biodiversity and controlling biopiracy. In *Proceedings of the International workshop on benefit sharing with local communities.* New Delhi, Dept. of Environmental Sciences: 6-11.
2. Asif, Mohammed (1998) Intellectual property rights and Biopiracy: Their implications for tribal medical traditions. *Social action* 48 (4): 375-391.
3. Fowler, Cary (1996) Biotechnology, patents and the third world. In Vandana Shiva and Mores, I (eds.) Biopolitics: A

feminist and ecological reader in biotechnology. London, Zed Books.

4. Narayan, Suresh (1999) Ayurveda needs urgent rejuvenation in Kerala. The Hindu. July 24 :22-23.
5. Patel, Aravind (2000) Ayurveda in foreign countries. In *Proceedings of the International Seminar on Ayurveda and other traditional medicines scope and challenges in 21st century.* Jamnagar, Gujarat Ayurved University: 82-83.
6. Ramachandran, K.V. (2002). Globalization: Threats faced by Ayurved industry. *Aryavaidyan*. 16 (1): 9-15
7. Singh, Ram H. (2000) Talking Ayurveda to the 21st century. The goal and challenges of globalization. In *Proceedings of the International Seminar on Ayurveda and other traditional medicine and scope and challenges in the century.* Gujarat Ayurved University. Jamnagar: 25-29.
8. Tara, C P (2002) Social relevance of Ayurveda. Kochi, In *Proceedings of the World Ayurveda Congress.* Kochi, Swadeshi Science movement: 31-35
9. Vandana Shiva, (2003) Keeping alive the science of life in the face of biopiracy. *Aryvaidyan* 16(2): 115-127.

16

INFORMATION SECURITY AND PRIVACY

Sudha A
Assistant Librarian
Kannur University Central Library
Kannur-670002

INTRODUCTION

Modern technology creates or improves better sensors and alarms to protect library collections. It blocks the potential criminals from achieving their goals and alerts the libraries. Information security puts the emphasis on protecting the information stored in or processed by the system. Today global libraries use network security policies to ensure the implementations of their security models in maintaining network security, protection of information loss, alteration, unavailability and the safe guarding of the organization's network from internal and external threats. Planned and correct security policy regarding the information in a computerised environment is not well developed. The result of a successful security policy lies in efficiency of user commitment towards organisational security and the implementation of a successful security strategy with management plan. The development and enforcement of a comprehensive security policy is needed for the effective implementation of security programmes in any institution. The security policy statement should describe what information should be protected and the extend of allowable distribution. The policy statement must also be unambiguous, so that no one can be exempted from the requirements.

Every staff member must perform security as a part of his/her job description. No devices and systems can protect our organization if the staff lacks the right attitude towards security. Careful planning and a continual state of vigilance is necessary for the security of libraries.

COMPUTER RELATED CRIMES WHICH AFFECT THE INFORMATION SECURITY

Computer crimes are committed by means of the special knowledge or expert use of computer technology. Technically expert computer hobbyist who use personal computers and modems to break into and tamper with computer systems are known as 'hackers'. The first reported case of computer abuse is in 1958.

1. **Data diddling:** Data diddling is a crime which involves changing data. This crime can be minimised by applying internal security controls.
2. **Trojan horse attacks:** Trojan horse involves the placement of unwanted computer instructions in a programme. So that the host computer will perform some undesired or unauthorised function. The instructions enter the target system hidden in some other message or programme, thus the name Trojan horse attacks. This crime can be minimised by implementing security control measures for all incoming data containing hidden content. So Trojan horse is defined as a malicious security breaking programme that is disguised as a screen saver, game, or attack, unlike viruses, Trojan horse do not replicate themselves . The most noted Trojan horse was the so called "Love Bug" in May 2000. It is in the form of a love letter. If it was opened, it would unleash the problems such as sending itself to everybody on your e-mail address book, erasing or modifying your files, and downloading

another Trojan horse programme designed to steal your passwords.

3. **Logic bomb:** Logic bomb is a computer programme executed at a specific time to cause damage to computer programmes or data. They often enter a computer system using the Trojan horse method, but differ because their presence is detected only after the bomb blows up. This crime can be minimised by using security methods that verify the system for inappropriate content.

4. **Impersonation:** The most common method to gain access to the system is to impersonate an authorised user. The impersonation usually requires that the intruder has access to the information of a) user ID b) password of the authorised user, and c) a dial port number, if access is attempted from a remote location.

5. **Internet and bulletin boards:** Internet and bulletin boards can be used by hackers to exchange information necessary to commit criminal acts on computer systems. Both the internet and bulletin boards allow users to communicate and exchange information on a wide range of topics. The systems access passwords are shared among the hackers, they may attempt to gain unauthorised access to the computer systems.

6. **Computer virus:** A computer virus is programme code which can attach itself to other programme and corrupt data and damage hardware. Software or hardware containing a virus can come from many sources such as public domain software, bulletin boards, the internet computer club software, a friend or colleague's diskette, or commercial packages. This crime can be minimised by incorporating virus scanning into the start-up of the computer system and scan any new software prior to use. No country has adequate laws to deal the heinous crimes of creating and propagating the computer viruses. According to Graham Cluley, senior technology consultant at Sophos, a leading anti- virus vendor, about 800 anti-viruses crop up every month.

The possible indications of a virus infection are i) the file size may increase when a virus attaches itself to the programme or data in the file. ii) an unexpected change in the time of last update of a programme or file may indicate a recent unauthorised modification. iii) if several executable programmes have the same date or time in the last update field, they have all been updated together, possibly by a virus. iv) a sudden unexpected decrease in free disc space may indicate the virus attack. v) unexpected disc accesses, especially in the execution of programmes that do not use overlays or large data files, may indicate virus activity.

7. **Trap doors:** Trap doors are a quick way into a programme by passing security

8. **Denial of service attacks:** Denial of service is the knocking off service without permission

9. **Threats:** Threat is something that can interrupt the operation or functionality of a system or can disrupt the integrity or availability of the information. There are four kinds of computer security threats interruption, interception, modification, and fabrication

   i) ***Interruption*:** These include any delay or disruption of normal operations.

   ii) ***Interceptions*:** These are unauthorized access to information, which may or may not result in the illicit use of data

   iii) ***Modification*:** Modification includes tampering with information once access has been achieved by changing software or hardware controls or the data itself. .

   iv) ***Fabrication*:** It is modification a way to benefit the intruder or to cause problems. It involves skillfully adding data or objects to the computer system such as transactions or additional files on a database.

10. **Remote login:** This is when someone is able to connect to

your computer and control it in some form. This can range from being able to view or access your files to actually running programmes on your computer.

11. **Application backdoors:** Some programmes have special features that allow for remote access. Others contain bugs that provide a back door or hidden access that provides some level of control of the programme.
12. **SMPT session hijacking:** SMPT is the most common method of sending e-mail over the internet. By gaining access to a list of e-mail addresses, a person can send unsolicited junk e-mail (spam) to thousands of users. These are done quite often by redirecting the e-mail through the SMPT server of an unsuspecting host, making the actual sender of the spam difficult to trace.
13. **Operating System Bugs:** Like applications some operating systems have backdoors. Others provide remote access with insufficient security controls or have bugs that an experienced hacker can take advantages of.
14. **E-mail bombs:** An e-mail bomb is usually a personal attack someone sends the same e-mail many times until the e-mail systems cannot accept any more messages.
15. **Macros:** To simplify complicated procedures many applications allow creating a script of commands that the application can run. This script is known as macro. Crackers have taken advantage of this to create there on macros that depending on the application can destroy the data or crash the computer.
16. **Spamming:** Spamming is harmless but always annoying. It can be dangerous. It is the electronic equivalent of junk mail. Quite often it contains links to websites. It should be careful of clicking on these because you may accidentally accept a cookie that provides a backdoor to your computer.
17. **Redirect bombs:** Crackers can use ICMP to change (redirect), the path information takes by sending it to a different routes.

This is one of the ways that a denial of service attack is setup.

18. **Source routing:** In most cases, the path a packet travels over the internet or any other network is determined by the routers along their path. But the source providing the packet can arbitrarily specify the route that the packet should travel. Crackers sometimes take advantage of this so that information appears to come from a trusted source or even from inside the network. Most firewall products disable source routing by default.
19. **Piggybacking:** Following an authorised person through a locked door, either a physical one or a computers security firewall.
20. **Dumpster diving:** Scavenging through materials that have been thrown away.
21. **IP spoofing:** Unauthorised access to computers where hacker sends messages to a computer with an IP (Internet Protocol) address indicating the messages is coming from trusted sources but in fact is a fake IP address. It is the act of fabricating an identity and is allowed access to information. Spoofing can be done at any layer
22. **Masquerading:** Where one person uses the identity of another to gain access to a computer.
23. **Password Suiting:** Automated guessing of phone numbers, user IDs and passwords
24. **Worms:** A stand alone programme that replicate itself on one computer and tries to infect other computers.
25. **Salami techniques:** An unauthorised programme that causes the unnoticed debiting of small amounts of assets from large number of sources.
26. **Hacking and Cracking:** Hacking and cracking happens when a stranger has broken in to your computer system without your knowledge and consent and has subsequently tempered with your confidential data and information.

27. **Software piracy:** Software piracy is a cyber crime that is to distribute illegal and unauthorised pirated copies of software online.

28. **Theft:** If the intruder is skillful and safeguards are not in place, the theft occurred will never be known. If measures to detect the intrusion and subsequent theft are not in place, theft will go unnoticed in most cases.

29. **Information Warfare:** Information Warfare is the ability to exploit, deceive and disrupt adversary information system while simultaneously protecting our own. It is the applications of destructive force on a large scale against information assets and systems against the computers and networks. The US Departments of Defence (DoD) Computers numbering over 2.1 million were victim of as many 2,50,000 cyber attacks in 1995. The Brown commission (US) defines information warfare as "Activities undertaken by govt. groups or individuals to gain electronic access to information systems in other countries as well as activities undertaken to protect against it".

30. **Attack (making resources unavailable):** This is one of the most difficult threats to over come. Hence the intention of hacker is to block access to the system and make information unavailable to the uses that need it.

THREATS TO INFORMATION DURING TRANSMISSION

Major challenges for securing information in transmission are to provide integrating and confidentiality. The following are the threats in their category.

Interception snuffing: Sometimes crucial information is not accessible to anyone else other than concerned parties. In the internet the threats of someone getting access to the information is high. This information has to be protected from unauthorised disclosures.

Modification: Information can be modified while in transit or it is possible that gets modified accidentally. There are threats to the integrating of the information. We cannot be sure that the information received is the same as what was sent.

Denial of action (Repudiation): It is possible that someone sends, receives or modifies information and later denies the action. This particular threat is very important in e-commerce, where a person can deny that he or she was responsible for the transaction.

Replay the information: A person can intercept information, modify it, and reply the information back to the sender.

INFORMATION SECURITY

Information secure involves any and all areas of protecting computers, information systems and online transaction. The issues which help the security concern in computerised environments are:

a) Apply all password recommendations and features.

b) Report any suspicious immediately

c) Never leave workstation unattended.

d) Take note any security documentation received

e) Scan data and files regularly for viruses.

f) Always attend all security meetings and courses

g) Never share user privileges

h) Do not exceed user rights.

i) Alert your superior if your identity has been revealed

j) Never repair security problems yourself

k) Apply all password recommendations and features.

All users should protect their workstation when leaving. Methods to protect workstations may include the use of a special hot button to enable the protective mode when out, or the use of a screen saver password. To keep up to date with security matters and findings, discussions groups and meetings should occur on a regular basis, to allow users to share their problems and solutions they discovered. The system should always be kept free from internal errors. When security problems have been addressed, it is better to avoid a subjective approach to the systems and it is advisable to use an external specialist. Their findings and recommendations are helpful to solve the problems. Important security topics in e-mails or weekly newsletters should regularly be reviewed for relevant information such as the active viruses on the system, unsafe internet sites, software that should not be downloaded, visual awareness methods etc.

DATA SECURITY

Data security is the result of effective day to day procedures with in the organization. They are the standards and procedures that protect data against unauthorized disclosure, modification, or destruction whether accidental or intentional. Physical security of data is the most basic form of data processing control. Data protection is used as a measure for data security, though it is not a strong control, it can be strengthened by writing a report to management detailing each system request for data protection override. The administration controls must be introduced to ensure that only authorised overrides are submitted by the console operator. If an attempt is made to write on that file prior to the expiration date a message will appear on the console log. The operator has the option of cancelling the job or of continuing by overriding the data protection. The sharing of data between many users and several applications systems creates a need for a central responsible authority with the ability to control the structure and content of database. All system requiring access to the database should use a common definition of each element in the data base and should apply standard edit and validation test for updating the database. The effective password controls is used as the security method of programmes of data in the computerised environment.

STAGES IN INFORMATION SECURITY

1. **User control:** The first step is the user authentication and control. User authentication ensures that the person at the

remote end is who he claims to be and he is able to see only that information which he is authorized to see.

2. **Security at the desktop level:** At desktop level, organizations adopt controls to restrict user misuse or unauthorised access via the desktop. The first step solutions are to implement desktop level antivirus solutions and proxy internet access. The control can be established at the desktop level with the following:

   i) Only authorised employees of the organisations get access to desktops.

   ii) Unauthorised access through password logging or sharing can be eliminated with the elimination of all static passwords

   iii) Movements of all users within the organisation's desktop servers and network should be monitored closely to profile user behavior

3. Security at the organizations level: Security considerations at this level include protection against attacks from the internet and intranet enabling trust and privacy protections for e-transactions, controlling access to systems and performing security management. A comprehensive security toolkit for organisations include several components including anti-virus software, firewalls, VPNs, intrusion detection and vulnerability assessment.

SECURITY SOLUTIONS

Security solutions should be affordable, flexible, interoperable, manageable modular and scalable.

Best practices that block most attacks.

i) Employ a layer 7 full inspection firewall

ii) Automatically update your antivirus at the gateway server and client levels

iii) Keep all your systems and applications updated.

iv) Hackers commonly break in to a website through known security holes, so make sure your servers and applications are patched and updated.

v) Turn of unnecessary network services.

vi) Eliminate unneeded programmes

vii) Scan networks for common back door services.

viii) Use intrusion detection systems, vulnerability scan and antivirus protect.

Password Security

For any computer system an appropriate password is of high importance. Password should be kept secret at all time never shared with anyone. It is better the password should be set to expire after a certain period. If a user enters an incorrect password more than thrice in a row the accounts should be locked out and reset only after verifying the users authenticity. All network devices like routers or firewalls should have different unique passwords. This is essential to keep one network device from compromising others. All passwords for systems purchased or developed externally should be changed immediately on handover.

Cryptography and Digital signature

Cryptography is the way keeping messages secret. Cryptography deals with all aspects of secure messaging, authentication, digital signature, electronic money and other applications. Today cryptography has become one of the main tools for privacy, trust, accesses control and security. In cryptographic terminology the message is called plain text or clean text. Encoding the content of the message in such a way that hides its contents from outside is called encryption. The encrypted message is called the cipher text. The process of retrieving the plain text from the cipher text is called decryption.

There are too many cryptography techniques. The first is single key cryptography or private key encryption which is based on a single key and is also known as symmetric key encryption. The second one is public key cryptography, which is based on combinations of two keys, secret key and public key and is also known as asymmetric encryption. In private key encryption, the decrypting device must use the same algorithm or method to decode or decrypt the data as the encrypting device used to encrypt the data. In public key encryption the standard for public key encryptions is known as RSA, named after the three founders of the protocol (Rivest, Shamir, Adelman). In a public key encryption, the encryption device encrypts a document using the intended recipient's public key and the originating party's private key. This public key is readily available in a public directory or is sent by the intended recipient to the message sender. To decrypt the document, the receiving encryption/decryption device must be programmed with the intended recipients own private key and the sending party's public key.

Digital signature encryption: Digital signature encryption provides an electronic means and guaranteeing authenticity of the sending party and assurance that encrypted documents have not been altered during transmission. By this method, a document's digital signature is created by the sender using and private key and the original document. Digital signature can also be used to timestamp documents that are a trusted party signs the document and its timestamp with his /her secret key, thus testifying that the document existed at the stated time. They can also be used to testify or certify that a public key belongs to a particular person.

To verify a signature, the recipient first determines whether it trusts that the key belongs to the person it is supposed to belong to and their decrypts the signature using the public key of the person. If the signature decrypts property and the information methods that of the message the signature is accepted as valid.

Virus Protection

1. Compare programmes or data files with backup version to determine possible integrity loss.

2. Write-Protect diskettes whenever possibie, especially when testing an untrusted computer programme.
3. Boot-diskette based system using clearly labelled boot diskettes.
4. Avoid booting a hard disk drive system from a diskette.
5. Never put untrusted programmes in hard disk root directories. Most viruses can effect only the directory from which they are executed, untrusted computer programs should be stored in isolated directories containing a minimum number of other sensitive programs or data files.
6. When transporting files from one computer to another use diskettes that have no executable files that might be infected.
7. When sharing computer programmes, share source code rather than object code, because source code can more easily be scanned for unusual contents.
8. Downloaded software should be prohibited or controlled and scanned.
9. Install virus scanning software at all points of attack.
10. All diskettes must be scanned before being loaded into network attached to clients or servers.

Virus can attack locally or remotely attached client platforms, server platforms, and/or the entrance to the organization network via the internet, all the points of attack must be protected. In fact 61 per cent of all viral infections are caused by infected diskettes. Virus scanning is the primary method for successful detection and removal. New viruses are appearing at the rate of nearly 200 per months. So it is necessary to update the anti virus software. Some virus scanners remove a virus from an infected file whenever others nearly destroying the infected files as a remedy.

Emulation technology attempts to detect the unknown viruses by examining the executing programme in a safe environment with a software emulation programmes known as virtual PC. The advantage of such programmes is that they identify potentially unknown viruses based on the behaviour rather than by relying on identifiable signature of known viruses. Due to their ability to monitor behavior of programmes, this category and antiviral technology is also known as activity monitors. These programmes are capable of trapping encrypted or polymorphic viruses.

Another category of anti virus technology is known as CRC checkers or hashing checkers creates and saves a unique cylindrical redundancy check character or hashing number for each file to be monitored. Each time that file is subsequently saved, the new CRC is checked against the reference CRC, If the CRCs do not match, then the file has been changed. These changes are then evaluated by the programme to determine the likelihood that the change was caused by a viral infection.

The precautions to be taken against Trojan horse before running the programmes are:

i) **Clear re-installation:** This will be the sure way to eradicate a Trojan. Back up your entire hard disc, reformat the disc, re-install the operating system and all your applications from original CDs if you are certain they are not infected, restore the files from the backup.

ii) **Shareware anti-Trojan programme :** Some of these programmes are effective against some Trojans, not against all Trojans.

iii) **IRC help channels :** It can be found Trojan/Virus removal help on IRC, such as dmsetup or Hackfix on Efnet. These experts will try to figure out which Trojans you have and offer you on how to fix it such as by using their own anti-Trojan script.

Firewall: It forces a security policy between a secure internal network and an entrusted network such as the Internet. A firewall allows only authorised traffic to pass. It is an immune to any sort of penetration and compromise. An ill configured or mismanaged firewall is much more dangerous than no firewall at all. Traffic originating from the internal network should appear to have originated from the firewall. So no one can see any internal machines address. All requests for any service, either for downloading on uploading any information should go through the firewall. No direct connection or contact with any internal machine should be possible. Firewalls must be configured to prevent spoofing attacks; where as external attacker sends malicious information as if it had been sent from one of your internal machines. Any connection to a third party network should be assessed for potential risks before it's allowed through the firewall. Restrict remote access to the firewall for administration to the internal network. If access from an external network is needed, it should be preceded by strong authentication. It is necessary to store firewall administrator's user account details, including their password. They can be used if the firewall needs to be accessed in an emergency. It is also necessary to develop and maintain complete documentation on the firewall, and keep it in a secure place. Regularly update it to include all changes made to the firewall rules. If administrator leaves the organization, staff with relevant skills should be able to follow the firewall rules and related configurations from this documentation. Any potential attack on the firewall indicated in the log must be classified as an incident. Any internal and external access that bypasses the firewall negates its purposed existence. It is necessary to take backup regularly and store them offsite, preferably on read only media, so information not over-written. They should also be secure, accessible only to authorised persons.

A firewall is protector that keeps away destructive forces from your network. Its job is similar to a physical fix wall that keeps fire spreading from one area to the next. A firewall is simply a programme or hardware device that filters information coming though the internet connection in to your private network or computer system. Firewall technology works hand-in-hand with antivirus protection on both the desktop and server which controls inbound and outbound traffic at critical end points .Microsoft deploys firewalls in Internet Security and Acceleration –Server 2000, Access Control to resources is integrated with Windows 2000 server. Key examples include role-based security as COM+ in Windows 2000 server, cryptographic security in Crypto API ,authentication in Windows 2000 Server Integrated Authentication, PKI-Certificate Server as part of the Windows 2000 server. Firewall use one or more of three methods to control traffic flowing in and out of the network.

Packet filtering: Packets (mall chunks of data) are analysed against set of filters. Packets that make it through the filters are send to the requesting system and all others are discarded.

Proxy Service: Information from the internet is retrieved by the firewall and then send to the requesting system and the vice-versa.

Stateful inspection: It is a newer method compares certain key parts of the packet to a data base of trusted information. Information travelling from inside the firewall to outside is monitored for specific defining characteristics. Then incoming information is compared to these characteristics. If the comparison yields a reasonable match, the information is allowed through, otherwise it is discarded.

Firewall, its functions: IP address: Each machine on the internet is assigned a unique address called an IP address. IP addresses are 32 bit numbers, normally expressed as for 'octets' in a dotted decimal number. A typical IP address looks like this:198.162.50.19.

If a certain IP address outside the company is reading too many files from server, the firewall can block all traffic to or from that IP address.

Domain names: All servers on the internet also have human readable names called domain names e.g.: *www@kucl.org*. A firewall can be installed on the computer to block all access to certain domain names, or allow access only to specific domain names.

Personal firewall: This is powerful desktop security software designed to protect a personal computer from internet crackers and prevent unauthorised access from an internal network.

Hack tracer: This is a personal firewall with integrated NeoTrace location and reporting technology. The purpose of a personal firewall is protecting one individual machine from unwanted or undesirable traffic. This traffic can be logged, and if traffic is deemed to be of a potentially threatening nature, it can be reported from further action. Hack Tracer allows it to see all traffic and to check it even gets to the TCP/ IP stack or the operating system.

File system authentication: File system authentication ensures integrity of the seized data and the forensic process. Before actually analysing the suspect disc, a message digest is generated for all system directories, files and disk sectors. A message digest is a signature that uniquely identifies the content of a file or disk sector. In the past, a 32 bit CRC 32 algorithm was used, but now more advanced one way hashing algorithm, MD5 a 128 bit hash is used, and SHA a 160 bit hash is used. These hashing algorithms guarantee the integrity of the processed data. The restored data should be analysed in a controlled environment in a forensic system. Everything on the system must be checked, starting with the file system and directory structure. The analyst should create an organisation chart of the disk file system. A number of commercially available utilities can be used to create a directory tree, list system files, identity hidden files, and to conduct keyword searches

It is more effective to make CD copies of the hard disk contents. This is more cost effective.

Virtual Private Network: VPN is a mean of transmitting information in a secure manner over an untrusted network. It achieves this by employing a combination of encryption, authentication and tunneling. VPNs cut down costs for organisations by allowing them to use the public network securely instead of having their own private networks. There are different technologies and implementations of the VPN protocol: PPTP, L2TP, IP sec or MPLS VPNs. Among these IP sec is the most popular technology which adds integrity authentication, reply protection, and encryption to IP packets.

Web security: Secure socket layer (SSL) and transport layer security (TLS) are the most popular mechanism in securing necessary web transactions. New technologies for securing web services are

XML Security, security in SOAP and securing the web services frame work itself using .NET, passport and UDDI.

Biometric Security: E-mail among the most popular internet application but it is very un-secure such as the disclosure of sensitive or proprietary information either in transit or in storage, and the modification of information during transit. The most deployed and popular solutions are PGP and secure multipurpose internet mail extension. (S/MIME).

Authorisation: The authorisation security software can be either server-based or workstation-based. The most well known combination authentication software is kerberos developed at the Massachusetts Institute of Technology and marketed commercially by a variety of firms.

Kerberos: Kerberos key exchange is a network authentication protocol, which is designed to provide for client/server applications by using a combination of both secret key and public key cryptography. Kerberos never transmit passwords on the network. It is not possible to secure all network servers, it is provided using a central secure server.

Intrusion Detection: Intrusion detection is the method of finding whether someone has already hacked or is trying to break into your system. An intrusion detection systems (IDS) detects unauthorised access to the system. Active IDS can create response on intrusions, such as blocking the traffic. Passive IDS records information about the intrusion in the form of audit logs. Host and network-based intrusion detection system give warning to administrators of real and attempted intrusions, both from inside and outside the organisations. Measures such as layered defence models, strong perimeter defence mechanisms, strong authentication and web filtering, fine-grained centrally managed security policy enforcement are the some of the solutions for the security of information.

Logical security: The term logical security refers to the software or hardware wired controls built into the system to prevent or detect unauthorised entry into the system.

Vendor Controls: Vendor controls ensure that data are not lost or amended during transmission from the media into main storage.

Parity-bit checking: Parity-bit is added to ensure that the count of "on" bits is odd of even depending in the type of computers.

File labels: Vendor-supplied software will generally attach header and trailer labels to data files created. The header labels can determine that the correct file is being used and can also protect the file from being over-written before a specified data.

Authentication of online users: An online system must device methods to identify the operating the terminal. Identification is usually made by the operator providing some kinds of password to the system. The passwords can be keyed into the system by the operator. Once an individual has been accurately identified, it is then possible to restrict that person's access to certain transaction of data files. The operator identification can be considered as known-secure information. The second stage concerns the authentication that the operator is who he says he is.

Testing: Several access control software packages are designed to protect data from unauthorised disclosure, modification, or destruction. Before new or amended programmes are placed in to the production environment, they must be tested. The two well-known testing facilities are regression testing facility and integrated testing facility.

Regression testing facility (RTF): Regression testing facility requires setting up a master file and transaction file containing all known conditions. Each record is documented stating the content of the record and its purpose during the running of a test. The documentation for the transaction file should also contain a section on the expected result after application of transaction. Tests of the system are run using these files. Whenever the system is changed, the tests can be rerun and the two sets of output compared. Output results can be compared either usually or by the use of an automated file- compare facility.

Integrated test facility (ITF): An integrated test facility entails the incorporation of certain records into the master file for use as a testing vehicle. The main advantages of an integrated test facility are in problem determination, auditability and training

i) Where an error condition is suspected the condition can be recreated in live situation without affecting the authentic records of the file.

ii) The auditors have the opportunity of submitting transaction for processing by the production system in its production environment without disrupting the run.

iii) Employees training on the system can use their dummy records until they have sufficient knowledge to work in the authentic records. A security education programme should be conducted to the personnel. An ITF combined with a regression testing facility can provide a powerful tool in ensuring that systems are property tested prior to their introduction into the production environment.

Security of telecommunication: Security of telecommunication includes the network control function, physical security of the equipment and lines use in the network, logical access controls over the applications and systems that run on the network, backup and recovery routines to ensure the continuity and reliability of the network.

Computer forensic: Computer forensic branch that deals with extracting evidence from the computer itself. Each forensic system must be able to conduct a disk image back up of the suspect system, to authenticate file system, to conduct forensic analysis in a controlled environment to validate software procedures. The disk image backup conduct a bit level copy of the disk, sector by sector rather than merely copying the system files. This process provides the capability to backup deleted files, unallocated clusters and slack space. The backup process can be accomplished by using either disk imaging hardware such as Image Master 1000, or though a variety of software programmes. Most of these programmes run under DOS or Windows and will backup most any type of hard disk or floppy disk, regardless of the operating system.

Integration with information system: Authentication product can be integrated with information system and applications development efforts. APIs (Application programme interfaces) are the means by which authentication product are able to integrate with Client/server application AT and T provides a software development kit that includes a library of C language security APIs and software modules for integrating digital signature and other security functionality into Windows NT and Windows 95 applications. Security dynamics, who market secure IDtime-synchronous token authentication products, software development kits known as BSAFE 3.0 and tool kit for Interoperable Privacy Enhanced Messaging. Microsoft's Crypto AH allows security service such as authentication, encryption, certificate management services and digital signature to be integrated with applications. GSS-API (Generic security service application programmes interface) allows applications to communicate with a variety of security authentication programmes.

Internet/ Intranet Security: All users should be educated about the damages of internet applications, and be familiarised of what content might he malicious with the necessary browser security settings in place.

There are the two primary standards for encrypting traffic on the World Wide Web, S-HTTP (Secure hypertext transport protocol) and SSL (Secure sockets layer). S-HTTP is a secure version of HTTP that requires both client and server S-HTTP versions to be installed for secure end-to-end encrypted transmission. It provides security at the document of application level. S-HTTP uses digital signature encryption to assure that the document possesses both authenticity and message integrity.

SSL acts as a wrapper to provide an encrypted envelop around HTTP transmissions. SSLversion3(SSL3) supports for more key exchange and encryption algorithm. It provides separate keys for authentication and encryption. Secure courier offered by Netscape another internet security protocol directed specifically towards securing and authenticating final transactions.

Password authentication protocol (PAP) is the authentication protocol designed for dial-in in communication. PAP repeatedly sends the user ID and password to the authenticating system until it is either acknowledges or the connection is dropped.

Challenge handshake authentication protocol provides more secure means for establishing dial-in communications. It uses a three-way challenge that includes the user ID, password, and also a key that encrypts the ID and password. Privacy enhanced mail(PEM) was the application standard encryption techniques for e-mail use in the internet used in association with WIT (simple mail transport protocol). An internet e-mail specific encryption standard also uses digital signature encryption to guarantee the authenticity, security, and message integrity of received e-mail is known as PGP(Pretty good privacy). Secure electronic transaction (SET) are a series of standards to assure the confidentiality of electronic commerce transactions. Secure multi purpose internet mail extension (S/MIME) secures e-mail traffic in e-mail applications. It encrypts and authenticates e-mail message for transmission.

Organisation network security: Single point of registration (SPR) allows a network security message to enter a new user or delete a terminated user from a single centralized location and assign all associated rights, privileges, and access control to organization resources from the single point. Single sign-on (SSO) also sometime known as secure single sign-on (SSSO) allows users to log into the enterprise network and to be authenticated from their client PC location. Single access control view allows the user's access from their client's workstation to only display those resource that the user actually has access to. Security auditing and intrusion detection is able to trace and identify suspicious behaviours from internal employees and potential intruders.

Intrusion Detection Systems (IDS)

Intruders who seek confidential information can steal or tamper with information can create anonymous files, carry out the desired crime. The used system configuration, a type of network connections, phone numbers, and access and authentication procedures are useful information to the intruders. Today intrusion detection system (IDS) are widely used to detect network intrusion. Active IDS can create response on intrusions, such as blocking the traffic. Passive IDS records information about the intrusion in the form of audit logs. Host and network-based intrusion detection system give warning to administrators of real and attempted intrusions, both from inside and outside the organisations. Measures such as layered defence models, strong perimeter defence mechanisms, strong authentication and web filtering, fine-grained centrally managed security policy enforcement are the some of the solutions for the security of information. Some important systems of intrusion detection are the following.

i) **Network-based intrusion detection system (NIDS):** An NIDS sits on independent machine watching all network traffic.

ii) **System integrity verifier(SIV) :** These monitor system files to detect when an intruder changes them and send alerts. SIV watch other components such as Windows registry and configurations. It may also detect when a normal user somehow acquires root/administrator level privileges.

iii) **Log file monitor(LFM):** LFM monitor log files generated by network services. These systems look for patterns in the log files that suggest an intruder is attacking.

iv) **Deception System (Decoys, lures, fly-traps and honey pots):** These are systems that look vulnerable from the outside, and hackers are trying to intrude. When hacker gets into the network it triggers an alarm at the same time.

Wireless network security: A wireless network is more vulnerable to attack than a wired network. So security is critical in WLANs (Wireless LANs). Using WEP (Wired Equivalent Privacy), using authentication services like a RADIUS (Remote authentication dial-in user service) server, providing access only through a VPN, restricting access based on MAC address etc are the options to provide security. The tools to break the WEP security were easily available on the internet.

WEP Security: In the WEP security model, the AP is the decision maker to allow people to access the WLAN. If the WEP key is correct, the user can access the network, if not he is denied.

MAC address based filtering: By using MAC addresses you can configure your wireless AP or route to accept packets only from known MAC address. Even if a person hits the correct WEP key, he still can't access the network. This method has its shortcomings. MAC addresses are very easy to fake or spoof and they flow in clear text over the air.

IEEE 802.11i and WPA

IEEE 802. 11i is a new generation security standard for wireless networks. It defines a new type of wireless network called RSN (Robust Security Standard)

Three party security model of WPA and IEEE 802.11i

The standard based on WPA describes a different a security model. When a user wants to connect to a wireless network he first connects to the AP. Then the AP connects to a separate AS (Authentication Server), which takes the decision whether a user should be permitted or not. Thus AP becomes the NAS (Network Access Server).

Wireless security EAP: In a WLAN to connect the network a user needs to identify itself to the AS and is done by using EAP (Extensible Authentication Protocol). Using EAP messages, the user provides his identity to the AP, which forwards it to the AS for Authentication.

REFERENCE

1. Building Fences on the Net. *Information Technology*. Nov.03:49-51
2. GauravVaidya. Securing anytime, anywhere Information. *Information Technology*. Sept.03: 57-60
3. Joy, Avinash. Firewalls: Keeping Intruders away. *Information Technology*. March03: 42-45
4. Kanter. Managing with Information. New Delhi: Prentice Hall of India, 1998
5. Mishra, R.C. Cyber Crime: Impacts in the New Millennium. New Delhi: Authorspress,2002
6. Nithin Kothari.Protect your Privacy on Windows 98. *Information technology*. May03: 34-36
7. Ramamurthy,C.R. Information Security: A source book for libraries. Delhi: Authorspress, 2001
8. Subramanian,Ganapathi. Security's Independence Imperative. *Smart Inc*.Jan03:15
9. Subramanian,Ganapathi. Watching those Viruses. *Smart Inc*.March03:22
10. Subramanian,Ganapathi.Beware when the Dead have Power. *Smart Inc* Vol2.5 May03:20
11. Surendra Singh. Web Security. *Information technology*. Feb03:69-70

PART III :

RESOURCE SHARING AND NETWORKING IN THE ELECTRONIC ENVIRONMENT

17

The Changing Trends in the Scholarly Communication World

M.G. Sreekumar
T. Sunitha
P. Sreejaya
Indian Institute of Management Kozhikode
Kunnamangalam, Calicut - 673 571

The concept of copyright had underwent drastic and dramatic changes over the past several years, especially in the scholarly communication world, where the value attached to the word is treated significantly. The advent of the Net and the Web and its family of distributed computing / communication technologies, the unprecedented proliferation of the digital documents in a variety of formats and standards, the increasing Web presence by almost all the publishers as an inevitable business strategy, the cultural revolution that has taken place in both authors as well as users, the corresponding changes - academic as well as cultural - experienced by the libraries the world over supplemented with the spiraling costs of published literature and the ever shrinking budgets etc. have contributed significantly to the changes in perspective and practice in the copyright concept. In the paper paradigm, the copyright had a definitive boundary whereas in the digital world it poses a variety of problems to publishers, authors and users as well. The word copyright assumes different connotations in the digital world which awards the buyer/subscriber with limited ownership or mostly with just access facilities. The scholarly communication system has been, for the past several hundred years, largely monopolised by the publishers. An exemption here would be the learned society publishers, who mostly do not handle scholarly literature with a profit motive. Of late the deprived stake holders in the scholarly communication ecosystem are trying out open archive alternatives for scientific publication and communication with a view to get rid of the clutches of the giant publishers. Open archive initiatives are poised to revolutionise the scholarly communication process where the copyright of the article will rest with the author himself, which is a large departure from the conventional publication process. This new form of electronic publishing could potentially and drastically alter the dynamism among authors, publishers and consumers of scholarly works. This paper discusses the above concepts in the changing paradigm as a case study at the Indian Institute of Management Kozhikode.

INTRODUCTION

Scholarly communication refers to the formal and informal processes by which the research and scholarship of researchers, faculty and independent scholars (freelance researchers) are created, evaluated, edited, formatted, distributed, organized, made accessible, archived, used, and transformed (Fig.1). Publishing is the formal system whose key players include faculty, publishers (including scholarly societies), and libraries. Building on the works of others, researchers first create and then give their research findings to publishers; publishers provide peer review, editorial improvement, and wide distribution; libraries acquire, organize, and provide access to primary resources and new materials and preserve them for future generations of scholars.

Over the past two decades dramatic changes have fundamentally reshaped the entire system of scholarly communication. The first and for most among these changes is the

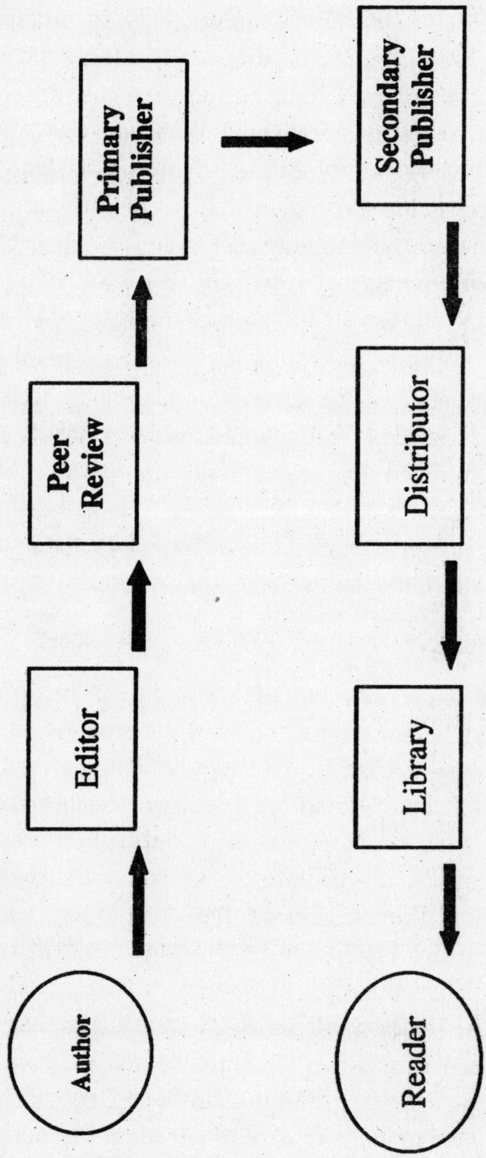
Author
Editor
Peer Review
Primary Publisher
Secondary Publisher
Distributor
Library
Reader

phenomenal increase in the body of published knowledge. It has been estimated that the number of published scientific papers doubles every five to ten years. The quantum leap in electronic and communication technologies has drastically altered the behaviour and activities of scholars. Libraries and their institutions can no longer keep pace with the increasing volume and cost of scholarly resources. The promise of the digital revolution to decrease costs and increase access has been eclipsed by commercial publishers interested in maximizing revenues through raising prices and restricting use in the name of copyright and IPR issues.

The principal set of vehicles for the communication of scholarly and scientific works are mainly scholarly journals, books, research reports etc. published by both commercial and not-for-profit ventures. For over several centuries the world of scholarly publishing has been monopolised by commercial publishers. The adverse effects on the scholarly communication system caused by the vast number of the stringent conditions enforced by these publishers are deepening and far reaching.

ELECTRONIC INFORMATION IN LIBRARIES

With the unprecedented advancements in Information and Communication Technologies (ICT) in the recent past, and with the advent and easy availability of powerful PCs at affordable rates, widening penetration of broad-band Internet connectivity all over, compounded with the uncontrolled outgrowth of scholarly information in almost all disciplines, we find that there has been a drastic growth in the production and distribution of scholarly information via electronic means. The predominant publication formats in vogue are mainly CDs, DVDs, VCDs, HDDs, Internet/ Web etc. Of the major publication types, we find that e-journals and e-books are outscoring the other information products. Interestingly the user community also have been influenced by these technologies to such an extent that there has been demands from users for providing such electronic information services in the libraries.

Put it briefly, the situation prevailing in the library scenario reveals that it has reached a critical mass both in terms of information products as well as the number of users. What is imperative at the moment is that the libraries are now forced to get equipped with state-of-art services for the benefit of the user community at large.

As a result of the above, libraries today buy licenses for an ever-increasing number of information resources from a range of different publishers and providers, and use a diverse set of technologies for information delivery [1]. As mentioned earlier, predominantly e-journals and e-books are the publication types used in scholarly communication.

Electronic Journals

Electronic Journals or simply e-Journals are the digital equivalent of their print counterparts. Whereas databases may contain only some full text or links to full text, electronic journals are literally the entire journal. For a good catalog of electronic journals currently available, see the World Wide Web Virtual Library: Electronic Journals [2]. An electronic journal is the whole journal, and libraries can subscribe to electronic journals from publishers or through a second party (e.g. vendors) just like they subscribe to print journals. This distinction between publishers and second parties is an important one, as these are the two ways libraries get electronic journals. Some companies create collections of entire journals and sell access to these collections.

Almost all popular journal publishers now have their Web / electronic version in addition to their print counterparts. Most of the renowned publishers provide online access to their current as well as retrospective contents. It is interesting to note that some of the journals publish only e-version. Some publishers consider e-version more significantly and they provide elaborate versions in the electronic form while their print counterparts maintain a compact approach. The process is popular as Electronic Long and Print Short (ELPS). For example, the British Medical Journal publishes long articles in the e-format whereas the p-format contains only short versions.

e-Books

e-Book or electronic book is a book in digital format that one can download to his computer and read using a software program. Depending on the specific format, the e-Book can be read on a computer, PDA, or dedicated reader device (sometimes typically called an e-Book too) with the proper software. Many e-Book readers, both open source as well as proprietary, are available for using e-Books at users' convenience. Many publishers now bring out e-Books as favoured format and many also provide access to content on licensing terms. A later development is the e-Book libraries such as the eBrary.com [3] which provide access to over 30000 e-Books through a single window at affordable costs.

COPYRIGHT AND IPR ISSUES

The economic system surrounding the scholarly publications is more or less strange. The researchers, most of the reviewers and many of the cost of the libraries are funded by tax payers, whereas strangely enough the copyright is given to the publishers. Or rather they make it a pre-condition to the author for publishing his research findings. It is to be bourne in mind that the authors are funded by their affiliating institutions and same is the case with the users – be they are a community like a library or individual users. Hence publishers have been enjoying a large stake in the game just because they facilitate the process as an intermediary. Since the other two groups are not united and they are distributed across, the publishing world has been able to exercise an upper hand over the authors as well as the libraries for more than centuries. The only exemption in this case is to learned societies and charities who do not have a profit eye while publishing scholarly content.

In the scholarly communication scenario the copyright assures reward for creativity, and protects the right of the creator to that reward. In the commercial setting, this reward is usually financial. In the not-for-profit, research environment, salaries and career advancement depend largely upon continued contributions to new knowledge. This regime lessens the need for scholars to receive direct payment from their copyrights.

Issues of copyright, intellectual property, and fair use are important to libraries, but librarians are struggling to make sense of all the issues in the new Digital Age [4]. We need to learn a lot about the "tricks of the trade" so that our hands are not burnt in the process. The number of accessible electronic journals are fast growing steadily. Studies are in progress the world over towards determining the trends in copyright policies among scholarly electronic journals. There are a number of issues which the Librarian should be highly careful while entering into digital subscriptions. Catches can come in multiple forms with the vague yet meticulously manipulated term "licensing". The audit and accounts are to be amply briefed about the problems and features of digital subscriptions. Proper measures and back-up agreements are to be ensured from the publishers/vendors.

In the case of free electronic journals, according to literature, the policies are found to be quite generous in the area of fair use and encourage sharing of information. Some of the salient features of copyright issues of a select set of freely accessible electronic journals are as follows: (1) copyright policies are informal, (2) policies are common to print and electronic titles, (3) contributing authors generally retain copyright, (4) noncommercial uses permitted include browsing, printing personal copies, and downloading, and (5) republishing is not permitted. Several of these journals admit library use.

ACCESS RELATED ISSUES

Access to E-Journals could be arranged from the respective publishers against UserID/Password or through IP authentication. For a wider audience, IP based access is mostly preferred, as the users need not have to bother about the UserID and Password every time. A useful alternative is to provide the UserID/Password in the library's portal / website so that users can pick them up during usage, and over a period of time, they also by-heart them. Libraries need to take care of the 'site license' aspects of content access, as some publishers lay stringent rules on this, making the life of the

Librarian miserable. Before jumping into such services, the Librarian should ensure necessary Internet bandwidth also, failing which complaints will pile up, resulting in a growing aversion against the electronic services in general. For full-text access to E-Journals and datasets published online, usually non-exclusive, non-transferable right and licenses are provided by the publishers. Unlimited access is provided to Tables of Contents, article abstracts, chapter summaries and websites for other Electronic Products. The most desirable access method, at least from IIMK's experience, is the unlimited access to full-text through IP authentication.

Another important aspect is the local administration of access management by the users. Users are to be properly oriented towards effective and efficient use of the Net as well as the journal sites. Unnecessary and unscrupulous hits, revisits and downloads can result in frequent choking of the Net connectivity, posing unwanted problems to the entire user community on campus, and also to LAN/Net system administration.

ONLINE ACCESS COSTS AND THE SWINGING PRICING MODELS

About 10 years ago when Electronic Journals first appeared the publishers didn't know how to sell them, nor librarians knew how to handle them. The technology scenario prevailing those days were entirely different too. Technology kept advancing and after 10 years, today the e-journals are sold as hot cakes in the developed world. The trends in the developing world also are equally encouraging, especially in India. This fast rate of embracing and change in mindset has taken many publishers by surprise. Earlier, negotiations that involved expanded access to electronic text usually began with print subscriptions as the bottom line of the deal. During the past couple of years, especially in the West, a number of consortia demanded that print and online be negotiated separately. They wanted online access at the core of pricing negotiations because their users clearly preferred online. Presence of robust IT infrastructure in most of the campuses/institutions may be the main reason behind this demand, which is not a reality in the developing world. They wanted an online-plus-print model, rather than print-plus-online. This is called "flip pricing" [5]. The reflections of the flip pricing has started crystallizing of late and most of the leading publishers have started offering flip price models to Indian libraries too, mostly under the consortia banner.

The evolution of the deeply discounted prices (DDP) model is yet another significant development in the journals pricing front in the recent past. As DDP has evolved, three models have emerged that govern the relationship between agents and publishers. First, the publisher requires the customer to place electronic orders directly with them; with the second version, customers may place their orders with agent or publisher, but customers are given an incentive to deal direct; and in the third scenario, customers are free to order either way.

In 2000, 75% of publishers offered online free with print, with the rest charging extra for online. But every year, publishers change their mind on this one issue, and last year the pendulum seemed to be swinging back in favor of charging extra for online with a print subscription. Of the 7,623 e-journals with set prices in EBSCO's reserve, 61% were offered free with a print subscription for this year (2001). The majority of major publishers still offer online "free" with print as a rule. The list includes Cambridge University Press, Elsevier, Emerald, Oxford, Routledge, Sage, Springer Verlag, and Taylor & Francis. Blackwell Science charges extra, but the other Blackwell imprints do not. University presses are split. Duke, Indiana, Johns Hopkins, and Penn State, charge; MIT, Chicago, and California do not. Society presses are also split, but the majority appear to charge for online with print. The list of STM publishers that charge extra include giants such as Academic, Wiley, Kluwer, Dekker, Nature, Plenum, and S. Karger.

Some of the other popular models include the "Base price plus consortium premium", the FTE (Full Time Equivalence) based pricing", "core subscription plus pay-per-view", "usage based pricing", "licensee membership fees" etc. Based on the nature of the subscription / licensing arrangements and the availability of funds a number of models can coexist in a practical library setting at the moment.

As regards IIMK's experience over the past five years, it has started with modest individual institutional subscriptions coupled with licensing services to a few electronic titles and later shifted to consortium based access to a wide range of titles under the IIM Consortium, one of the practical and successful consortium in the country operational since 2000.

THE IIM CONSORTIUM

The year 2000 was a landmark in the history of IIMs, with the formation of the IIM Consortium. The objective was to ensure among the IIMs, optimum utilization and enhancement of the resources, and to minimise the expenditure by consortia based subscriptions to the commonly subscribed databases and journals. The idea was to approach publishers of Electronic Journals and CD-ROM Databases to begin with, as a consortia, for better pricing and services. The consortium meetings were proved to be very productive and successful. The bottom line of the concept was thus collectively "to pay a little more and get a lot more" in an effort to build up a strong information resource base in all the IIMs. The additional burden while accessing all the electronic titles across the IIMs for the individual print subscriptions at each Institute was shared equally by working out the license charges for the Enhanced Access License (EAL). During the first meeting itself, a host of journals and databases were jointly subscribed at very competitive prices, and a number of others promised supply of their products at a nominal cost.

The end result has been highly praiseworthy, that online access to over 900 E-journals are being accessed by all the IIMs from major international publishers such as Elsevier [6], Kluwer [7], John Wiley [8], Blackwell [9], Taylor & Francis [10], and MCB University Press (Emerald Full-Text Intelligent Library) [11].

The success displayed by the IIM Consortium was observed by the Ministry of Human Resource Development (MHRD) Government of India and in the year 2002 the Ministry launched the INDEST (Indian National Digital Library in Engineering, Science and Technology) Consortium[12]. All the MHRD set up institutions such as the IISc., IITs, IIMs, NITs, RECs, IIITMs, NITIE etc. are beneficiary of this successful consortium.

UPCOMING SCHOLARLY COMMUNICATION MODELS: AUTHOR SELF-ARCHIVES (E-PRINT ARCHIVES), OPEN ARCHIVES INITIATIVE, OPEN ACCESS / PUBLISHING

At this juncture it is worth mapping out the prevailing scholarly communication scenario. Technology now very much provides a drastic change and endless support to scholarly communication, though commercial journal publishers are not keen in exploiting the situation in apprehension of revenue loss or fear of losing control over the domain of publication or for whatever reasons only known to themselves. One key issue to which the commercial publishers attribute all their vested interests in increasing profit and monopolising the publication domain is "copyright". At the time of accepting the manuscript itself they take away the copyright from the author and take full control of the rest of the value chain, which in the case of formal scholarly publication is very long, with several links between author and reader. (Eg., author, editor, peer review, primary publisher, secondary publisher, distributor, library, and reader). It is reasonable to conclude that this chain, with various inefficiencies, is not sustainable in its current form. The rate of penetration of computers and communication technologies in the society especially among the educationally elite and the academics has resulted in a demand hike for instant publication procedures and speedier information services. Ultimately the hitherto "publisher centered" scholarly communication process is now being shaken by the innovative concept "author self-archiving" or the e-print archives.

A revolution in the scholarly communication system is brewing with the goal of returning choice back to authors [13]. Efforts to give authors control over the communication and distribution of their work, in the form of electronic author self-archiving systems, are gaining ground. Author self-archiving allows authors to deposit their papers or preliminary drafts into an archive and thereby speed up the communication process. Submissions for publication and peer review follows later, if desired by the author. These archiving alternatives, typically organized by subject domain or organizational entity, are growing and rapidly gaining acceptance.

The first and most important preprint server and archive is Los Alamos National Laboratory's physics preprint archive[14] which expanded to support mathematics, nonlinear sciences and computer science (formerly known as xxx.lanl.gov). Created by Paul Ginsparg in 1991 to speed the delivery of high energy physics preprints, the arXiv has become the global repository for research in physics. The arXiv contains over 170,000 papers and receives about 2,500 new author submissions monthly. Mirrored in 15 countries, it receives constant and heavy usage, supporting an average of 120,000 daily connections. The impact of this model in the scholarly communication value chain is illustrated in the Figure2.

In October 1999, a meeting was held in Santa Fe, USA to discuss mechanisms to encourage the development of E-Print solutions and the integration and interoperability among the existing distributed and scattered e-print archives. The group at this meeting was united in the belief that the ubiquitous interconnectivity of the Web provides new opportunities for the timely dissemination of scholarly information. The result of this meeting was the formation of the Open Archives Initiative (OAI) and beginning of work on a framework facilitating the federation of content providers on the Web [15]. Since that first meeting, the OAI has undergone a period of intensive development both organizationally and technically. The original focus on E-Prints has broadened to encompass content providers from many domains (with an emphasis on what could be classified "scholarly" publishing), a refined and extensively tested technical framework has been developed, and an organizational structure to support the Initiative has been established.

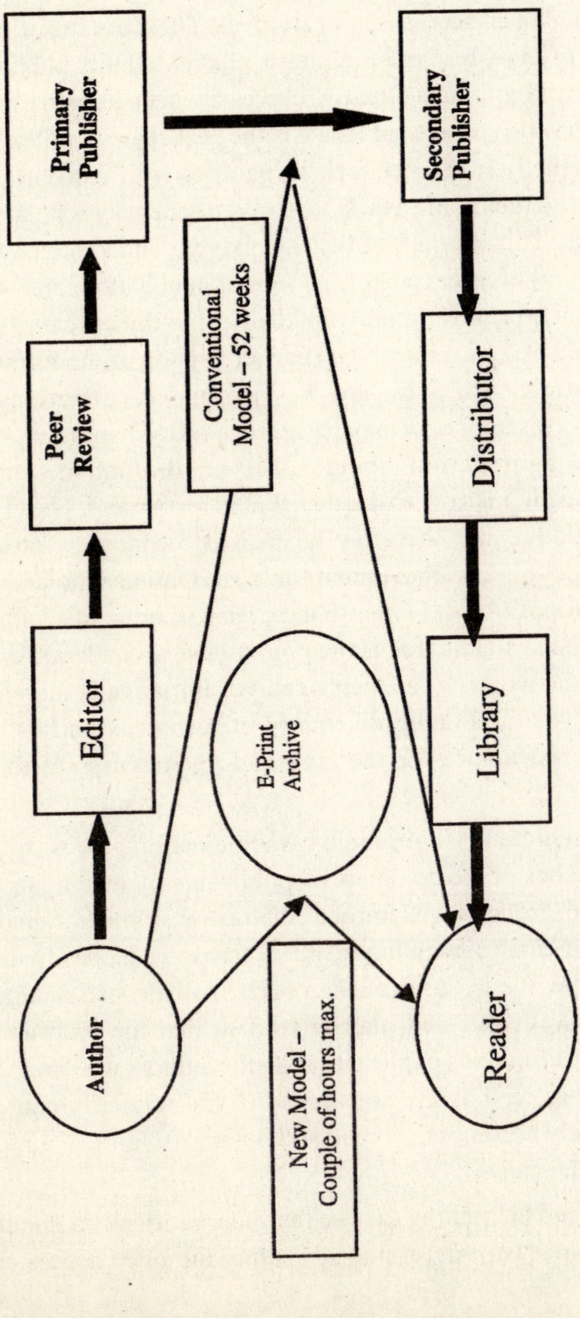

Fig.2 Upcoming Models of Scholarly Communication Value Chain

The Open Archives Initiative is therefore to support the development of open access e-print archives. These are specifically aimed at the primary research literature, conventionally published in peer-reviewed journals. Open Archives are seen as providing a mechanism in which papers published in the peer-reviewed literature can be published on the network in parallel with conventional publication, and thus made available for free access by scholars on a global basis. This e-print publication may be undertaken either before (preprint) or after (postprint) formal publication; and what is published in e-print form may be identical to the article as it is formally published, or it may be an earlier version of the formally published article. Archives may be aggregated collections of information by discipline, or may be aggregated by institution, with the resource aggregation being achieved through metadata aggregation (with links out to the distributed resources). The Open Archives Initiative may therefore be seen as forming an integral part of the "open access" movement for "Free Online Scholarship" (FOS). The proposition of FOS is that the work of academic authors should be made available free at the point of use to academic users anywhere in the world. The Open Archives Initiative is therefore seen not only as facilitating discovery of resources but also as providing infrastructure for the free and open access to those resources.

The recent trends in research communication process to get rid of the clutches of the commercial publishers by leveraging on technology and through a well formed cultural transformation among the scholarly research community spanned across the globe is indeed a welcome move. We are sure a number of technologies and strategies will continue to evolve and play around so that the proprietary publishers' unscrupulous exploitation on the authors who are both the producers as well as the consumers of the scholarly content which ultimately becomes the bread and butter of a limited number of players in the game.

It is indeed heartening to note that internationally a number of initiatives are fast progressing spreading the open access and open publishing philosophy of scholarly communication. There are three major categories upcoming predominantly, viz., author driven initiatives, commercially driven initiatives and collaborative projects. Examples of author driven initiatives include the e-print services such as the physics e-print archives and the PubMedCentral [16]. The earnest efforts of e-prints.org [17] software development team and the Free Online Scholarship Movement aiming the open access to journal literature by freeing authors from publishers' monopoly etc. are laudable initiatives. The Public Library of Science [18] aim to use author-power to make *commercial* publications freely available by Influencing commercial publishers.

The "BioMed Central" which provides open publishing facility for the biomedical researchers, "CrossRef", a publisher-linking service promoted by over 170 publishers the world over, are examples of commercially driven initiatives. BioMed Central is an independent publishing house committed to providing immediate free access to peer-reviewed biomedical research [19]. All the original research articles in journals published by BioMed Central are immediately and permanently available online without charge or any other barriers to access. This commitment is based on the view that open access to research is central to rapid and efficient progress in science and that subscription-based access to research is hindering rather than helping scientific communication.

Examples of collaborative endeavours include the ICAAP, SPARC, High-Wire Press and many more. The ICAAP (International Consortium for the Advancement of Academic Publications) does wonderful job and publishes a number of journals for the developing countries. SPARC (Scholarly Publishing and Academic Resources Coalition) an alliance of universities, research libraries, and organizations is built as a constructive response to market dysfunctions in the scholarly communication system [20]. These dysfunctions have reduced dissemination of scholarship and crippled libraries. SPARC serves as a catalyst for action, helping to create systems that expand information dissemination and use in a networked digital environment while responding to the needs of academia.

HighWire Press is a division of the Stanford University Libraries, which produces the online versions of high-impact, peer-reviewed journals and other scholarly content [21]. Recipient of the 2003 ALPSP Award for "Service to Not-for-Profit Publishing", HighWire partners with influential scholarly societies, university presses and publishers have created a collection of the finest, fully searchable research and clinical literature online. Together, these partners produce nearly half of the 200 most-frequently-cited journals publishing in science. HighWire Press hosts the largest repository of free full-text life science articles in the world, with more than 600,000 free, full-text articles online. Since 1995, with the launch of the Journal of Biological Chemistry (JBC), to the continuous online production of hundreds of prestigious journals, such as Science Magazine, the New England Journal of Medicine, PNAS and JAMA, HighWire has established an outstanding reputation for helping to disseminate primary scientific information on the Web.

ELSSS the ELectronic Society for Social Scientists[22], INASP (International Network for the Availability of Scientific Publications)[23], Open Journal Systems (Public Knowledge Project)[24], Electronic Publishing Trust for Development (EPT) [25] are other international initiative promoting open publishing and open access systems.

CONCLUSION

Scholarly communication has been the prerogative of the publishers, commercial as well as learned societies, for centuries now. It is an established fact that the paper paradigm had been following this tradition though there were many instances where the role of copyright and the intellectual property rights (IPR) were debated for want of clarity between publishers and the creators of thought content. Somehow the economics of scholarly communication went into the hands of publishers owing to their institutional / infrastructure capabilities and in lieu of the service they rendered to authors for their visibility. In other words both of them had been drawing their strength from each other and they both needed each other's contributions for continued sustenance. Recent advancements in technology and the advent of computers, Internet and communication technologies have revolutionised the scholarly communication scenario drastically. Though publishers across the globe argue that the copyright and IPR are still valid and should be complied in the new digital paradigm too, the ground reality is that they are utterly shaken by the endless capabilities of these technologies in enabling the end users. One example could be that with the Internet / WWW publishing facilities, one can publish his/her content and announce to the entire world with just few resources and very low investments. One big reason for this paradox may be that they simply failed in providing the doctrine of "fair use" clause in line with the changing social and technological demands. We have also witnessed several examples displaying the power of intellectual capital. It is therefore imperative that scholarly publishers must resort to newer models of revenue and copyright strategies with a view to meet the challenges posed by the digital paradigm. Scholarship can no longer be under the clutches of few commercial publishers whose primary motto is profit, though there are a few exemptions. A total reengineering has therefore become highly inevitable for the electronic publishing industry to sustain the demands that are put forth by the scholarly community spanning the globe. Publishers cannot have double standards in terms of services and subscriptions to the powerful developed countries against their weak counterparts. Publishers also should not impose undesirable and unscrupulous subscription, licensing and access conditions to libraries which are already facing the onslaught of many other challenges such as the unprecedented cost hike of information, unscrupulous budget cuts, alarming inflation rates in currencies etc. The consortium approach resorted to by libraries to source scholarly journals in bulk by jointly negotiating with the scholarly publishers is yet another welcome model. This is a win-win situation to both the publishers and the libraries. Open access and Open publishing models, Open archives initiative, Open source software systems and the Open linking systems are really welcome developments towards curbing the anomalies existing in the commercial publishing scenario. It is hoped that the emerging Open Philosophy models shall be able to address the above issues in a befitting and aggressive manner and that the scholarly world will be able to get a deserving position and stake in the digital publishing ecosystem of tomorrow. The library fraternity's euphoria is that only then we will be able to bridge the digital divide and eliminate the disparities of information access and delivery.

ACKNOWLEDGEMENT

The authors wish to express their sincere gratitude to the Director, Indian Institute of Management Kozhikode for the encouragement and support in the preparation of the manuscript.

REFERENCES

1. Terry, Ana Arias (2000). *How today's technology affects libraries' collection choices.* Computers in Libraries Vol. 20, No. 6, pp. 51-55.
2. World Wide Web Virtual Library- Electronic Journals : http://www.edoc.com/ejournal
3. http://www.ebrary.com/
4. Orsdel, Lee Van; Born, Kathleen, *Doing the Digital Flip.* Library Journal (2002) Vol. 127 Issue 7, pp.51-55.
5. Pavliscak, Pamela (1996). *Trends in copyright practices of scholarly electronic journals*. Serials Review 22 (3): 39-47.
6. Elsevier Science Direct : http://www.sciencedirect.com/web-editions
7. Kluwer Academic Publishing : http://www.kluweronline:com
8. John Wiley & Sons : http://www.wiley.com
9. Blackwell Scientific Publishing: http://www.blackwellpublishing.co
10. Taylor & Francis : http://www.tandf.co.uk/journals/default.asp
11. Emerald Library : www.emeraldinsight.com/ft

12. INDEST Consortium : http://paniit.iitd.ac.in/indest/
13. http://lib-www.lanl.gov/lww/articles/oai_nasig2000.htm.
14. http://www.arXiv.org
15. http://www.openarchives.org
16. http://www.pubmedcentral.com
17. http://www.eprints.org
18. http://www.plos.org
19. http://www.biomedcentral.com
20. http://www.arl.org/sparc/
21. http://highwire.stanford.edu
22. http://www.elsss.org.uk/?current=The+solution%3A+EPT
23. http://www.inasp.info/
24. http://www.pkp.ubc.ca/ojs/
25. http://dspace.dial.pipex.com/bioline/page3.htm

18

Trends of Information Networks and its Role in Libraries

Dr. Rabinarayan Mishra
P G Dept. of Lib.&Inf.Science
Sambalpur University
Jyoti Vihar- 768 019 (Orissa)

PROLOGUE

Libraries and Information Centers have since long been acknowledged as an indispensable organisation to nourish the academicians, specialists, scientists, research scholars, students, and society at large with required information. Further, neither the Libraries nor the Information Center could accomplish the versatile need of the user community in the present era with the handful information available in shape of printed documents such as, books, reference books, encyclopedias, manuscripts etc. To cope up with the altering environment, the Libraries along with the Information Centers adopted the means of accumulating information in electronic form using various means with the help of Information Technology, which has emerged as a vehicle of rapid change in the growth of a society. The spectacular developments made in the last fifty years especially in the field of electronics, computer, telecommunications, communication satellites with optical fibers sparked off the most significant revolution in the creation of information, its storage, distribution and above all its use. The communication technology has proved to be the most effective and competent instrument for leading a better standard of service in the Libraries. The incredible amplification of information in varied fields and fiscal constraints of the Library put under compulsion to extend cooperation with the global sector that became imperative through computers, consortia, cooperation and above all networks. (Trezza; 1981;p.101). The Network, according to Webster's Encyclopedic Unabridged Dictionary of the English Language (1989;p.960) is a device embodying telecommunication, computers technologies where telecommunication acts as a system for receiving and transmitting information, based on computers, computer terminals, printers, and or interconnected telephone lines. Network signifies promoting scientific and related information in a subject field through communication technology. The Webster's New World Dictionary defines network as a group, system etc. of inter connected cooperating individuals. Thus, Networking signifies interconnection of autonomous computers so as to facilitate exchange of information through copper wire, laser, and microwave or through communication satellites. In the era of information revolution, scientific and technical literatures in printed form as well as electronic form has been increasing widely with a very faster rate. Considerable growth of electronic form in the field of Information Technology involving computers and telecommunication has brought a sweeping change in the service sector in the Library. Linking of computers with telecommunications has revolutionized the expansion of information systems, commercial vendors of information and networks. Added to this, on-line information has also become imminent for getting transformed, authentic, and instant information by the users. The impact of computer has permeated all sectors of librarianships and information retrieval. The information storage and retrieval problem has become progressively more serious in recent years particularly in the areas of Technology and Science, where the volume of data and information is increasing at an unprecedented nearly exponential rate. Further, as the amount of data available in any Library or in any Information Center is not sufficient enough to explore research, it became essential to adopt computerization and networking though computer becomes imminent.

GENEALOGY OF NETWORK

The Internet, a network of networks worked out from the Arpanet that was conceived in the year 1969 by and for the Pentagon's Advanced Research Projects Agency. This was conceptualized as a National Computer Network to link Scientists and Universities doing Defense Research, Computer Science and other governmental funded projects. Over the network they not only could above exchange information and data, collaborate over a distance but also could become co-author of research papers. The Arpanet, the first network was restricted for its use with in limited professionals and as well as for a limited period that was winded up in 1990 and this venture of network gave birth to World Wide Web (WWW or W3). The World Wide Web was introduced by a group of Physicists at the CERN European Laboratory for practical Physics in Geneva, Switzerland as an online documentation resource which is now the world's most powerful tool on the Internet (Patnaik; 2001;p.172). They created a protocol, Hypertext Transfer Protocol (HTTP), which standardized communication between servers and clients. At the outset, Internet was proficient to propel electronic mail service. World Wide Web, i.e., the Web in the present environment caters a leading and most commanding information retrieval service of the Internet making up the worldwide computer network. Moreover, the Web countenances the users to access to a gigantic array of documents without any geographical circumscribe through Hypertext or Hypermedia electronic connections that link related pieces of information to permit a user for easy access to them. The history of the Internet has been depicted in Table-1 as under (Hobbes; Internet Time line, v.6).

Table 1. History of Internet

Year of Inception	*Description*
1957	USSR launched Sputnik, the first artificial Earth Satellite
1958	US formed ARPA with in the Dept. of defense to establish US lead in Sc.& Tech. applicable to Military.
1961	First paper on Packet Switching Theory entitled, "Information Flow in Large Communications Nets" by MIT – based scientist Leonard Klein rock was published
1962	Two MIT – based scientists, JCR Licklider and W.Clark jointly published a paper, entitled, "Online Man – Computer Communication" to boost the idea further.
1962	US senator Edward Kennedy sends a congratulatory telegraph to BBN for Million Dollar APRA contract to build "Interfaith Message Processor (IMP)
1962	A Network working Group (NWG) headed by Steve Crocker developed host-level protocols for communication over the ARPANET. As a result, Tymnet was built as a part of Timeshare service.
1969	ARPANET was finally commissioned by DOD for research into Networking initially with 4 nodes:
30.8.69	NODE-1at UCLA (the first host to IMP connection).
1.10.69	NODE-2 at Standard Research Institute (Augmentation of human Intellect)
1.11.69	NODE-3 at Univ. of California, Santa Barbara (Interactive Math)
1.12.69	NODE-4 at Univ. of Utah (Graphics)

A network from the Library point of view is a formal agreement between two or more different types of libraries who share with their mutual users materials, information and services without any geographical restrictions. Computer and telecommunication technologies use to play a pivotal role in promoting communication among the libraries. Swank has defined the network concept as the development of cooperative systems of libraries on geographical, subject or other lines, each with some kind of center that not only coordinates the internal activities of the system, but also serves as the system's out let to and inlet from the enters of other systems (Swank; 1967;p.51).

The Network, according to UNESCO (1985;p.11) is a compact arrangement or an administrative configuration that links a group or individuals or organisations that have established to work together and/ or have assets. Information Networking entails the sharing of resources so as to smooth the progress of information needs to both actual and potential users of information. UNISIST-II in 1979 has defined Information Network as a set of interrelated information systems associated with communication facilities, which are cooperating through more or less formal agreements and institutional arrangements in order to jointly implement information handling operation, with a view to pooling their resources and to offer better services to the users.

CHARACTERISTICS OF NETWORKS

The characteristics of a network can be portrayed as below. Swank (1971; p.19-20), the stalwart in the field has acknowledged the characteristics of Information Network as:

* Information Resources which concerns with collection of documents or data and database;
* Readers, who usually are at the remote places from the main source of information;
* Schemes for intellectual organisation of documents or data which act as directories for use by readers;

* Methods for the delivery of resources to readers is the output;
* Formal organisation of cooperating or contracting formations, representing different databases;
* Bi-directional communication Networks which is the requirement preferably through high speed, long distance electrical signal transmission with switching capabilities and computer hookups.

According to Atherton (1994;pp.138-39) the information network has been divided into following components.

* Organizational structure that provides for fiscal and legal responsibility, planning and policy formulation which requires commitment, operational agreements and common purpose among the cooperating agencies;
* Collaborative Development of resources;
* Identification of nodes which provides for designation of role specialization as well as for geographical configuration;
* Identification of primary patron groups and provision for assignment of responsibility for information service to all with in the network;
* Identification of levels of service that provide for basic needs of patron groups as well as special needs, and distribution of each service type among the nodes with the provision of transfer of document, data and information;
* Establishment of communication system that provides 'conversational mode' format and is designed to carry the desired message load at each level of operation;
* Common standard message code that provides for understanding among the nodes on the network;
* Switching capability that provides for interfacing with other network and determines the optimum communication path with the network;
* A central bibliographic record that provides for location of required items with the network;

* Guidelines for selection of what is to be placed on the networks;
* Evaluation criteria and procedures to provide feedback from users and operators and means for network evaluation and modification to meet specified operational utility; and

However, Cesar Mercado (1982; p.12) has acknowledged the following characteristics of information network.

* The members are located in different places such as, regions, states, provinces or districts;
* They have ways of organizing and transmitting information or data (e.g., the collection of data based on standard classification system or the use of computerized storage/ retrieval system;
* They have ways of organizing and transmitting information or data
* There is two way communication and transfer of information among the members; and
* They have information resources and produce publications and documentation for members.

Thus, in addition to above characteristics of information network, the following are some of the major components that add a substantive value in promoting network among the Libraries and Information Centers.

(f) It is a decentralized multilateral arrangement for the sharing of information;

(g) It is a completely voluntary arrangement with autonomy;

(h) It strengthens interdependence among the participating nodal organisations;

(i) It promotes greater accessibility to information and more amenable to users;

(j) It reduces expenditure on building up huge complex infrastructures and thus, proves cost effective;

(k) It accelerates standardization in the organisation and free flow of information with least time and supports the decision-making system.

(l) It also sparks off the usage of resources which include all types of media and formats such as serials, monographs, documents in printed form and also non-print materials including on-line databases of the organisation;

(m) Extending of integrated of services of all types of libraries and segments of the information and library community including abstracting and indexing services;

(n) The rapidly changing and expanding technologies in the fields of communication through networks accelerate research and development in many areas.

TYPES OF NETWORKS

The functions and components are the building blocks of various types of data networks that exercise it competency with more effectively. Principally, the data networks are classified into four types such as,

1. Wide Area Network (WAN);
2. Metropolitan Area Network (MAN);
3. Local Area Network (LAN); and
4. Value Added Network (VAN).

Wide Area Network

Wide Area Networks, established in 1960 specifically meant for promoting academic research project. Wide Area Network, a telecommunication network connects computers and smaller networks to larger networks over greater geographic areas, including different continents. In Wide Area Network, the system provides an ability for hosts at geographically scattered sites to communicate with one another. The host computers are generally on Local Area Network which are connected to regional networks which inturn are interlinked with routers to form World Wide Network (Patnaik; Ibid: p.152). They may link the computers by means of cables, optical fibers, or satellites, but their users commonly access the networks via a modem (a device that allows computers to communicate over telephone lines). However, the function of Modem is to modulate the signal from Analogue to Digital and vice-versa. The largest Wide Area Network is the *Internet*, a collection of networks and gateways linking millions of computer users on every continent (Encyclopedia Britannica CD). Based on the communication infrastructure, they are classified as Terrestrial Data Networks (TDNs) or Satellite based Data Networks (SBDNs). In TDNs, data communication is organized using cables, fiber optic lines or radio links (IGNOU; 1995;P.40).

Metropolitan Area Network (MAN)

A Metropolitan Area Network interconnects computers with a metropolitan city. Community Antenna Television (CATV) cables, twisted pair wires or shielded lines, optical fibers, radio link are provided as the communication medium for MAN. This network is generally applied for multimedia applications.

Local Area Network (LAN)

The Local Area Networks, which came in to existence in 1970 are restricted to a particular area such as, a Library, different departments of the University or College. LAN normally transmits data in a digital form with typical transmission speed of up to several megabytes per second. LANs connect computers and peripheral devices in a limited physical area, such as a business office, laboratory, or college campus, by means of permanent links (wires, cables, fiber optics) that transmit data rapidly. A typical LAN consists of two or more personal computers, printers, and high-capacity disk-storage devices called file servers, which enable each computer on the network to access a common set of files. LAN operating system software, which interprets input and instructs networked devices, allows users, to communicate with each other; share the printers and storage equipment; and simultaneously access centrally located processors, data, or programs. The Local Area Network is consisted of different work stations not only share the tangential devices but also the work stations are connected with gateways so as to provide access to other networks. A schematic diagram of Local Area Network is depicted below.

The application of Local Area Network especially in Library and Information Centers has proved to be most worthy and cost effective as it provides benefit of Personal Computing, Sharing of Equipment, Sharing of Personal Files, Sending of Messages, Sharing of Databases, Office Automation, Fire and Security problem. Process control and above all administer common sharing of Software.

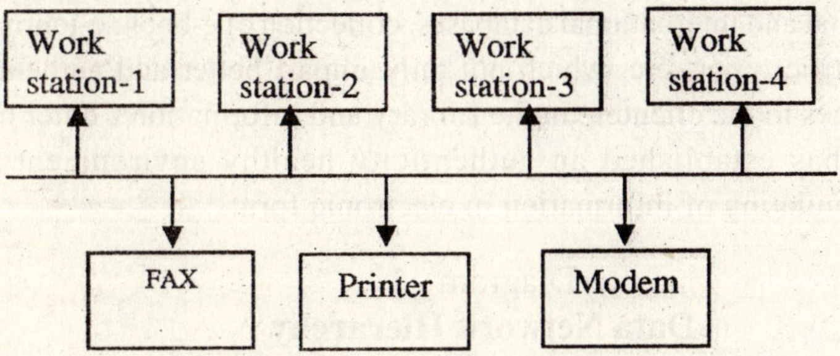

(Schematic Diagram of Local Area Network)

Value Added Network

The Value Added Network yields a better result in the network sector as this is applied primarily in a commercial service sector. As the Library and Information Center are non-profit organisations, hardly VAN is applied in these organisations. However, the intellectual value is added through VAN in the Library for better understanding the value of a theme. This type of network promotes the business sectors such as bank, insurances to satisfy the customers. The difficulty of keeping Wide Area Network networks operating is one of the principal reasons for using VANs that are public data networks which 'add value' by transmitting data and by providing access to commercial databases and software. The Library and Information Centers cannot be excluded from this network system as reputed firms have started creating commercial databases pertaining to various scientific and technological areas. This adds a substantial value for promoting research and development in an academic well as special institution. As VAN is cost effective, many companies which are lacking the technical expertise opt for it. Added to this, VAN provides a convenient access to data that would not otherwise be available.

Local Area Network, Metropolitan Area Network and Wide Area Network are generally interconnected in a hierarchical manner to form a global network that has been depicted in Diagram No. 1 (IGNOU, ibid; p.41). The global network has proved to be the most effective means of transmission of information, accessing of different national and international databases, collection of e-book, e-journal, scientific report etc. which not only impart better and authentic services to the clientele in the Library and Information Center but also has established an authenticity healthy environment in accumulating of information in electronic form.

Diagram –1
Data Network Hierarchy

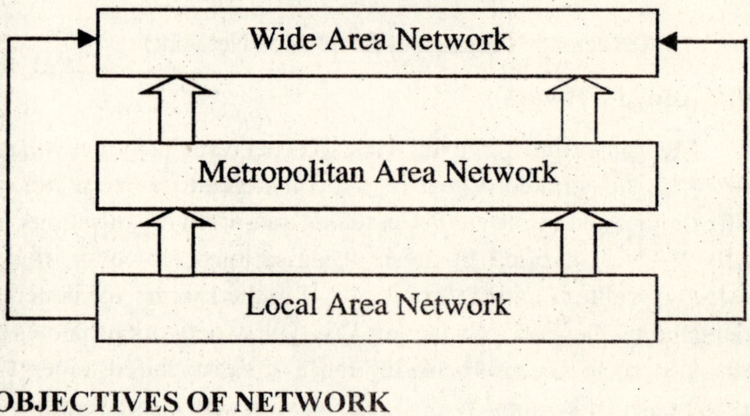

OBJECTIVES OF NETWORK

The primary objectives of a library network in a digital environment can be spelled out as follows (INFLIBNET; 2003;P.72):

i. To increase the availability and accessibility of resources. The resources of the Library are transferred from one destination to other through the modern technological means;

ii. Resource sharing encourages building specialized collection in the networked Libraries and avoids possession of duplicate documents which facilitate to provide effective services to the clientele;

iii. Resource sharing advocates the exposition of availability of reading materials to the readers of different libraries;

iv. Network also promotes in Cooperative Acquisition, Exchange of Data or Information, Storage of Documents, providing Documentation Services etc.;

v. Network also boosts for preparation of Union Catalogue, Bibliographical Control, Exchange Agreements, Document Delivery Service, Exchange of Information with cooperative networks, Creation of Authority Files, stimulates the improvement of library facilities and services and above all, the fiscal control;

vi. Optimum utilization of library materials, Current Awareness Service, developing a State Standard for Information handling and research and development etc. are viable in a networked Libraries and Information Centers.

IMPLICATIONS OF NETWORKING

In the electronic environment, it has become the necessity of the hour to provide the electronic services to the users of the Library and Information Centers by providing a vast array of information irrespective of the fields. The application of computer and network has become indispensable in the library as it enhances the capability of :

* Policy Development;
* User Feedback Analysis;
* Performance Analysis;
* Procurement sources;
* Order preparation and control;
* Transaction control like additions and deletion;

* Online Public Access Catalogue;
* Remote login;
* Cataloguing of network resources;
* On line Catalogues
* World Cat (OCLC);
* Web OPAC; and
* Metadata Standards- Dublin Core;
* Cooperating Cataloguing;
* Standardization; and
* Marketing;

However, the networking plays a pivotal role in serials control in the Library, as serials control is one of the complex and expensive procedures in any Library system. An automated serial control though computerization and networking perform:

* Establishment of policies and procedures;
* Subscription control;
* Providing e-journal;
* E-publishing;
* E-Atlas;
* Creation of Databases;
* Providing of CAS Service;
* Extending of SDI Service;
* Preparation of Bibliographies;
* Thesaurus construction.
* Document Delivery Services;
* Inter Library Loan;
* Resource Sharing;
* Database Access
* Bibliographical; and
* Full Text;

CONCLUSION

Library and Information Networks endow with a platform for distribution of information resources and proficiency. Individual Libraries in a specified area are strengthened in Network environment which, not only prove to be the one of the best means to activate the optimum use of Library resources but also cost effective access to a wider range of information resources. It also throws dissemination of information to the target audience in a wider scale.

The applications of telecommunication and computer technology have a splendid impact on these centers that led to the availability of important networks in Indian environment. INDONET, NICNET, ERNET and other networks could be established through network. ERNET i.e, Education and Research Network, a project supported by DOE was established to link the educational and research institutions in India, whereas, SIRNET, Scientific and Industrial Research Network came into existence which links Council of Scientific and Industrial Research and other research institution. NICNET was setup by National Informatics Center that proved to be a nationwide network. INDONET was established for commercial distribution computer network to provide access to the considerable computing and software resources of CMC Limited which is a public sector company in India (Raghavan & Vijayalakshmi; 1997;p.273). Thus, networking in Libraries and Information Centers has become essential to cope up with the present digital environment. The networking further could facilitate for on-line searching of national and international databases that are also accessible through CD-ROMs and these are updated continuously. The target of the networking is to widen a widespread full service network which should not be restricted to bibliographical information or computerized data but should encompass all methods and techniques to improve access to information available around the globe. A full service network covering scope, depth, quality and quantity should be built up in regional basis to satisfy the desire of the clientele in an effective and well-organized manner.

REFERENCES

1. Atherton. Characteristics of Network. *In.* Changing Frontiers of Library & Information Science. 1994. by S.F.Rab. Ess Ess Publications, Delhi; pp.138-39.
2. Encyclopedia Britannica 2001 Deluxe Edition CD.
3. Hobbes 'Zakon. Hobbes' Internet Timeline V6.1
4. IGNOU. Application of Information Technology. MLIS-06.1995. IGNOU; New Delhi; p.40-1
5. INFLIBNET. Inflibnet Regional Training Programme on Library Automation- 2003. INFLIBNET; Ahmedabad; p.72.
6. Mercado (Cesar). Information Networking Concept and Models. Quexondity; Institute of Mass Communication, University of Philippines. 1982.p.12.
7. Patnaik (S). First Text Book on Information Technology. 2001. Dhanpat Rai and Co. (Pvt) Ltd., New Delhi. pp..152-172.
8. Raghavan (J) and Vijayalakshmi (S). Electronic Information Sources and Access Mechanisms. *In.* Access to Electronic Information. SIS, Bhubaneswar chapter; 1997. p. 273.
9. Swank (R C). Interlibrary Cooperation under title III of the Library Services and Construction Act. 1967. Sacramento; California; p.51.
10. Swank (R C). Interlibrary Cooperation, Interlibrary Communications, and Information Networks- Explanations and Definition. *In.* Interlibrary Communications and Information Networks. *Ed. by* Joseph Becker.1971; ALA; Chicago; p.19-20.
11. Trezza (Alphonse). How Information Networks may develop and accommodate to future trends. Strategies for Meeting the Information Needs of Society in the year 2000. Libraries Unlimited; Littleton, Colorado; 1981; p.101.
12. UNESCO. Information Networking in Population Education.

Bangkok. UNESCO Principal Regional Office for Asia and Pacific. 1985; p.11.

13. UNESCO-UNISIST-II. Intergovernmental Conference on Scientific and Technical Information for Development, Main Working Document. Paris; 1979. Unesco; Paris.

14. Webster's Encyclopedic Unabridged Dictionary of the English Language. Gramercy Books; New York; 1989;p.960.

19

Resource Sharing in Digital Environment some Concerns

A.K. Sobhana Devi
Assistant Librarian
Cochin University

INTRODUCTION

The amount of information and the multitude of formats in which it is recorded have been growing exponentially over the last few years. Without consistent and reliable access to information sources from both the past and the present a society cannot keep on advancing. No programmes can be materialised with out sufficient information. Libraries play a crucial role in transferring this very ingredient to progress. Individual libraries can never satisfy the increasing demands of the user and no library can be self reliant in terms of its own resources. But what ever be the constraints there cannot be any compromise on the satisfaction of user needs. So it has become crucial to turn to the alternative of providing information by sharing the resources a library have with a network of libraries. Easy access to information in print and electronic medium is possible by network and information is a resource that is to be shared between those who cannot access it.

RESOURCE SHARING AND LIBRARY COOPERATION

Resource sharing

The term resource includes all that libraries have or use to disseminate information from reading materials in print and non-print, staff expertise and even technology.

Sharing of resource is the reciprocal agreements negotiated between individual libraries to help in the enhanced access to collection at least for onsite reference. In fact the modern concept of resource sharing overflows the boundaries referred above and includes cooperative acquisition, cataloging and classification, cooperation in training and development of professionals; cooperative acquisition of equipment and machines. The traditional way of collection management and resource sharing is being changed significantly by the advent of electronic resources. Resource sharing is being considered as an important element in the package of services provided to users under the present changing environment.

The factors that make resource sharing necessary for libraries for resource sharing are the rising volume of information, decreasing budget and escalating price of information sources, impact of technological advances and increasing needs of the users. Libraries cannot be deaf to the demands of users. It is possible to share the resources among a network of libraries to satisfy the increasing needs of the users.

Effective resource sharing presupposes an infrastructure which enables users to locate materials of interest in both print and electronic medium with in a library and also with sharing libraries. The ability to locate and identify materials implies that users must be able to interact with the database of the sharing libraries. The three major components of resource sharing are co-operative collection development, bibliographic access, interlibrary loan and document delivery.

Library Cooperation

Library cooperation is a means of mobilizing total library

resources to meet the needs of the users without specific regard to the library to which they belong. The early objective of this alliance was associated with exchange of catalogue records and print based document delivery. These functions are now facilitated by electronic exchange of records and record keeping. As individual libraries are increasingly unable to provide all their services by themselves they are banding together into cooperative alliances and consortia. Library cooperation can be on the areas of collection development, classification and cataloging, interlibrary lending, preservation and storage of information materials of print and electronics for present and future use.

Co operative Collection Development

Cooperative acquisition is aimed to acquire high quantity information materials from anywhere through cooperative bargaining power of consortia for the use of the member libraries at minimum cost. The questions like which library is collecting what, whether to subscribe in electronic or print or hybrid and what is the most economical way of subscription are some of the areas where consenses is needed for effective collection development.

The selection decision concerning electronic resources and print should be made with in an explicit collection development policy. The policy should include the statement of the mission of user groups, objectives of the cooperative institutions, size of the collection including books, periodicals, monographs, e-resources etc, the budget each library can utilize and the existence of cooperative agreement for collection. Cooperative acquisition can help in purchasing materials from wherever published and it is aimed to increase the national provision of research level materials to rationalize holdings wherever necessary and to identify current gaps in provision. To ensure availability, accessibility and easy flow of information is the relevance of co operative acquisition and resource sharing

Selection of Print and Electronic Resources

The two terms selection and acquisition form the concept of collection development. It is the process of developing the resource by assuring the quality of collections. The traditional effects of selection criteria for print such as author, publisher, content and format continue to be central issues in the selection of electronic resources also. Access to all materials legally obtainable should be assured to the users and policies should not unjustly exclude materials. The basis of selection is an understanding of readers, why they come or do not come to the library what they find or do not find and to what uses they put the information.

Librarians are very well aware of the criteria of selecting print resources. In the non-print market the reputations of both the producers and distributors are equally important in the selection process which is absent in print medium. Producers and distributors are often the same in non-print media. In the electronic medium the creators of search software and database designers take in new importance.

A major difference between print and electronic products lies in the profusion of product choice available to the selector. The electronic products of the print version may easily be sliced and repackaged into a variety of products. Many times content available in the electronic product is not the same as the print product. Librarians must thoroughly examine all purchase options and determine the most appropriate version for the library.

The primary factors influencing the selection criteria for electronic products are technology options licensing issues and the items format. Libraries should select only those electronic products for which they have the applicable technology. Most of the license agreements explicitly deny many rights defined by the copyright law and the publishers introduce new issues of user identity, product capabilities and restrictions on use.

The formats of e-resources have a considerable impact on selection of print. The organization and presentation of text greatly influence selections. The binding options and special feature such as bibliographies, indexes, tables and appendixes quality of paper, type case etc play significant role in selection.

For non-print products the format compatibility is key to the selection decision. The items user friendliness in terms of loading accessing and operating the equipment is deciding factor in selection. Once the library has committed to a specific format the collection is built to its standards. The selector must examine command structures, screen displays system responses and help screens to assure responsible functionality and selection decision of electronic resources must be based in the principle that the library has adequate equipment to view or provide access to the product. Electronic products should assure a user-friendly interface. It is essential to evaluate the basic features such as menu driven functions, consistency in screen displays, online help, Boolean search capabilities and response time. Preview copies or test discs are excellent methods of determining how user will respond to the product.

Licensing Limitations

Contract negotiations are basic in managing electronic resources in a consortia environment. Before selecting e–resources it has to determine if a license exists, what impact the license will have on the selection and acquisition process and whether the rights assigned by the license are adequate for the library's purpose. Issues of user definition, users access and user rights, copyright and interlibrary loan restrictions, 3rd party liability, renewal and price payments, termination of agreement by either parties, definition of sites/ institutes, full descriptions of product (content, features, timelines) usage reports, performance warranty, technical standards (ex. Z39.50) are some of the issues that are to be discussed among libraries before negotiating license agreement.

By contract law any right not expressly granted in the license agreement are reserved to the product supplier. Many times agreements are stated in certain vague terms which are misinterpreted by libraries and this leads to denial of certain rights to libraries by producers. Hence it is the responsibility of the consortia to assure that the desired rights are granted in the license. The provision for returning outdated CD Rom discs, restrictions on the assignment of passwords, restriction on granting the provider the right to audit uses of the product at any time are some other areas where libraries must be careful while making a license agreement.

Inter Library Loan and Document Delivery

The key element in access to information in library cooperation and consortia is document delivery and interlibrary lending. Any cooperative or network library program is effective if there is a provision of successful delivery of documents in print or electronic media. There is a need for a number of local, national and international union lists and bibliographies in machine readable databanks given rapid access to records of what is available in each library.

In simplest form document delivery is the transfer of a photocopy of requested document to the end user. Since information is produced in different formats there are different options for document delivery such as directly to the end user or library as intermediary, the medias such as CD- Rom, Fax, E- mail, on line etc. The print based document delivery is now being supplemented by electronic document delivery.

Most of the request for document delivery a library has to deal is for journal articles. Since there is a huge increase in the information available on the web there is a corresponding increase in the price of the journals and this has posed libraries with limited resources a challenge in terms of subscriptions. The shift from holdings to access has led a grater demand for website. At present electronic journals are often in a trial phase and libraries maintain print subscription for archival purpose.

Library consortia can provide a lower cost method of delivery of scholarly journal articles. For the academic libraries consortium delivery and decrease in the number of journal subscriptions is worthwhile.

Shift to Access

The task of library to provide information is being shifted largely from ownership to access of information outside its four walls. The possibilities of IT in accessing information in a-multitude of ways have changed the entire concept of library and the patrons began to demand and approach libraries for more service. Access has become a core question for resource sharing in a network-based system. The availability of diffuse and diverse nature of resource on the web have forced libraries to reassess their role in the digital age. In fact it is apt to say that the demand of the users have changed the age old concept of library and library as an institution has transformed itself into a resource gateway for local and remote access.

Libraries have built up collections with care and effort to know the preference, special needs and requirements of their known users and now they have begun to serve audiences unknown to them and this invest new roles and responsibilities to libraries. There is a number of non library venues that a customer can have access and as such libraries are in a situation in which they do not control the services themselves. This has necessitated the importance of resource sharing to give improved access to information. Libraries are challenged to design measures of user behaviour that help them make good decisions about what materials should be added to collection that support user needs.

Access cannot be denied simply on financial reasons. Hence resource sharing in considered by many libraries to be a solution to the financial problem. The potential of sharing digital resources is to control cost and give access to more information through net.

LIMITED SUCCESS OF RESOURCE SHARING

Resources of an academic librarary is driven by teaching and research needs. These are liable to change due to change in courses and change in syllabus. Collaborative collecting is likely to centre in the elite few and this will further reinforce the gap between information haves and have nots which could be politically sensitive. Improved resourcing of specialized collections would be desirable at this point.

Institutions are very keen to guard their autonomy and may have very different missions. The amount of budget allocation will also differ. Institutions which have high budget allocation and those which have different sources of funding would like to have an upper hand in framing policies and sharing. Hence a consensus is necessary among libraries to serve the purpose of resource sharing ie. "Serving ones own and helping others"

Libraries provide more service and resources through multiple delivery methods. Virtual users do not browse the stacks as do physical users. Not all of a libraries collection is available in digital format. In some cases a service or resource is available only in electronic format.

Electronic resources especially in a networked environment involves a very different set of circumstance than those in the print resources. The technology for the delivery of the information resources is constantly changing and that in turn affects the services a library can deliver. The mental satisfaction that a user gets from a physical visit to a library is very much higher than a visit to library's web site. Leased services are not truly the services of the library rather library acts as gateway to such resources and this results in poor response from the publishers to render service.

Lack of leadership in planning and implementing programmes in a consortial environment greatly affects the quality and services provided by libraries. Monitoring the work of the participating libraries, checking the violation of license agreements, arguing for access to information against unnecessary restrictions by copyright laws, restringing the unnecessary expenditure on acquisition all need careful supervision under an able leadership. Leadership is the factor that brings together all other areas in successfully implementing the programmes. Lack of this kind of leadership is a factor in the limited success of a consortia.

The difficulty of administering consortial programmes outside of a relatively limited geographical range, lack of sufficient authority in many regional and national programs are some other reasons for the limited success of resource sharing.

COPYRIGHT ISSUES

The copyright is a bundle of legal right for a limited period given to the authors of works recognised and protected by law for a monetary gain. The laws of copyright are framed in order to protect an author against piracy of his work.

Libraries have always been in the for front of efforts towards universal access to information. Libraries are given certain rights to copy from works for the use of the patrons under the fair use principle of copyright. Libraries can down load a portion of database or can make another copy for library use. CD Rom and multimedia which are extensively used in a library environment enjoy copyright protection and down loading a portion of them is allowed. Licensing drew more attention in electronic field. Some licence agreements do not allow library to provide for multiple use. User and usage restrictions under contract are imposed on libraries by publishers in the name of copyright. Some publishers prohibit inter- library lending and document delivery of the electronic resources. The question of ownership of data, the fair use principle, the vague terms in license which do not express the libraries rights etc prohibit libraries in providing sufficient access to information.

Copyright, freedom of information and data protection have changed significantly in recent years. Copyright continues to be a battleground between copyright owners and users. The Internet culture that is openly antagonistic to the entire concept of copyright means that problems associated with copyright are likely to increase rather than decrease in the future. Information professionals find themselves in an awkward position between the competing factors.

CONCLUSION

The availability of scholarly and scientific literature in print and electronic media has profoundly altered the needs of the user.

The introduction of IT in retrieving information with in seconds through a mouse click made the user to go out of the four walls of the library to get what he wants. The need for access to high quality information has resulted in the realization of the importance of an authoritative physical institution in disseminating information. More over libraries are becoming a wall less institution where the need and importance of a librarian is very much shrinking. To recognize this is very important for the existence of library as an institution and librarian as a professional.

In the current digital environment libraries have almost covered the transition from the scholarly communication of print to digital, which has become a primary vehicle for research now a days. Library services must be restructured to present high quality trusted information in digital form to meet the needs of the users. Vision and planning must be there on the needs of resources and services to be provided to the user, whether the library's customers receive value out of the communities investment in library services, what should be the real or perceived quality of library service and the impact of services to the community that the library serves etc are some factors to consider to assess the quality of services given in libraries.

In a circumstance of ever decreasing funding and growing digitization, the factors of resource sharing such as cooperative collection development, interlibrary lending document delivery, licensing agreements etc. are to be better understood. The emphasis on cost effectiveness/ performance measurement requires resource sharing essential for better service. As libraries struggle to identify, define and articulate the benefits derived by customers through the use of library services and resources, librarian must educate the communities regarding the issues associated with network based information content to establish the democratic nature of library in providing access to information

REFERENCES

1. Bertot McClure: "Out comes assessment in the networked

environment "Research quertions. Issues, considerations and moving forward" – library trends / spring 2003

2. Katz, William A. Collection development the selection of materials for libraries, 1980
3. Muir, Adrienne and Oppenheim, Charles "National Information Policy Development world wide 11: Universal access – addressing the digital divide" – Journal of Information science 28 (4) 2002.
4. Miller, Ruth. H. Electronic Resource and academic libraries 1980 – 2000: A historical perspective.
5. Oppenheim, Charles – "Does copyright have any future on the internet" – journal of documentation. Vol 56 (3) may 2000
6. Sounders, Laverna M. "Transforming acquisitions to support virtual libraries" information technology and libraries Vol: 14 (1) March 1995.
7. "The evolution of selection activities for electronic resources" Library Trend Vol: 45 (3) winter 1997. P: 392 – 395.
8. Thornton, Glenda A. – "Impact of electronic resources on collection development, the. Roles of librarians and library consortia" Library trends 48 (4) spring 2000.

20

RESOURCE SHARING AND NETWORKING AMONG LIBRARIES IN KANNUR DISTRICT : A PROPOSAL

Dr. S. Humayoon Kabir
Project Officer
Kerala Women's Commission
Trivandrum - 14

INTRODUCTION

We call our society as information society. Information society is a post-industrial phenomenon. In such a society more stress is given to information activities than anything else. It includes information generation, information recording, information processing and dissemination of information. All these were done manually in the last few decades are now being done with the help of machines. Automation in the above mentioned activities helped in the improvement of library and information services which intrun helps in carrying out research and educational activities at a higher speed. Today many of the libraries information centres are striving hard for achieving the goal. Many obstacles are there - Information deluge, multidisciplinary nature of subjects, spiralling cost of documents etc, are some of them. To keep pace with all these, policies for resource sharing should be formulated and building network among libraries in particular area/region is essential. Infact the advancement of information technology and automation led to the networking concept.

Networks opened up new horizons for speedy communication, dissemination, storage and retrieval of information in wide subject areas. A glance at the libraries in Kannur show that they are ill - equipped to handle, retrieve and provide information services to the users at a satisfactory level. The practice of issuing books on interlibrary loan is the only resource sharing activity existing. Most of the libraries information centres in this area are facing inadequate financial resources as well as space. Some of the libraries have installed the computer and started computerising the library and information activities. Many of these libraries are using CDS/ISIS package for their IR activities since it is cheap and having network compatibility. Many libraries in this area have reprographic facilities. Thus we can see a favorable environment for networking in this area with a little effort.

DEFINITION

Resource Sharing

The term "resource" applies to any thing, person or action to which one turns for aid in time of need. The word "sharing" connotes apportioning, allotting or contributing something that is owned to benefit others. Resource sharing in its most positive aspect entails reciprocity, implying partnership in which each is willing and is able to make available the materials when needed[1].

Network

Special Libraries Association (SLA) of USA defined networks "as a formal arrangement whereby several libraries or other organisations engage in exchange of information, materials, services etc[2].

Library network may be defined as "A distribution system composed of two or more libraries and/or other organizations engaged in a common pattern of information exchange through communications, for some functional purpose[3].

A library network is defined as a "set of inter-related information system associated with communication facilities which adhere to more or less formal agreements, in order to jointly implement information handling operations with a view to pooling the resources and serving the users better[4].

NEED

Resource sharing activities help to lay strong foundations for effective library and information services. There is an urgency now for paying greater attention to it in our country. The current UNESCO approach to information resource systems is to develop them as national information systems. For this purpose, the 'Universal Availability of Publications (UAP) programs have been sponsored by IFLA and UNESCO. The district under study has several libraries in various subject fields. They hold information resources in the form of macro, micro, audiovisual etc. They should be maximised in use by devising schemes and services to put them to widest access and circulation.

FIVE LAWS OF LIBRARY SCIENCE: as stated by Ranganathan are: -

i) Books are for use
ii) Every book its reader
iii) Every reader his book
iv) Save the time of the reader, and
v) Library is a growing organism.

These laws emphasise the need for resource sharing.

AIMS AND OBJECTIVES

i) To evolve a network of library and information centres in and around Kannur initially and in other parts of the Malabar region later.

ii) To facilitate sharing of resources among the participating libraries and promote information dissemination through computerised network.

iii) To bring about co-operative working among the participating institutions through computerised network.

iv) To establish linkages with regional, national and international networks at a later stage.

BENEFITS

- Utilisation of library holding within the budget.
- Large volumes of literature can be accessed without additional finance.
- Improved user Services.
- Avoids unnecessary duplication
- Reduced investment
- E-mail, Remote Login service can be availed.
- About 1000 international databases can be accessed.

EXAMPLES OF NETWORKS

Some of the selected networks (global, regional, national and local) and those in various stages are the following : -

Global and Regional

a) APINESS (Asia – Pacific Information Network for the Social Sciences)

b) ARIS-NET (Arab Regional Information System Network)

c) ASTINFO (Regional Network for the exchange of Information in Science & Technology in Asia and Pacific)

d) CARIS – SEA (Current Agricultural Research Information System for South East Asia)

e) ChIN (International Chemical Information Network)

f) DEVINSA (Development Information System)

g) GULFNET (Network for the Arab Gulf Region)

h) IARC – NET (International Agricultural Information Centres Network)

i) NTFS (Network of Tropical Fisheries Scientists)

j) NTAS (Network of Tropical Agricultural Scientists)

k) IDIN (International Development Information Network on Research in Progress)

l) INFOLAC (Programme for co-operation in Information for Latin America and the Carribbean)

m) PADIS (Pan-African Development Information System)

n) PANGIS (Pan-African Geological Information System)

o) TIPS (Technology Information Pilot System)

National and Local

a) INDONET

b) ERNET (Education and Research Network)

c) SIRNET (Scientific & Industrial Research Network)

d) INFLIBNET (Information and Library Network)

e) CALIBNET (Calcutta Library Network)

f) DELNET (Delhi Library Network)

g) MALIBNET (Madras Library Network)

h) MYLIBNET (Mysore Library Network)

i) PUNET (Pune Library Network)

j) BONET (Bombay Library Network)

k) BALNET (Bangalore Library Network)

l) NAGNET (Nagpur Library Network)

Non – Bibliographic Networks

a) OILNET (Oil and Natural Gas commission Network)

b) SAILNET (Steel Authority of India Limited)

c) COALNET (Coal India Limited)

d) RAILNET (Indian Railways)

e) BANKNET (Bank Network)

METHODOLOGY TO BE ADOPTED

a) Identification of the Institutions in the Kannur Region

The first thing to be done is to identify the institutions existing in the Kannur area. After that establish contact with all the head of the institutions / libraries and ascertain their views on establishing KANLIBNET. A thorough data collection regarding the details of the institutions of the area should be done. The information should be collected by visiting each and every institution / library in the locality personally. After identifying the institutions, the detailed data regarding the nature of the collection has to be done with the help of the questionnaire.

b) Questionnaire

The questionnaire should contain the following to elicit information on:-

i) Type of documents in libraries

ii) Number of documents in the libraries

iii) Funding agencies

iv) Infrastructural facilities

v) Availability of computer hardware and software

vi) Information services provided by the institutions

vii) Dependence on other institution

viii) Willingness of the parent institution to share finance.

ABOUT KANNUR

Besides being famous for its scenic beauty, Kannur occupies an important position in the political scenaria of the state. It is an educational and cultural centre of the malabar region. A random survey / observation showed that the libraries in this area have been growing in number and size. A number of institutions of importance are there. The Kannur University has been established recently which cater the educational needs of the people in the malabar region. It is also having a number of research institutions with vast information sources. Many of the libraries possess hardware, which is essential for networking. Some of the libraries have already computered their activities.

TYPES OF LIBRARIES

The libraries existing in Kannur can be grouped into the following categories :

i) School Libraries
ii) Public Libraries
iii) College Libraries (General)
iv) Medical / Homeo / Ayurveda College Libraries
v) Engineering College Libraries
vi) Agricultural colleges / institutes / research centres
vii) University / University Department Libraries
viii) Special Libraries
ix) Government Libraries
x) Industrial / Technical Libraries
xi) Libraries of Voluntary Organisations

FORMATION OF A SOCIETY FOR KANLIBNET

The KANLIBENT should be registered as a society which will have the advantage that even in the absence of funding from the government / other sources, the network can work effectively and efficiently.

The structure should be as follows :

a) The Vice – Chancellor of the Kannur University should be made the ex-officio chairman of the society. In the absence of the VC, the Pro-Vice Chancellor of the Kannur University will function as the chairman. The chairmanship should not be restricted to a particular individual but to the officers holding the position. This will enable continuity and the smooth functioning of KANLIBNET.

b) The Principal of the Medical College should be made the Vice- Chairman of KANLIBNET.

c) One expert nominated by the Syndicate of Kannur University.

d) Member representatives of the participating institutions in the area (Medical college, agricultural centres etc.)

e) The office of the KANLIBNET should be situated in the Kannur University Library and the University Librarian (or in-charge) of Kannur University should be made the member secretary.

The society should be registered under the provisions of the Registration of Societies Act, 1860 with its constitutions, bye-laws and rules governing the organisation and management of these societies. Care should be taken while drafting the constitution to safeguard the interest of the university / research organisation.

FINANCIAL RESOURCES

An essential factor in a network is the finance. Continuous cash flow programme should be planned. There is not much difficulty to initiate the network. But the difficult part in it is to maintain the continuity of its service. So the finance required for KANLIBNET has to be worked out. DGSIR, NISSAT, DST or other bodies should be approached for grants. The Kerala State Government could also be approached to allocate funds to the state government institutions participating in the network. Parent departments / establishments may also help for this good cause.

TRAINING OF MANPOWER

Since the networking activities are to be done by information professionals it is essential to train information professionals towards the perception, planning, execution and implementation. The University Library (since there is no Library & Information Science Department) should conduct courses in computer applications in libraries & information centres frequently. NISSAT should be approached for providing financial assistance for computer training and also experts for the courses / workshops.

HARDWARE AND SOFTWARE REQUIREMENTS

Hardware Requirements

The central node should have the following hardware specifications with additional disk space.

i) PC – AT / 486 (minimum 33 MHz)

◇ Minimum 8 MB RAM

◇ 1 X 1.44 MB FDD (Floppy Disk)

◇ Drives

◇ 2 X 1.2 MB FDD

◇ 2 X 300 MB HD (Hard Disk)

◇ Mono-monitor, with 101 standard

◇ Key board and with SVGA card

◇ Serial ports

◇ Parallel Port (Minimum one)

◇ Real Time Clock

ii) PC – AT / 486

◇ Minimum 2 MB RAM

◇ 1 X 1.2 MB FDD

◇ 1 X120 MB FDD

◇ Mono-monitor with 101 standard

◇ Key board with SVGA card

◇ Minimum 2 serial ports

◇ Minimum one parallel port

iii) Other Requirements

1. Fax
2. Modem

3. Telex
4. CD-ROM drive
5. Minimum two printers
6. One laser printer
7. Cartridge type drive
8. Tables, Chairs
9. Separate room partition in the library hall, glass panel, push back door
10. Telephone connection.
11. Electricity fittings and fixtures
12. Switch board with 3 way pins
13. AC, UPS

The participating libraries with at least 20,000 documents must have the following minimum hardware facilities.

i. PC – AT / 486

◇ Minimum 4 MB RAM

◇ 1 X 1.44 MB FDD

◇ 1 X 1.2 MB FDD

◇ 2 X 200 MB Hard Disc

◇ Mono-monitor, with 101 standard

◇ Key board and with SVGA card

◇ Serial ports

◇ Parallel port (minimum one)

◇ Real Time clock

ii. Other Requirements

1. Fax
2. Modem
3. Telex
4. CD-ROM drive
5. Printer

6. Tables, Chairs
7. Separate room with partition in the library hall, glass panel, push back door
8. Telephone connection.
9. A fan, one stool
10. Electricity fittings and fixtures
11. Switch board with 3 way pins
12. AC, UPS

Software Requirements

<> DOS and / or UNIX

<> LAN, Software for E-mail

<> Word Processors, DBMS Packages

<> Library Automation Packages (Like Libsys etc)

<> Programming Languages (i.e. C or Pascal)

NISSAT has been distributing the UNESCO software CDS/ISIS to Indian libraries with a nominal charge. The Computer Maintenance Corporation (CMC) is having a software called MAITRAYEE. It is better to create the databases for libraries in the Kannur region in the CDS / ISIS package.

CONCLUSION

Advancements in Computer and Communication technologies have made available a large number of computer based systems in various sectors for information storage, retrieval and dissemination. This has facilitated sharing of information resources distributed over various geographic locations using computer based communication networks aimed at information exchange among various institutions and organizations. A well designed computerised library and Information system can help in providing the right information to the right user at the right time.

A proposal for establishing KANLIBNET is highlighted in this paper. It is aimed to alleviate the major problems of services and resource crunch prevailing in the libraries and information centres of the Kannur region. The network will definitely provide a solution for the problem of accessing primary and secondary literature in the local area as well as outside. Once the feasibility study is done establishing KANLIBNET will not be a distant dream.

REFERENCES

1. Encyclopedia of Library & Information Science, New York, Marcel Dekker, 1983. P.293.
2. Samuelson, K and others. Information systems and networks. North-Holland, 1977. P.121.
3. Paskoff, Beth M. Networks and networking. How and why should special libraries be involved Special Libraries. 80; 1984; P.94.
4. Raghavan, R and Raghavan, J. Notable features of MALIBNET. DESIDOC Bulletin of Information Technology. 16,2; 1996. P.47.
5. Mehta, Surendra Nath, Resource sharing: co-operative acquisition of documents by research libraries in India. DRTC Annual Seminar, 19, 1982; P.1-21.
6. Samuelson, K. Information Systems and Networks, 1977.
7. Turner, F. Facilitating resource sharing in an automated environment. An update on the National Library's Interlibrary Loan Protocol, Canadian Library Journal, 47, 5; 1990; Oct. P.347-52.
8. Laguardia, C and Dowell, C.C. The structure of resource sharing in academic research libraries. Reference Quarterly: 30, 3; 1991, Spring PP.370-376.
9. Dobrovits, Peter. Resource sharing and retrospective conversion. Australian Library Journal. 41,2; 1992, May: P.118-120.

PART IV :

INFORMATION PROCESSING IN THE ELECTRONIC ENVIRONMENT

21

USER INTERFACES DESIGN IN WEB OPAC

Veerankutty Chelatayakkot
Junior Librarian
Cochin University of Science and Technology

INTRODUCTION

Online Public Access Catalogues (OPAC) began to appear in libraries in the early 1980's. The OPAC quickly gained wide acceptance among the public who preferred them to their traditional card catalogues. The first generation online catalogue had limited capabilities and was simple an extension of the card catalogue. The traditional OPACs provided users with a few access points like author, title, and subject headings. They used character-by-character, matching algorithms to retrieve bibliographic records. Users were not given any display options.

Boolean searching, proximity operations, keyword access, and shelf list scanning, different display options and help faculties characterized the second generation OPACs. Although these OPACs offered many more features than their predecessors, most of them were limited to text-based command driven interfaces.

Current advances in computer technology and distributed networking have contributed to a surge of interest in the development of a new generation of OPACs that are ultimately intuitive and require a minimum of instruction. Remote access through internet, the client/server model, and standards such as NISO, Z 39.50 have opened new doors for vendors and researchers to propose innovative OPACs .

The WWW, developed as a hypertext and multimedia retrieval system for distributed information, has emerged as the most popular information delivery platform on the Internet. Because the WWW handles multimedia information, it is highly interactive and is implemented on a global scale, user acceptance of the WWW presents library management with the opportunity to implement a unified information infrastructure on behalf of its end users. The WWW offers the potential to make online catalogues accessible through the use of gateways.

The expansion of the WWW since early 1990 has been truly amazing. Once simply communication medium for scientists and researchers, its many and pervasive tentacles have spread deeply into business, organization and homes around the world. By the result, our OPAC automatically being converted to WEB OPAC.

USER INTERFACES IN WEB OPAC

User interfaces is one of the important quality of any software especially in WWW. Unlike earlier text based and graphical user interface systems, the web's root was the design of navigation and presentation of information. It is about content, not data. The web is a navigation environment where people move between pages of information, not an application environment.

Qualities of Good User Interfaces

A good design of user interfaces must possess some qualities.

1. Aesthetically pleasing
2. Compatibility with user needs, task and job
3. Comprehensibility
4. Consistency
5. Control i.e., actions should result from explicit user request, action should perform quickly

6. Efficiency i.e. minimize eye and hand movement
7. Familiarity
8. Simplicity

The design of user interface depends upon the purpose and application of the software. In web OPAC, searching and navigating are two major activities. So while designing the user interfaces in web OPAC, we should give special consideration to navigational and searching tools.

COMPONENTS OF WEB NAVIGATION SYSTEM

To move between web sites information fragments necessitates the creation of navigation links. They are contained within a framework of tools or controls, including the browser's command buttons, textual phrases, website navigation bars and website command buttons.

All the navigational tools must posses some qualities like

1. Make a sense in the absence of site context.
2. Be continually available.
3. Be obvious and distinctive
4. Be consistent in appearance, function and ordering.

The web browser have its own navigational tools to move from one website to another, and it should be differentiated from the website's navigational tools in which the second helps to navigate within a website.

As like user interface design, the alignment of interfaces in screen is also important. A well designed screen should reflect the capabilities, needs, and task of its users and be developed within the physical constraints imposed by the hardware and capabilities of software. A simple test for screen design is whether all screen elements like field caption, data, title, heading, text, types of controls and can be identified without reading the words that identify or comprise them. If this is so, a person's attention can quickly be drawn to the part of the screen that is relevant at that moment.

SCREEN DESIGN IN WEB OPAC

All elements of a screen must have meaning to users and serve a purpose in performing tasks or fulfilling needs. The screen posseses visual clarity when the elements are organized and presented in meaningful and understandable ways. Clarity is influenced by a multitude of factors like consistency in design, a visually pleasing composition, a logical and sequential ordering, the presentation of the proper amount of information, groupings, and alignment of screen items.

Some Samples of Screen and Interfaces in Web OPACs

Opening Screen

Beverly Hills Public Library Web Catalog

Search for Library Materials By

AUTHOR

TITLE

AUTHOR/TITLE

MAGAZINE & NEWSPAPER TITLES

SUBJECT

Keywords

CALL NUMBER

(Fig.1) (INNOPAC)

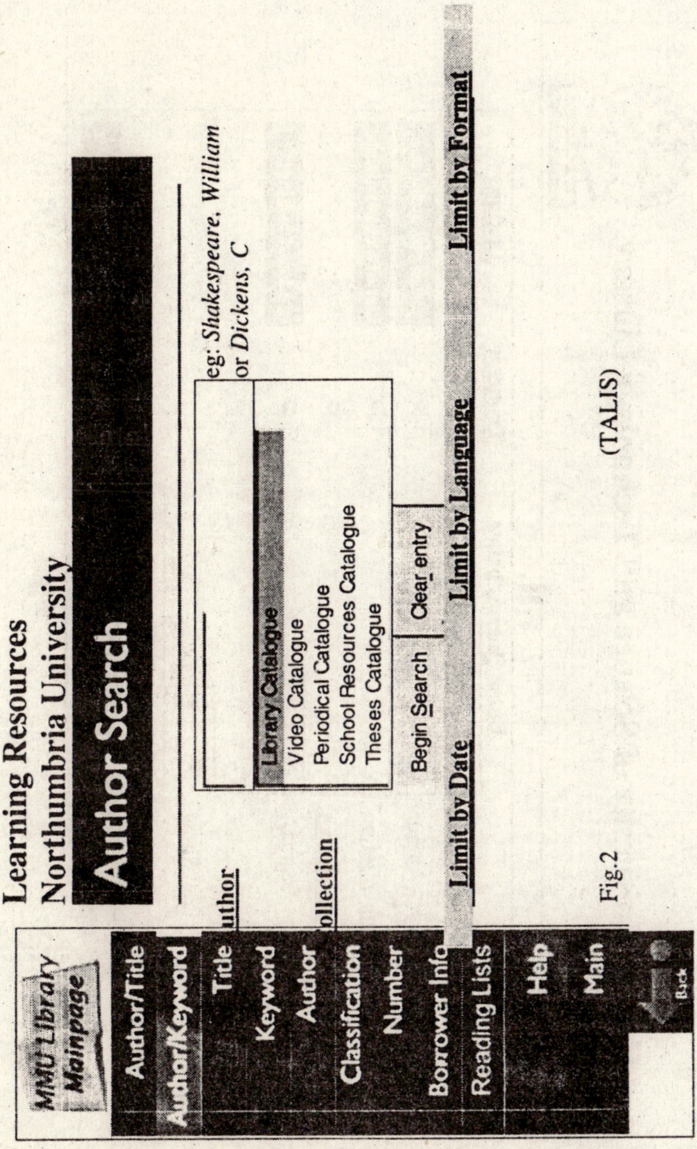
MMU Library Mainpage
Author/Title
Author/Keyword
Title
Keyword
Author
Classification
Number
Borrower Info
Reading Lists
Help
Main
Back
Learning Resources
Northumbria University
Author Search
eg: Shakespeare, William or Dickens, C
Library Catalogue
Video Catalogue
Periodical Catalogue
School Resources Catalogue
Theses Catalogue
Begin Search
Clear entry
Limit by Date
Limit by Language
Limit by Format

Fig.2 (TALIS)

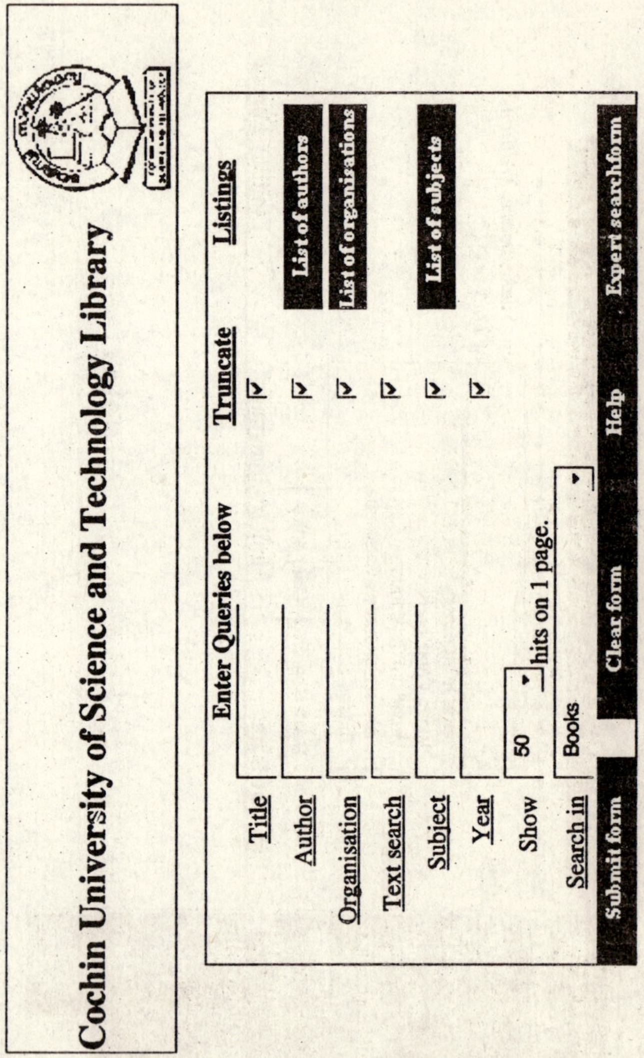

Cochin University of Science and Technology Library
Enter Queries below
Truncate
Listings
Title
Author
Organisation
Text search
Subject
Year
Show
50
hits on 1 page.
Search in
Books
List of authors
List of organisations
List of subjects
Submit form
Clear form
Help
Expert searchform

Fig.3

(ADLIB)

Display of the Search Result Screen

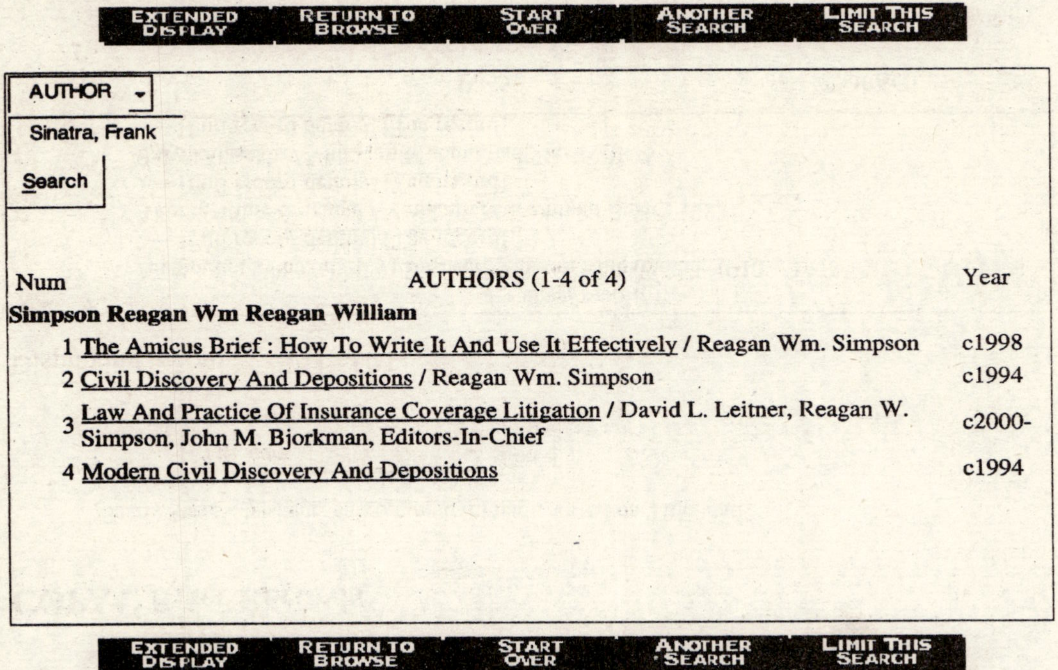

Fig.4 (INNOPAC)

Search Menu | History | Download | Previous Next

COPAC Brief Records

Search terms: basheer, vaikom muhammad ; sorted on Title, date.

Sort by [Title, date ▾] [Sort]

Displaying records 1 to 21 of 21.

No.	Tag	Brief record
1.		Anapputa : kathakal / [by] Basheer, Vaikom Muhammad, 1910- . 1975 — [Full record details] [Tag record]
2.		Anuragattinte dinangal / Vaikkam Muhammad Basir . 1983 — [Full record details] [Tag record]
3.		Balyakalasakhi / Vaikkam Muhammad' Basir . 1976 — [Full record details] [Tag record]

Fig.5 (COPAC)

Bibliographical Details Screen

Detailed presentation of retrieved records

1 **Title description**

Book

JSP: the complete reference / Phil Hanna . -New Delhi : Tata McGraw-Hill, 2001 . - xxiii, 876p.

Dept. of Computer Applications.

ISBN 0-07-044527-3

Keywords

Java Server Pages (JSP)

Web Development

Programming language

Classification codes

004.43J

Copy details

Copy number
Status
Loan category
Shelf mark
Location

CA003100
available
Book
004.43J HAN
Computer Application

CA003101
available
Book
004.43J HAN
Computer Application

Search again

Fig.6 (ADLIB)

PREVIOUS RECORD | NEXT RECORD | RETURN TO BROWSE | ANOTHER SEARCH | START OVER

EXPORT | REQUEST

AUTHOR | Shakespeare | Search

Author
Shakespeare, L. M. (L. Marguerite)

Title
A question of risk / L.M. Shakespeare

Publ&date
New York : St. Martin's Press, c1989

LOCATION	CALL NO.	STATUS
ADULT	FICTION Shakespeare	AVAILABLE

Edition
1st U.S. ed

Descript
287 p. ; 22 cm

Note
"A Thomas Dunne book."

"First published in Great Britain by Macdonald & Co., Ltd."--T.p. verso

PREVIOUS RECORD | NEXT RECORD | RETURN TO BROWSE | ANOTHER SEARCH | START OVER

EXPORT | REQUEST

Fig.7 (INNOPAC)

ANALYSIS

The opening screen of web OPAC should present the name or names of libraries with search options. In Talis web opac software(Fig.3), the opening screen is designed into two vertical frames . The left frame works as main menu in which all search options and links are arranged.In INNOPAC (Fig.4) the search options frames have also provided in all pages so that the user does not need to use 'back buttons'to refine his/her search.

In the display option, all most all software provides brief records with link to full bibliographical records. In COPAC there are provisions for sorting the search result. Users can sort the search result by title/date,author/title and by date. In bibliographical details screen display ADLIB and INNOPAC(Fig.6 and 7) provide full details with location and availability status.

CONCLUSION

A model web OPAC should have some of the qualities given below.

1. The opening page should display the name of the library with search options
2. There should be navigation buttons in the OPAC other than in the web browsers.
3. There should be search options in all pages so that users may not need to use back buttons to refine his search in the main menu.
4. There should be options to sort the search result by title/ date., author/title, date
5. There should be options to display related entries in such a case where no exact match was found.
6. The full bibliographical record should display the availability status and location marks.

REFERENCE

1. Beheshti, Jamshid (1997) The Evolving OPAC *Cataloging andClassification Quarterly*,24,163-185.
2. Cooper,Alan(1995).*The Essential of User Interface Design* India:Wiley Dreamtech.
3. Galitz,Wilbert O. (2002) *The Essential Guide to User Interface Design* (2nd.ed.)India:Wiley Dreamtech.
4. *http://12.164.240.5/search.*
5. *http://mmu.ac.uk/library*
6. *http://opac.cusat.ac.in*
7. http://catalog.jmls.edu/search
8. http://copac.ac.uk/copac/

22

CURRENT TRENDS IN AUTOMATIC CLASSIFICATION WITH PARTICULAR REFERENCE TO DDC

K.S. Chudamani
H.C. Nagarathna
JRD Tata Memorial Library
Indian Institute of Science
Bangalore-12

INTRODUCTION

Library automation is known as modernizations of library house keeping operations by computerization. It is a phenomenon based on computerized information processing of day to day operation of library system and library services. Automation delineated on a set of control procedures adopted in libraries. Library automation includes both house keeping operations as well as information handling; house keeping where computers are extensively used are acquisition or book ordering, classification, circulation, stock taking and serial control. Automated library system perform some intellectual processing. Information analysis had been attempted by researchers from time to time.

CLASSIFICATION-AUTOMATION

Classification of documents involves three major processes. The first two processes define a structure of categories and determining a basis for the classification decision that are casually performed by a classificationist, while the third, the process of classifying documents into categories is performed by a classifier.

The present computer programs perform the general and third process.

1. Programmes that help the classificationist.
2. Programmes that help the classifier.

Classification is an activity where a significant level of human expertise, abstract thinking and understanding is needed and this is not easy to substitute by artificial intelligence or expert systems. A growing number of research projects and experiments are taking to support knowledge and structuring activities on the net.

The effectivity of classification into on-line is yet to be fully exploited. Methods and projects which stick closely to automatic routines connected with the usage of established library classification system in internet services are:

a. Automatic classification of WAIS databases using UDC
b. Project Gerhard
c. Project Scorpion
d. Colon classification

Automatic Classification of Wais Databases Using UDC

First project to apply simple methods of automatic classification in order to improve the discovery and retrieval of internet resources. It is based on a coherent single type of resource. About 700 WAIS databases Automatically extract more or less a detailed descriptions of content from the internet. The project deals with automatic indexing and classification of WAIS databases. Classifications are decided using a heuristic method based on the accumulated weights for each proposed classification and on the number of proposed classification. The methodology is not tied to UDC, but could be used with other classification schemes like the Library of Congress Classification to produce different views of the resources.

Project Gerhard

This project deals with automatic classification of WWW resources in a robot generated index using computer linguistic methods. This project is run by Olderburg universities library.

GERHARD intends to create a robot general index of WWW resources in Germany and to automatically build a browsing structure by subject. GERHARD uses a similar, but linguistically more advanced method than the Nordic WAIS-WWW project. Computer linguistic methods are used to match the natural language content of the indexed documents to a library classification system. The relevant parts of the documents contents are indexed, together with the resulting classification notations, into a database open to direct searching.

Project Scorpion (OCLC)

Automatic classification and indexing using DDC Scorpion is a research project at OCLC exploring the indexing cataloging of electronic resources. Since subject information is the key to advanced retrieval, browsing and clustering are the primary focus of scorpion in the building of tools for automatic subject resolution based on well known schemes like the Dewey Decimal system (DDC).

DDC was first produced by Melvil Dewey in 1876. Originally produced for a small North American college library. Currently 21st edition is published by Forest-press. DDC is distributed in MARC record produced by the LC. DDC is also used in the national bibliographies of the UK, Canada and other countries. DDC was a suitable tool for browsing, first for library catalogues, there for the internet. Internet search was also under taken for the terms 'Dewey Decimal' or DDC.

In scorpion, the document requiring indexing is treated as a query against a DDC. Knowledge base analysing of vocabularies, notations, structure and relations of the classification system. The results of the search, using ranked retrieval, will then become the subjects of the document and can then for instance be used by a human cataloguer for classification support. The knowledge base for DDC is the Electronic support system (ESS) used by the electronic Dewey for windows CD-Rom product from OCLC forest press. The intention is to increasingly exploit linkages between Dewey classes and LC subject headings as well as other subject schemes gathered from different database and conversion programs. So far, the project has explored the use of DDC as a concept definition source. DDC was deemed very suitable for the task because it demonstrated a high degrees of class intensity meaning that subject definitions are unambiguous and well defined. DDC would therefore be a suitable system for automatic classification.

Synthesis of Class Number in Colon Classification

Neelameghan and Venkatraman conducted experiments in India in 1968 on the synthesis of class number by computer in which kernel terms expressing a subject in the natural language are given.

Also, Mr. Satyapal has developed a software for classifying documents according to postulational approach. He has developed a semi-automatic method of general of CC Number for these studies of colon classification (CC).

This study was divided into the following phases.

a. Preparation of the CC schedule on tape.

b. Reading in kernel terms.

c. Distribution of kernel terms.

d. Synthesizing the class number.

e. Printing out the class number.

DDC-INTERNET SITES THAT USE DDC

* EXPANDING UNIVERSE - Specialized in astronomy resource.
* PICK-Resource for information and library studies.
* **Net first** - browsing structure since October 1996. DDC notations had been present in their links from the start of the service.
* **Blzled** is a subject services for business education, based at the university of Bristol and organizations, including Elib.

TRADITIONAL USAGE AND OTHER ONLINE SERVICES

1. DDC is used by more library than any other classification scheme. In 135 different countries are currently used.
2. It has been translated into 30 languages.
3. It is used by the LCC services in the bibliography records, it creates, alongside the LCC.
4. DDC classification also appears with LCC and library of congress subject heading (LCSH) in the cataloguing in publication. (CIP) dataproduced by the library of congress, (more about this is in section)
5. OCLC is now the owner and publisher of DDC and the computer maintains a web page for forest press.

MULTILINGUAL CAPABILITY

DDC notation, because it consists solely of digits and decimal points, is language independent. Translation of DDC exists in French, Italian, Spanish Turkish and other languages.

DDC AND THE TREE OF KNOWLEDGE

The DDC has been likened to giant tree of knowledge: the trees branches are the DDC's classes. Its leaves are the DDC's subclasses and its fruits all the DDC's sub subclasses.

DDC IS LIKE GIGANTIC OUTLINE

The DDC is like a gigantic outline in which the broadest topics (classes) are followed by more specific topics (subclasses and sub-subclasses) and indented in the outline.

1. Broad Class I
   a. Broad subclass 1-A
   b. Broad subclass 1-B
2. Broad Class II
   a. Broad subclass II-A
      1. Specific sub-subclass-a-I
   b. Broad Subclass-II-B
      1. Specific sub-subclass II-B-1
      2. Specific sub-subclass II-B-2

STRENGTHS AND WEAKNESS OF THE SCHEME

The first edition of DDC was published in 1876. As such it was a product of instance and was imbibed with a western Christian pre-technological age view point. Subsequent revisions have done much to try and alleviate this; for example, in 21st edition such a major revision of the life sciences in 560-590 has been carried out. Which saw a move away from the organism centered approach in earlier version of DDC towards an orientation concentrating more upon processes. The scheme is updated more frequently than any other universal schemes.

INTEGRATION BETWEEN CLASSIFICATION SCHEME AND OTHER SYSTEM e.g. CONTROLLED SUBJECT-HEADING

a) DDC numbers are linked to LCSH heading by most major bibliographic services to the extent that their bibliographic records contain certain LCSH headings together with DDC and LCC classification data.

DDC 21st classification numbers have also been mapped to LCSH, using statistical mappings between the two systems generated from the OCLC database.

b. Linking DDC to third party classification system, including LCC, UDC and NLM.

DIGITAL AVAILABILITY

The DDC classification is maintained using an editorial support system which has first used to create edition 20th in 1990. Subjects of this database have been made available under license for certain projects.

An online summary of the first 3 digits of DDC 21 numbers is available on the WWW at: (URL: http://WWW. ocio.ors/ocic/tp/ddc/ddesum21/dde21 sml.htm). The scheme has been made available to internet users on an experimental basis with the intention of encouraging authors and other relevant people to use DDC to classify Materials on the internet.

Edition 21st is the latest revision under gone constant and sometime radical revision from within it has remained structurally recognizable and constituently useful. When devised, DDC was an enumerative scheme. Subsequent revisions have absorbed and made use of the significant challenges and contributions of classification theory chiefly the structure and methodology of faceted classification and the use of facet analysis. As a result, subsidiary tables and divide like devices that reflect and express many aspects of complex topics have been expanded, even though DDC is not a faceted scheme. DDC stands ideologically or theoretically between its two major counterparts. Decidedly more flexible than the library of congress classification and certainly simple than UDC.

DDC is well support by an extensive explanations and Iranians literature. Its simple notations has accumulated considerable user familiarities over the long span of its existence. Dewey editors are trying to code the nature of the relationship between class number and subject headings to see if it is possible to develop classifier and retrieval assistance tools.

WEBDEWEY

Webdewey, the latest development in Library Classification, has been attempting to classify documents automatically.. The problem of lots of information on many different topics: people communicating their ideas on so many different topics. The problem of lots of information in many different format: Authors, performers, artists, musician companies and composers love so many ways of communicating their ideas, data, and art causes the problem of finding the information. Finding exactly what you want is very difficult because there is so much information out on so many different topics and in so many different formats. It also enables the users to use the dewey for day to day classification. For this purpose a multimedia tour has been provided.

DDC multimedia tour is designed for: Different subject, Different formats and Different Topics.

The DDC makes a place for every topic under the sun. It also locates related topics near each other. This is handy because we might also be interested in those topics DDC is a hierarchical classification system that divide knowledge from the broadest to the most specific topics.

SOCIAL SCIENCE

POLITICAL SCIENCE

SYSTEMS OF GOVERNMENT and STATE

DEMOCRATIC GOVERNMENT

Webdewey provides four alternate numbers to select from. While selecting, one can go back to the schedules and views the hierarchy. Thus, webdewey paves the way for automatic classification.

CONCLUSION

Automatic classification process is a necessity if large robot-generated services are to offer a good browsing structure for their documents or advanced filtering techniques as well as proper query expansion tools to improve the search process. DDC provides the starting point for such a venture through its webdewey.

REFERENCE

1. http://www.oclc.org/support/documention/worldcut/cataloguing/interguide2
2. ukoln.ac.uk/metadata/desine/classification
3. Satyapal, B.G. and Satyapal, N. Sanjivini. (2002). Postulational approach to classifying documents: use of satsan auto-matrix version 1-program for synthesis of colon class number. *Information Studies*, 8(2).
4. mldforum. org/volume 1/issue2/role classification.html/
5. http:/www.lita.org/template. htm
6. http://www.ub2. lu.se/autoclass,html.

23

USER BEHAVIOUR TOWARDS CATALOGUE : A STUDY CONDUCTED IN THE C H M K LIBRARY

T.M. Vasudevan
Lecturer
Department of Library and Information Science
University of Calicut

Jesbira.M
MLISc Student
Department of Library and Information Science
University of Calicut

INTRODUCTION

Library catalogue is a systematic list of documents of a library or a group of libraries. It is arranged according to a definite order containing specific bibliographic data for the purpose of identification and location of the documents catalogued. It is an essential and important tool in the library.

Different methods were followed for achieving this function. With the development of other activities in the libraries, the catalogues used also underwent changes. In whatever form and type the catalogue may be, it is required to show what is available, where is it located.

Further the catalogue has to satisfy approaches through authors, titles, series, etc.,

IMPORTANCE OF THE STUDY

Catalogue use studies in university libraries have assumed added significance due to proliferation and complexities of publications, users and their diversified demands. Study of users' approaches to find and locate a document helps to improve the effectiveness of catalogue. The study will have practical utility as it surveys the existing catalogue facilities. The study will enable the authorities of the libraries to have better understanding of catalogue using habit of the users. This study will also help the authority to understand the extend of the problems faced by the catalogue users and find out the solution to the problems. This will enable the authority to take necessary steps to meet the requirements of the users.

The study covers the use of OPAC and card catalogue in the C.H Mohammed Koya Library, which is the central library of the University of Calicut. Post graduate students, teachers, research scholars and the staff of the university are included in the sample taken for study. Catalogues in the university library was computerized two years back. This fact gives more significance to the study. This will help the authority to understand how the users receive the matter of computerization of library catalogue and how are the users benefited from the computerization of catalogue. It also helps to understand the reasons for nonuse of OPAC or Card Catalogue and to take appropriate measures for increasing the use of catalogue. Thus the study of catalogue use helps to improve the effectiveness and use of catalogue, which is an indispensable tool, which facilitate the use of library materials.

OBJECTIVES

Following objectives were laid down for the study.

1. To determine what proportion of users of the library make use of the Catalogue.
2. To determine who uses the catalogue, for what purpose, in

what way, with what degree of success and satisfaction.

3. To find out which form of catalogue is more preferred by users.
4. To ascertain the proportion of users who know how to use OPAC/Card Catalogue
5. To ascertain the need for training in use of catalogue
6. To find out whether they are satisfied with the information given in the catalogue
7. To examine the necessity of keeping two forms of catalogue in the same library

METHODOLOGY

Types of Catalogue (OPAC and Card Catalogue) and category of users have been used as the variables. A sample of 100 users were selected on the basis of Random sampling technique. There were four strata, viz: research scholars, teachers, staff and students. Sample includes a minimum of 10% of the total from each category. Questionnaire method was used for the collection of data. Collected data were analyzed by statistical technique and percentage method.

Most of the users (59%)located the books of their interest by direct search on the shelves. 48% users located the books of their interest with the help of library catalogue while 10% located with help of library staff and 20% with the help of their friends. The underlying motive or cause of using the catalogue may be different for each individual depending on the strata to which one belongs. Whatever may be the motive for which the search is attempted the purpose must be either one or more than one of the following;

1. To find out whether a particular document is available or not
2. To select books with the help of bibliographical details provided in the catalogue
3. To locate an available document by noting call number

Fifty three percentage of users use catalogue for all the purposes, i.e., either to select a book or to know its availability or to know its location. 14% of the users use the catalogue to select a book while 17% used it to know the availability of book and 13% used to know its location.

AWARENESS IN USING OPAC AND CARD CATALOGUE

Among the users 33% of teachers,60% of research scholars 45% of students and 93% of staff were aware of using OPAC and 86% of teachers, 100% of the researchers, 83% of students and 86% of staff know how to use card catalogue. Thus it is seen that most of the users know only about the traditional catalogue.

PREFERRED FORM OF CATALOGUE

The study shows 24% of users give equal preference to both OPAC and card catalogue, 30% of users prefer to use only OPAC and 36% prefer to use only Card Catalogue.

The following table shows the preference of users to one or other form of catalogue.

It shows that most of the teachers prefer to use card catalogue. 40% each of researchers give preference to either OPAC or card catalogue. Larger number of students prefer card catalogue, where as larger number of staff preferred to use both card Catalogue and OPAC. In general larger number of users prefer to use card catalogue than OPAC.

REASONS FOR PREFERRING CARD CATALOGUE

The study reveals that 38% of users prefer card catalogue only because of that they don't know how to use OPAC. 20% prefer card catalogue because of ease of use while 23.33% prefer card catalogue for which there were no reason., 18% not responded.

FINDINGS

The following are the findings evolved from the study.

Table 1

Preferred form of Catalogue

Form of catalogue	Teachers	Researchers	Students	Staff	Total
OPAC	2 (13.33)	4 (40)	18 (30)	6 (40)	30 (30)
Card Catalogue	8 (53.34)	4 (40)	22 (36.67)	2 (13.33)	36 (36)
Both	2 (13.33)	2 (20)	13 (21.67)	7 (46.67)	24 (24)
Not respondent	3 (20)	-----	7 (11.67)	-----	10 (10)
Total	15 (100)	10 (100)	60 (100)	15 (100)	100 (100)

Figures given in the brackets represent respective percentages

Table 2

Reasons for Preferring Card Catalogue

Reasons for preferring card catalogue	Teachers	Researchers	Students	Staff	Total
It is easy to use	2 (20)	1 (16.67)	7 (20)	2 (22.22)	12 (20)
Don't know to use OPAC	5 (30)	3 (50)	14 (40)	1 (11.11)	23 (38.33)
There is no reason	1 (10)	1 (16.67)	10 (28.57)	2 (22.22)	14 (23.33)
Not responded	2 (20)	1 (16.67)	4 (11.43)	4 (44.45)	11 (18.34)

(Figures in brackets indicate percentages)

1. Most of the users locate books of their interest by direct search on the shelves. Most of the Staff and researchers locate books of their interest with the help of library catalogue while most of the students and teachers locate the books by direct search on the shelves.
2. Most of the users use catalogue for all important purposes, such as to select books, to know its availability and to know its location.
3. Compared to OPAC larger number of users know how to use card catalogue
4. Comparatively larger number of users prefer to use Card catalogue than OPAC. This is mainly because of the unawareness in using OPAC.
5. Most of the OPAC users prefer it because of all the four qualities of it, ie, ease of use, simple arrangement, speed and no need to move from one place to another.
6. Most of the users need training in the use of OPAC but most of the users do not need training in the use of card catalogue.
7. Most of the users were satisfied with the given information in OPAC.
8. Most of the users used author and title access points to search through OPAC.
9. Most of the users got all required information from OPAC and card catalogue.
10. Most of the users of both card catalogue and OPAC are satisfied. Users who are not satisfied or somewhat satisfied are those who had not got training in use of catalogues.
11. Most of the users were in favour of introducing some more nodes of OPAC.
12. Most of the users were in favour of keeping two types of catalogues.

CONCLUSION

From the study it is seen that most of the users belonging to different categories in the library are using OPAC. But a good number of users are still using and preferring the traditional card catalogue. This is only because of lack of training (unawareness) in using OPAC. So training is required for users in using OPAC. Most of the users are satisfied with the information given in OPAC. Most of the users are in favour of keeping both catalogues. Alternative to giving training in the use of OPAC is to print small leaflets and sign boards explaining the step by step procedure in using OPAC for author, title and subject searches. However it is better to keep both forms of catalogue, viz., card catalogue and OPAC because of frequent current failure.

24

OPAC: An Effective Information Retrieval Tool to the Distance Learners

Manzoor Babu V.
Research Scholar
Department of Library and Information Science
University of Calicut

INTRODUCTION

A knowledge society can be one of the foundations for a vision for the nation: Developed India. Knowledge has always been the prime mover of prosperity and power. The acquisition of knowledge has always been the thrust area throughout the world and sharing the experience of knowledge is a unique culture of our country. During the last century the world has undergone a change from agricultural society to industrial and to knowledge society.

IT AND LIFE-LONG LEARNING

Information has become the most valuable entity in the modern information society. It is due to the application of recent electronics and telecommunication in the handling of information. The Information Communication Technologies (ICTs) have affected all aspects of human society especially higher education and life-long learning.

Education and learning has become a life long process. Since it is impossible for the modern society to depend on formal educational methods for their life-long learning, people began to depend more on distance learning methods. Life-long learning can be considered a process inherent and natural to human existence. However the pace and mode of learning changes according to the manner and mode in which the individuals are positioned in the society.

DISTANCE EDUCATION

Distance education has become the globally accepted mode of education. In the modern time the distance learning has attained more coverage and communication techniques enable distance-learning courses to give greater educational content to the students. As a result distance education has gained acceptability as a flexible system of education.

Distance education, which started as correspondence or off-campus mode of education, has now widened its scope to on-line education. Distance education institutions have been in the forefront of adopting new technologies to provide increased access to education of masses. Network technologies facilitate learning at anytime and anywhere. As a result our educational systems are gradually changing from closed systems to open systems. Accordingly there should be a transmission from a closed society to an open one.

INDIAN SCENE

The population of India has crossed one billion, and literacy rate has tremendously increased to 64%. Opportunity of higher education is yet to reach large segments. Ten Open Universities and about 62 distance education schools attached to conventional Universities together have contributed enormously for the higher education of the masses. The Open and distance education have now over 2 million enrolment and in coming years we will witness that they will surpass the conventional universities in diversification of the academic programmes. This will be possible only with high bandwidth Internet and large-scale network facilities. For that the Open Universities and distance education schools have to acquire the reputation of the society by improving the standards of distance learners through the strict quality control. IGNOU, the national open university has a decisive role in this regard.

LIBRARY AS A SUPPORTING SYSTEM

Library is the very important instrument for academic growth of students. The importance of library within any academic system can be realized only in the context of the philosophy of education of the system. The main purpose of open systems of learning is to disseminate knowledge and information by new means including the use of modern communication technology. This is likely to provide opportunities of education to those who live in remote and interior areas. Library is the most important student supporting system of open learners. So the open institutions of learning like Open Universities and Virtual Universities should provide efficient library services with the help of Internet and other communication media.

Unfortunately most of the Universities and correspondence schools in the country are not providing efficient on-line library services and most of them are not well equipped with even conventional libraries. Even the national Open University, IGNOU has not arranged adequate library services to its students. Thus the students are compelled to use conventional university libraries for the preparation of their assignments, project works, reference and for other information retrieval purposes.

ON-LINE INFORMATION RETRIEVAL

An important alternative before the Open learners, as well as the conventional regular learners, is to depend on on-line databases for the retrieval of knowledge and information. Various search engines in the Internet play a vital role in on-line information retrieval. But most of the browsers provide too much information, which may confuse the learners or make them in trouble in getting correct information. Moreover they are not designed in such a way as to satisfy the particular approaches of the learners. In other words there is a need for an effective tool for the retrieval of information. OPAC (Online Public Access Catalogue) with Internet support is the most useful in this regard.

OPAC: AN EFFECTIVE TOOL

OPACs were introduced in the United States in the late 1970s as an offshoot of the on-line real-time circulation system, which had been available from the early years of that decade. As part of the circulation system, some form of enquiry module was provided for library staff and, as this facility was developed and became more powerful, it was a logical step to extend the provision to the library user. The honour of being the first library to use OPAC most probably goes to the University of Hull, which introduced OPAC with its circulation system.

Early On-line Public Access systems were designed to run on a mini computer, but later network of microcomputers and linking OPAC with Internet began to provide most effective library services. Development of OPACs can be grouped into three generations. In the first generation, access to catalogue records was restricted to author and title data. Only short bibliographic records were displayed in a format that resembled the catalogue card. No subject access via either keyword or controlled vocabulary was provided. Without full records, subject access authority based searching with cross references, and meaningful browsing facilities, first generation on-line catalogues were understandably classified as inferior to traditional non-automated library catalogues.

In the second-generation online catalogues, which appeared in the mid-1980s, represent a qualitative leap of progress over 1st generation on-line catalogues. Today's state-of –the-art, second generation OPAC is a far more affective form of the library catalogue than earlier form due to the following functions.

1) **More access points :** Any field or word or symbol in the bibliographic record can become an entry point

2) **More browsing options :** For those who cannot describe what they want, or for those who wish to explore the unknown, perhaps via links and trails it leads to books of interest and related materials

3) **Multiple catalogue arrangements in a single place :** Dictionary, divided, classified, etc.

4) **Better search results :** Broad search results for browsing "mini-catalogs", or very precise search results through the careful use of Boolean search capabilities

5) **Remote access :** Consultation from locations near or far from the library. It is this function that makes the OPAC as most suitable to the distance learners.

6) **Material status and availability information :** Interfaced to a circulation system, it provides specific-copy loan status; with an acquisitions system, "on order" and "in process" information may be displayed

7) **Access to the resources of other Libraries :** Either through a shared database or system-to-system linkages

8) **Increased utilization of Library resources :** Both human and material resources

9) **Greater user enjoyment and satisfaction :** With the search process and search results

Although some first-generation OPACs can still be found in libraries, most have been replaced by today's state-of-the-art second-generation systems. The features defining second-generation OPACs are listed below. The majority of installed OPACs satisfy these criteria.

FEATURES OF SECOND GENERATION OPACS

* Card Catalog-Like Alphabetical Searching
* Subject Access Via Library-Assigned Headings
* Keyword Access
* Boolean Searching

* Index Term Browsing
* Shelf List Review/Scan
* Full Standard Bibliographic Records
* Multiple Display Formats
* Two or More Dialogue Modes
* Interactive Search Refinement/Modification
* Search Results Display/Print Manipulation
* Help Facility, Context-Sensitive
* Informative Error Messages
* Action and "How To" Option Prompts

Improved card catalog-like "main entry" searching and browsing-by-heading capabilities have been joined with the conventional IR keyword and Boolean searching approaches. Much of the power and flexibility familiar to online database search specialists which enable the "post-coordinating" of search concepts and terminology have been brought to the online catalogue searcher. Many online catalogs support the ability to restrict searches to specified record fields, to perform character-masking and/or right-hand truncation, and to limit the results by date, language, place of publication, etc. These developments have, increased the usability of these catalogues by untrained users. Acquiring an adequate conceptual understanding of present-day OPACs is further complicated, because they are hybrid card catalog/Boolean search systems.

Recent developments with OPACs, including the advent of the networked OPAC, encouraging as they are, must be kept in proper perspective. Progress has been made along some, but not all, dimensions of potentiality. Improvements to the user interface have made second-generation OPACs more usable for the untrained user, and new graphical user interface (GUI) techniques like windows and point-and-click buttons hold the promise of rendering the search process both more intuitive and more direct.

THE E3 OPAC

Extended third generation catalogues typically provide value-added access beyond the conventional online catalogue by providing expanded entry points, augmented information resources, access to locally mounted and/or remote periodical index databases, and gateway functions to local, regional and national telecommunication networks. Third generation OPACs are called E3 OPACs because it has ***Enhanced*** functionality, ***Expanded*** access and ***Extended*** network linkages.

The studies conducted by the students of various departments of the Calicut University also stress that on-line catalogue is easy to use and students prefer on-line catalogue to card catalogue.

Nowadays most of the libraries of the advanced countries have on-line catalogue which can be referred anywhere from the world. Most of them are providing indexing and abstracting services, and some of them even provide the full text retrieval services. LC (Library of Congress), and OCLC (Online Computer Library Center), of USA provide On-line catalogue services through networks. The British Library Automated Information Service (BLAISE) is also worth mentioning.

The organizations working at national and international levels like Commonwealth Of Learning (COL), International Council for Distance Education (ICDE), Association of Asian Open Universities (AAOU), Distance Education Council (DEC), etc. are trying for the globalization and internationalization of education. Therefore information scientists should be capable of meeting information requirements of On-line Open learners. This will be possible only through networking all the available information sources and by facilitating free flow of information among them. Here OPACs can play the role of a valuable tool of information retrieval. Thus it can be a great supporting system for the online distance learners.

The Union Catalogues like COPAC (Co-operative Online Public Access Catalogue), which is a union catalogue of 24 University libraries in U.S.A., have a great role in on-line information retrieval.

Similar examples such as JANET (Joint Academic Network) are there in UK. also.

CONCLUSION

In short the importance of distance education as an alternative to the regular system of education is increasing day by day. In order to meet the information requirements of the distance learners, access to the library resources should be given to them through the network of libraries. In such a system OPACs linked with Internet is the most suitable information retrieval tool before the access oriented distance learners.

REFERENCES

1. Bates, Marcia J. "Subject access in online catalogs: a design model. *Journal of the American Society for Information Science*, 37(6, 1986) P.357-376.
2. Hunter, Rhonda N. "Successes and failures of patrons searching the online catalog at a large academic library: a transaction log analysis". *Reference Quarterly*, Spring, 1991: 395-402.
3. Kalam, APJ. "Teachers should be the best minds in the society" Convocation address. *CU news*, Calicut: Calicut University, 2003.P.4–8.
4. Kochar, RS and Sudhakaran, KN "Library automation: issues and systems" New Delhi: APH Publishing, 1997. P.268-314.
5. Laxman Rao.. et.al, *ed.* "Globalization of Library and Information Science education". IATLIS seminar papers. Hyderabad: Iatlis, 2003. P.134-141.
6. Leigh Gernert "A text book of Cataloguing" New Delhi: Dominant publishers, P.267-272.
7. Parameswaran, M. "Creation of bibliographic database and use of on-line catalogue in CHMK Library: A case study" In Electronic information environment and Library services: A contemporary paradigm. *Seminar papers.48th All India*

Library Conference. New Delhi : Indian Library Association, 2003. P.415- 421.

8. *www.BLPC.org*
9. *www.LC.org*
10. *www.OCLC.org*

INDEX